THE COLD WAR
AMERICAN WEST, 1945–1989

THE COLD WAR
AMERICAN WEST, 1945–1989

Edited by
KEVIN J. FERNLUND

Historians of the Frontier and American West
RICHARD W. ETULAIN, SERIES EDITOR

University of New Mexico Press
Albuquerque

Published in cooperation with the
University of New Mexico Center for the American West

For my Father,
Douglas W. Fernlund

© 1998 by the University of New Mexico Press
All rights reserved. First edition

Library of Congress
Cataloging-in-Publication Data

The Cold War American West, 1945–1989 /
edited by Kevin J. Fernlund.
p.   cm. — (Historians of the frontier
and American West)
Includes biliographical references (p.   )
and index.
ISBN 0–8263–1984–X (cloth). —
ISBN 0–8263–1985–8 (pbk.)
1. West (U.S.)—History—1945–   .
2. West (U.S.)—Social conditions.
3. Cold War—Social aspects—West (U.S.).
I. Fernlund, Kevin J.   II. Series.
F595.C69   1998
978'.033—dc21   98–23804   CIP

CONTENTS

LIST OF ILLUSTRATIONS   vii

LIST OF TABLES   ix

ACKNOWLEDGMENTS   xi

INTRODUCTION   1
Kevin J. Fernlund

1. Landscapes of the Cold War West   9
   María E. Montoya

2. Migrants, Immigrants, and Refugees:
   The Cold War and Population Growth in the American West   29
   Kevin Allen Leonard

3. Containment and Emancipation:
   Race, Class, and Gender in the Cold War West   51
   A. Yvette Huginnie

4. The Great Cantonment:
   Cold War Cities in the American West   71
   Ric Dias

5. The Legacy of Containment:
   The Military–Industrial Complex and the New American West   87
   Michael Welsh

6. Pro-Defense, Pro-Growth, and Anti-Communism:
   Cold War Politics in the American West   101
   Timothy M. Chambless

7. Crusaders Against Communism, Witnesses for Peace:
   Religion in the American West and the Cold War   119
   Mark Stoll

8. From the Beat Generation to the Sanctuary Movement:
   Cold War Resistance Cultures in the American West   139
   Steve Fox

9. The Cold War West as Symbol and Myth:
   Perspectives from Popular Culture   167
   Charles Kupfer

10. Alaska and Hawai'i:
    The Cold War States   189
    John Whitehead

    Epilogue: The Cold War West—A New Image?   211
    Kevin J. Fernlund

    CONTRIBUTORS   215

    INDEX   217

ILLUSTRATIONS

❧

PHOTOGRAPHS
View of Rocky Flats from Majestic View Park, Arvada, Colorado   10

MAPS
Jacqueline V. Nolan, Cartographer

The Cold War West Major Military Installations   8

Alaska Major Cold War Military Installations   190

Hawai'i Major Cold War Military Installations   191

TABLES

2.1 Population Growth of "Mild-Winter" Western States, 1950–1990   36

2.2 Population Growth of "Hard-Winter" Western States   37

2.3 Increase in African American Population of Western States,
   1950–1990   38

2.4 Increase in American Indian Population of Western States,
   1950–1990   39

6.1 Number of Military Bases in Western States for Three Time
   Periods   102

ACKNOWLEDGMENTS

I wish first of all to thank the contributors to this project. It was a privilege to work with such a dedicated and agreeable group of individuals. I would also like to express my appreciation to Larry Ball at UNM Press and to Richard W. Etulain at the University of New Mexico's Center for the American West for their support and encouragement from the book's inception to its completion. Special thanks go to Donald Worster and Virginia Scharff for their sage advice at a very early stage in this book's development; to María E. Montoya for advice and comments along the way; and to Sharon Corn Krueger for her advice and criticism. I wish also to thank my colleagues and students, especially Jian-Zhong Lin and Michael Seth. Finally, I wish to acknowledge my deep indebtedness to my parents, Douglas and Shirley Fernlund, who taught me things about the Cold War that are not found in books.

INTRODUCTION[1]

~

KEVIN J. FERNLUND

In the fall of 1989 the German people tore down the Berlin Wall, a momentous event signifying the reunification of Europe. The surprisingly peaceful dismantling of this barrier, which had divided the U.S.-led western alliance and the Soviet-backed Warsaw Pact, ended decades of hostility and conflict. The Cold War, as this period of superpower rivalry and international tension has been called, began in Eastern Europe with the failure of the Yalta Agreements. Fittingly enough, it ended there, too. Yet, the Cold War was never far removed from the everyday lives of Americans. The U.S. government *waged* this non-war as much within its borders as abroad. Directly or indirectly, this ideological conflict influenced the country's politics, economy, society, culture, and environment. Very little in American life, in fact, remained untouched by this lengthy and costly struggle.

Perhaps nowhere in the country was the effect of decades of cold war felt more intensely than in the lands west of the Mississippi River. During this period, the American West's open skies and diverse landscapes of mountains, deserts, canyons, and plains bristled with airfields, army bases, naval yards, marine camps, missile fields, nuclear test sites, proving grounds, bombing ranges, weapons plants, military reservations, training schools, toxic waste dumps, strategic mines, transportation routes, lines of communication, laboratories, command centers, and arsenals. From the Dakotas to California and from Washington to Texas, the federal government armed the American West with the apparatus of massive destruction. Moreover, the American West lay at the center of the U.S. strategic network that extended to every corner of the globe. In the geography of the Cold War, little distance separated the Rocky Mountains from the Urals.

As important as the Cold War was to the history of the region, western historians have yet to study the Cold War's broader implications on the people and the environment. Until the Cold War in the West becomes a major subject of inquiry, the story of the region in the last fifty years will remain incomplete in a number of important respects. And until students of the Cold War take into account the unique experience of the American West, their histories of Soviet–American rivalry will be lacking as well. These undertakings will involve nothing less than showing how the central events of twentieth-century Western civilization shaped, and reciprocally, were shaped by the American West. By the same token, the region, as the staging area for the Korean and Vietnam Wars—the two major armed conflicts of the Cold War—was an important variable in recent Asian history. How historians judge these complex and ambiguous relationships will, no doubt, produce some of the most significant interpretations that we have seen in a generation of scholarship on the modern American West.[2]

In terms of the region itself, the key question is whether the Cold War transformed or deformed the American West. In 1985, the historian Gerald D. Nash wrote the first volume of a pioneering study on World War II in the American West.[3] Nash argued that no other event in western U.S. history did more to "transform" the region than the global war against Germany and Japan. Nash used the term "transform" to suggest that the West experienced both dramatic and positive change. As Nash put it, the struggle against fascism compressed into four years what "might have taken generations to accomplish."[4] According to Nash, then, the war was a benefit for the region, in the sense that the war put the American people back to work and ended the Great Depression. In Nash's words:

> In 1945 the West emerged from the war with a burgeoning manufacturing complex, a bustling service economy, and a bevy of aerospace, electronics, and science-oriented industries that heralded a new phase of economic development with the rise of a postindustrial economy. In four years, the war had transformed a backward colonial region into an economic pacesetter for the nation. And the *pattern* [italics mine] created by the war dominated the western economy for the next three decades.[5]

What sustained this "pattern," of course, was not inertia but rather four long decades of cold war. Without the decision of the United States to challenge and counter the Soviet Union in the postwar years, the region's development would have been very different indeed.

In writing the history of the Cold War in the American West, one starting point might be to ask whether this postwar pattern of development was, in any sense, beneficial for the region. The militarization of the region certainly enabled the United States to make good on its commitment to defend the free world. But that is a different point. The issue here is did the Cold War continue the transformation of the region—in the positive sense of that term—that Nash argues began with World War II. As yet, the case "for" the Cold War in the American West has not been made, the strong implications of Nash's work on this point notwithstanding. Nor, for that matter, has the case "against" it been made. Of course, since the 1930s western scholars, such as Bernard De Voto and Walter Prescott Webb, have challenged the triumphalist or nationalistic narrative of western history. And more recently, Richard White, Donald Worster, and Patricia N. Limerick have offered their own influential critiques of the triumphalist narrative of the region's past. But no one has yet written a history of the Cold War distinctly from the regional perspective of the American West, one that looks at the environmental, political, social, economic, and cultural costs and benefits of the war for the region.

Relevant to any discussion of the region is the broader, global perspective of George F. Kennan, the ninety-two-year-old historian, diplomat, authority on the USSR, and architect of the U.S. policy of "containment." In his recent book, *At a Century's Ending* (1996), Kennan characterized the twentieth century as "tragic," for both East and West. Kennan observed that this "sad century" began with the Great War, which was "not only in itself a tragedy of immeasurable dimensions, but one that lay at the heart of a great part of the subsequent misfortunes of the century." A major consequence of the Great War, according to Kennan, was that "great orgy of wastage of human and material resources" known as World War II. Moreover, that international conflict manifested its own major problems, namely, the Cold War, the development of nuclear weapons, and an international community ill suited to managing the collapse of Europe's colonial empires. Adding to these global problems, Kennan identified two other dire postwar developments, global environmental deterioration and overpopulation. In view of this history of wasted energy, failure, and lost opportunity, Kennan reflected:

So here we all stand—we of the Western World—at the end of this sad century; still partially crippled, genetically and morally, by the injuries we brought to ourselves in the two internecine wars of the earlier decades, and confronted now with emerging global problems for the solutions to which neither our ingrained habits nor our international institutions have prepared us.[6]

From Kennan's perspective, it is difficult to find anything positive, or "transformative," about the era of global war. Kennan does not refer specifically to the American West, or to any other country or region, for that matter. But the implication of Kennan's view for the region is clear. The region's human and material resources, like those in the former Soviet Union, were spent on war or in preparing for war instead of being used to build a better, more inclusive, and just society.

The purpose of this volume of essays on the American West is to extend to the Cold War the same regional perspective that Nash boldly applied to the Second World War, while evaluating both sides of the historical ledger. What we need is a balanced view and sober judgments. To this end, the ten commissioned essays survey the Cold War in the American West from the end of World War II to the fall of the Berlin Wall. Researching and writing these essays has been no small task, given the paucity of secondary literature, on the one hand, and the vastness of primary source material, on the other. Despite these difficulties (or perhaps because of them), each participant agreed to essay a single, large topic, ranging from politics to popular culture. In the end, they reached as many conclusions about the Cold War's significance as there are essays. Predictably, at this early stage in the scholarship of the Cold War West, no "consensus" has emerged. What has emerged, I believe, is an engaging introduction to a new area of inquiry in western history.

Opening the collection is María E. Montoya's essay, "Landscapes of the Cold War West." The author provides a satellite image of the enormous environmental transformation that the western people and landscape underwent as a result of decades of cold war—a point that is neatly illustrated by the accompanying interpretive map by Jacqueline Nolan. The second essay is no less broad: Kevin Leonard's piece on "Migrants, Immigrants, and Refugees: The Cold War and Population Growth in the American West" charts the vast demographic changes the West experienced as a result of Cold War polices, from the influx of uranium miners to the Colorado Plateau in the 1950s to the arrival of political refugees from El Salvador in the 1980s. A. Yvette Huginnie organizes her essay on western society during the Cold War around the dual themes of social containment and emancipation movements. She focuses her discussion on the early period of the Cold War, employing the descriptive and analytical categories of race, class, and gender. Next, Ric Dias makes the compelling argument that the Pentagon's administration of three hundred western military bases and installations during the Cold War had a significant impact on the region's urban growth and development. In his essay, Michael Welsh shows how, for over four decades, the military-industrial complex secured the economy of the American West by raising it above the vicissitudes of the free market.

In "Pro-Defense, Pro-Growth, and Anti-Communism: Cold War Politics in the American West," Timothy M. Chambless makes the case that the Cold War produced a political alliance that made sure defense dollars went west. Mark Stoll, in his essay, notes that the religious response to the Cold War, with the obvious exception of the Mormon Church, was national rather than regional. Stoll identifies three distinct religious periods during the Cold War—anti-Communist unanimity, post-Vatican II doubt, and Reagan-era schism—and demonstrates how churches in the West, whether they were liberal or conservative, figured in this religious response, with easterners taking the lead in faith-based opposition to the Vietnam War in the 1960s and 1970s, and westerners leading the opposition to Cold War policies during the 1980s. Next, Steven Fox explores the largely secular resistance to the Cold War. In doing so, he discovers that American opposition movements had a distinctly western, and especially Californian, flavor. Charles Kupfer discusses the Cold War West as it was expressed in popular culture, from film to comic books to sporting events. According to Kupfer, the American West was endlessly re-imagined so that it could speak to audiences experiencing the harsh and frightening realities of cold war. In the final essay, John S. Whitehead argues that Alaska and Hawai'i should be seen as extensions of the American West and that these states are, in fact, integral to any discussion of the Cold War West. Of particular significance is Whitehead's argument that Cold War considerations were a vital part of the successful statehood movements in these last two western territories.

The Cold War ended only a few years ago, and arguably it is still being fought in Asia. Indeed, many individuals have grown up in the American West taking the Cold War for granted. But the events that precipitated and sustained the Cold War, so fresh in all of our memories, have now passed into history. In my own case, in 1964 my father was stationed at Davis Monthan Air Force Base in Tucson, Arizona, having completed his training at Sheppard Air Force Base in Wichita Falls, Texas. He served as a missile combat crewmen in the Titan II program, which ran in Arizona for twenty-two years from 1962 to 1984. There were fifty-four Titan II missile sites: eighteen in southern Arizona; eighteen in the vicinity of Little Rock Air Force Base in Jacksonville, Arkansas; eighteen around McConnell Air Force Base in Wichita, Kansas; and an additional three testing and training sites at Vandenberg Air Force Base in Lómpoc, California. The Titan II's, incidentally, were aptly named. They were 110 feet long, 10 feet in diameter, and with fuel weighed 330,000 pounds; at a speed of 17,000 miles per hour, they could reach their destination 6,000 miles away in thirty-five minutes.[7]

For obvious security reasons, my mother and I were never permitted to visit my father at his command post. Today, however, the sites have been deactivated and I am now able to visit the very missile silo, Complex 571–7, where he carried out "alert duties," because that particular installation has been converted into the Titan Missile Museum. For the price of admission and in the company of tourists, I can now enter, in Barbara Kingsolver's words, the "belly of the beast," where my father and many other crewmen over the years kept a constant nuclear vigil.[8] The Cold War, of course, touched the lives of millions of other westerners in countless ways. In fact, in numbers alone this long conflict affected many more people than did the fur trade, the mining rushes, the overland crossings, the Indian wars, and all of the other classic nineteenth-century western experiences combined.

The task at hand is to begin to define the Cold War in the West by studying its wide impact on the lands and peoples of the region. All of my life I have tried to understand the many forces that brought my father to the Santa Cruz Valley, where he waited beneath the cacti and creosote for the president of the United States to give the emergency war order to fire an ICBM at a Soviet target halfway around the world. There is still much more that we should know about the Cold War West. But the following collection of essays have helped me, and I believe will help others, realize how significant the Cold War was, and will continue to be, to western history.

Kevin Fernlund
Stillwater, Oklahoma

NOTES

1. The author wishes to thank María Montoya, Michael Welsh, and John Whitehead for their comments, and Rita Napier and Kent Blaser for their helpful criticisms of the paper "The American West in the Era of Global War, from 1914 to 1989, a Historiographical Assessment," which was read at the Mid-America Conference on History in 1996. This paper served as the basis for the introduction and epilogue to this volume.

2. For thoughts on writing twentieth-century western history, see Howard Lamar, "Westering in the Twenty-First Century: Speculations on the Future of the Western Past," and Michael E. McGerr, "Is There a Twentieth-Century West?" both in *Under an Open Sky: Rethinking America's Western Past*, ed. William Cronon, George Miles, and Jay Gitlin (New York:: W. W. Norton & Co., 1992); and Richard W. Etulain, "Prologue: The Twentieth-Century West: A New Historiographical Frontier," in *The Twentieth-Century West: Histor-*

ical Interpretations, ed. Gerald D. Nash and Richard W. Etulain (Albuquerque: University of New Mexico Press, 1989).

3. Gerald D. Nash, *The American West Transformed: The Impact of the Second World War* (Bloomington: Indiana University Press, 1985), and *World War II and the West: Reshaping the Economy* (Lincoln: University of Nebraska Press, 1990).

4. Nash, The American West Transformed, vii.

5. Nash, World War II & the West, xii.

6. See the foreword of George F. Kennan, *At a Century's Ending: Reflections 1982–1995* (New York: W. W. Norton & Co., 1996).

7. Titan Missile Museum (Green Valley, Arizona) informational materials: "Putting the Titan II ICBM into Perspective: A Brief History of Air Force Ballistic Missiles, From 1955 to 1975" and "Titan II Takehome Tour."

8. See Barbara Kingsolver, "In the Belly of the Beast," in *High Tide in Tucson: Essays from Now or Never* (New York: HarperPerennial, 1996; 1995), 207–21.

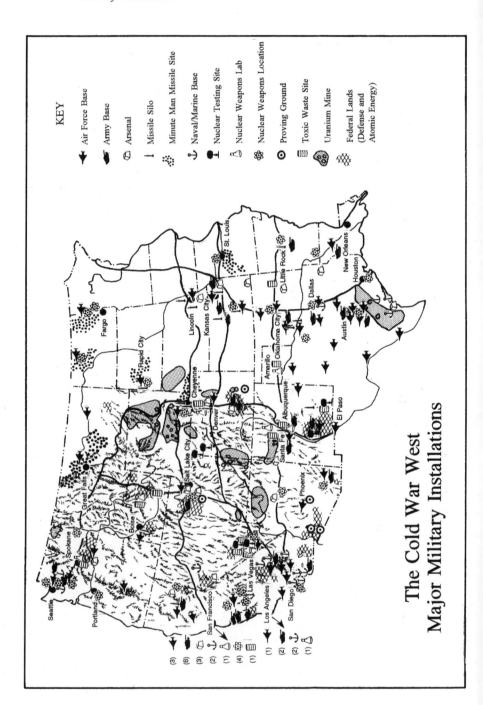

The Cold War West
Major Military Installations

CHAPTER ONE

LANDSCAPES OF THE COLD WAR WEST

❦

MARÍA E. MONTOYA[1]

One image of my childhood still haunts me. Every evening as I went to bed, I stopped at my bedroom window and gazed upon the foothills of the Rocky Mountains along Colorado's Front Range. What struck me most was not the majesty or beauty of those mountains. They were not unusual in that landscape; they simply belonged. What I noted was the orange glow of a small city. Rocky Flats, or Rocky Flats Environmental Technological Site, as it is known today, housed the place where the U.S. federal government chose to assemble plutonium triggers for its nuclear weapons arsenal. Rocky Flats also employed my father for most of his career and drew my family to this northwestern suburb of Denver, Colorado in the late 1960s.

What now fascinates me most about that view from my window is that then it never bothered me in the least. Rocky Flats was a part of my own personal geography: it determined much about how I placed myself, physically and mentally, in the American West. Only recently have I stopped to think about how living next to a nuclear weapons facility altered the way we lived, and how my father's life changed because he worked in one. The U.S. military-industrial complex's ability to alter the landscape and people's lives, however, no longer eludes me. I do not take for granted that view of Rocky Flats from my bedroom window—and all that the view implied. I now realize that not every child had a similar view.

1. I would like to thank Mike Droeger, Pablo Mitchell, and Alexander Shasko for their research assistance. I also want to thank Larry Ball, Kevin Fernlund, Rick Hills, Kevin Leonard, Ken Orona, Daniel Salmanson, and Virginia Scharff for their comments.

View of Rocky Flats from Majestic View Park, Arvada, Colorado. (Photo by Frederick D. Montoya, 1996.)

For instance, today when I compare my childhood view with the one my parents had in their youth, I find the contrast striking. Both my mother and father grew up in the San Luis Valley of southern Colorado, a high plateau that has remained sparsely inhabited throughout the twentieth century. Outside their windows, both saw mountain ranges (the Sangre de Cristos and the San Juans), which enfolded, even isolated, their day-to-day lives. When I return to that rural, enclosed place, I imagine how comforting it must have been as a child to feel so protected by that natural geography. When one stands in that valley, it is as if one is in the center of this world: nothing seems to lay beyond those mountains. The view from my window differed so dramatically from my parents' because mine was dominated by a human presence. I, too, saw majestic mountains, but what stuck in my mind was the less-striking foreground of Rocky Flats. My view, this human-constructed vision, has had far-reaching consequences across Denver, the state of Colorado, the American West, and even the world. That view outside of my window truly sat at the center of the

Cold War. My landscape, unlike that of the insular world of my parents' childhood, did not offer isolation from the outside world but instead tied me and my life to worlds far away.

The Cold War continued what World War II had begun in the development and exploitation of the western states. If, as Gerald Nash argues, World War II was the watershed event in the history of the American West, then, I would argue, the Cold War assured that the legacy of World War II would be preserved. The Cold War imbedded the remnants of war, whether hot or cold, in the landscape of the American West from Washington to Texas and from California to North Dakota. No state in the American West escaped the imprint left by America's technological and diplomatic struggle with the Soviet Union (see map 1).

On a micro level, the story of my family's journey to Rocky Flats and Denver reflects the story of the American West during the Cold War era and the dramatic consequences of that forty-four-year struggle. The Cold War changed the probable direction of my parents' lives. Instead of becoming subsistence farmers and wage laborers, they traveled a new road as suburban dwellers and white-collar workers. The Cold War drew my father into a technical career that he probably never could have imagined as a child. It turned my mother into a suburban car driver, a role which she never intended for herself, but one which she now embraces daily as she heads east from her home in the suburbs to her job in downtown Denver. The Cold War altered our physical living space and influenced the way I thought about place, nature, and my relationship to them.

My personal and familial experiences reflect the more general experience of westerners in the late twentieth century. From a broader perspective, this essay will examine three processes by which the Cold War shaped the landscape of the American West. First, the war's military-industrial complex physically transformed large sections of empty landscape. It made deserts into proving ranges and testing grounds. It tucked secret military hideouts into mountains, and it created places so poisonous that it will be thousands of years before humans can ever inhabit those landscapes again. Second, the social and economic culture of the Cold War era, with its emphasis on consumption and the single-family dwelling, had a profound effect on the landscape in terms of resource exploitation and suburbanization. Finally, the Cold War has influenced how Americans, particularly westerners, think about the landscape around them, and their relationship with it. The direct physical impact of military use, the secondary effects of resource development—the suburbanization associated with the Cold War era, and the changing mental images of the West's landscape are the legacies of this war on the American West.

Gerald Nash and other scholars of the twentieth-century American West have pointed out the oasislike features of the twentieth-century American western landscape. Postwar immigrants congregated around human-made bodies of water to create cities like Denver, Phoenix, Salt Lake City, Omaha, and Los Angeles. Available water and burgeoning industry combined with technological advances such as central air conditioning drew people into densely populated areas. One hundred years ago these cities never could have sustained such intense development. These high-density population centers, surrounded by hundreds of miles of "open" and "unused" space, distinctly mark western geography. Today's westerners, then, are immigrants who have learned to live where nature suggests, if not dictates, they should not.

Nearly a century before the Trinity detonation in July of 1945, some people already considered vast portions of the American West empty space devoid of much functional use. Early-nineteenth-century explorers, and Stephen Long in particular, labeled the Plains the Great American Desert. Long and his contemporaries apparently did not notice, or label significant, the thousands of Native Americans who made their homes on those Plains. Not until the late nineteenth century, after thousands of overlanders had passed through the area making their way to the Far West of California and Oregon, did European Americans stop to challenge Long's label of the Great Plains as arid desert. Cattleman from Texas were the first to recognize and market the area's grazing potential. As their longhorns and other breeds spread north, the buffalo quickly disappeared from their native environment, and with them went the main resource that sustained the Plains Indian cultures. These cattlemen transformed the hinterland into America's grazing fields for domesticated animals, which could feed into the ever-demanding "porkopolis" of Chicago. Next came the "sodbusters," who began to claim the land from Native Americans and cattle ranchers. They stripped the Plains of their natural grasses and planted imports like wheat, alfalfa, and oats to feed the expanding nation. By the early twentieth century, America's Midwestern desert had been transformed by technology into economically productive land for an industrializing nation that demanded a steady and inexpensive source of food.

Throughout the twentieth century the Midwest has remained one of America's largest food-producing regions. The region, with its sprawling fields and scattered communities, has also provided the United States with the perfect location for missile sites—from the Minutemen to ICBMs to the MX. The West's cold warriors, who searched for quiet, out-of-the-way locations in which to place warheads, easily adapted their missile sites to the human-shaped environment of the rancher's and farmer's seemingly empty world. What better place to put a missile than in an area surrounded by the most vernacular of farm structures—the silo? The missiles lay far away from major population centers and thus provided secrecy and isolation in the event of an attack or an accident. Even nicknames like the Minuteman and Peacemaker made the missiles seem at home in this American place.

The arid environment of the Southwest proved even less inviting to European Americans than the Great Plains. Names such as Death Valley and Jornado del Muerte only served to label what European Americans knew about the Southwest: it was ugly, stark, lethal, and uninhabitable. The idea of desert conjured images of a lifeless wasteland: yucca plants, gila monsters, and rattlesnakes just accentuated the inhospitality of the environment to humans. The Spaniards endured the harsh environment only because they believed they would find riches on the northern side of the wasteland. When the gold of Quivera and the Seven Cities of Cibola proved elusive, however, they were the first government to see the potential of the region as an area devoted to national defense. The Spanish government, through the military, settled this far northern province as a protective measure against further European or Indian encroachments on their successful interior settlements. The environment, however, proved much too harsh for the Spaniards and their Mexican and American followers. No European Americans seemed capable of creating a truly prosperous or growing society prior to the late nineteenth century.

The strangeness and "otherness" of the desert that European Americans perceive results from its apparent isolation from the relative lushness that marks the American landscape. The desert is dry, hot, and, unless you look closely, apparently barren of life. This seeming emptiness and vast unoccupied space has provided an opportunity for humans to experiment, to free themselves from the confines and demands of the normal cycles of family and society that existed in the farms and cities of Europe and the eastern United States. The desert has also been one place for old people to seek refuge from society, to isolate themselves from the demands of their families. The desert has provided a place where the sick, particularly tuberculosis sufferers, have come to recover and isolate themselves from the unhealthy climate of the East and Midwest. It has also been the place where avant-garde artists, like Georgia O'Keeffe, have come to isolate themselves from the Euro-centric art of the East and to find inspiration in the landscape. The very term, avant-garde, a French military phrase, refers to the soldiers beyond the trenches of the front line. It is not surprising, then, that the avant-garde in military technology should join the artistic avant-garde in seeking refuge from the presence of humanity to test their new and destructive creations. Whether in leisure, art, or military technology, the avant-garde has always instinctively sought this seemingly empty, lifeless, unconfined space we know as the desert. The desert's openness seems to beg for transformation.

Whether for artists looking for inspiration, military leaders looking for isolation, or "snowbirds" seeking refuge from children, familial responsibility and the cold, the desert became a magnet for twentieth century seekers of empty places in which to develop their alternative art, land use, and lifestyle. Consequently, despite the fact that desert environments are and always have been teeming with life—human and otherwise—Cold War engineers have come here to look for places to put waste and to place testing sites. Federal sites such as Yucca Mountain in Nevada and WIPP (Waste Isolation Pilot Project) in New Mexico share their desert environment in common, and government officials chose these locations as dumping grounds precisely because of their landscape.

The Nevada Test Site and White Sands Missile Range exemplify this phenomena most clearly. White Sands sits astride the Jornada del Muerte, and the Nevada Test Site rests in the Great Basin Desert. Except for the few buildings used for observation, the areas exist devoid of most human habitation. The federal government labeled some land uninhabitable and turned both landscapes to, what the government perceived, as its highest utilitarian use. The desert land, its flora, its fauna, and its human inhabitants have been sacrificed so that the federal government could test its weapons and Americans could sleep safer knowing their country's potential to protect itself.

What we realize now, long after aboveground testing has ceased and the damage done, is that no matter how secluded we believe an area, there exists no such thing as complete isolation from humanity. Just ask the inhabitants of Saint George, Utah, who suffered the consequences of fallout from the Nevada Test site, or Terry Tempest Williams, whose essay, "The Clan of the One-Breasted Women," details the effects of living on an irradiated landscape, or Mary McDonald, who has lived next door to the thundering jet noise of White Sands for years. They know the consequences of living on such a "deserted" landscape. The Cold War's effects on land and people no longer allows Americans to hold onto the illusion that they live unconnected from the rest of the world. Technology intruded into people's lives, as the far-reaching (in terms of geography) and long-term (in terms of time) consequences of nuclear technology and testing eventually rained down on the heads of westerners.

Los Alamos, New Mexico, the site of the Manhattan Project, presented a somewhat more difficult problem for those looking for an "empty" place to conduct high-tech, secret investigations: this site actually had people living a secure life on its proposed location. Robert J. Oppenheimer, the lead scientist for the project, had been visiting the Pajarito Plateau and the Los Alamos Boys Ranch since his younger days and had come to love the high desert landscape and isolation of the area. He was often quoted as saying, "My two great loves are physics and New Mexico. It is a shame that they can not be combined." Perhaps unluckily for New Mexico, Oppenheimer got his wish when the Manhattan Project established Los Alamos as its central locale. General Leslie Groves and Robert Oppenheimer chose the plateau because of its seeming isolation from "civilization." That they did not consider important the lives of the thousands of Pueblo Indians and Hispano villagers who lived at the foot of that plateau says a great deal about what the two considered uninhabited, civilized, and isolated.

For the last fifty years, the Los Alamos laboratories have spread across the high plateaus and steep valleys of the Rio Arriba area of the Rio Grande valley. No longer confined to the secluded top of the Pajarito Plateau, the labs have expanded their secret hiding places to other locales and further intruded on local fauna, flora, and human residents. The laboratories of Los Alamos have almost doubled the size of land they occupy on and near the plateau. New communities, like White Rock, have sprung up to accommodate the sprawling population that flocks to Los Alamos looking for work. Since the 1980s, Los Alamos has had one of the highest population densities in the state, second only to Albuquerque, which is a more spread out and diversified city.

The federal government and its contractors who run the labs have intruded not only on the natural landscape but also on the aesthetics of the built environment. Los Alamos remained a closed city through much of the Cold War—no one but authorized, badged workers and residents could enter—with the government owning and controlling all of the land within the city. The U.S. government allowed no private property or home ownership within the facility. Even when the city opened to the public in 1957, the federal government maintained control over large parcels of land and made most of the decisions about land use on the plateau. Federal contractors went for function over aesthetics, and created circa 1950s, federal-style buildings. These bleak and sterile structures stand out as eyesores in a state that prides itself on (and lures tourists with) its historic and romantic adobe architecture.

Zoning and land-use regulations typically belong under state and local governments. And New Mexico valiantly attempts to maintain its supremacy in regulating land use: Santa Fe and Taos aggressively require everything from the Sheraton to the Texaco station to be given a regulation adobe brown exterior, molded from chicken wire and concrete. These aesthetic regulations maintain the merchants' collective myth of a secluded outpost dependent only on locally generated clay to produce their buildings and store fronts. Reality intrudes nonetheless at Los Alamos, where the federal government has immunity from state and local law. Consequently, the labs are concrete boxes with hospital green interiors. They are the physical manifestation of a legal and economic fact: northern New Mexico is not the adobe Brigadoon that time forgot but rather a field office of the Pentagon and the Department of Energy, a creation of the national military, rather than local geological necessity.

While many protest the existence of the labs, their expansion, and the eventual highway path that will truck away the site's waste to WIPP (Waste Isolation Pilot Project) some three hundred miles to the southeast of the state, many local residents value the tangible benefit of a Los Alamos paycheck. For most New Mexicans growing up in the Española Valley, Los Alamos National Laboratories have become an essential component of their economic landscape; it remains one of the largest employers in the region. Moreover, the labs have created a stratified economic environment that eerily corresponds to the landscape. Up on the hill, where the labs are located, Los Alamos boasts of a per capita income of $22,900. Ninety-eight percent of its population graduates from high school and 50 percent have bachelors' degrees. Only 1.5 percent of its families live below the poverty line. Eighty-five percent of the residents are White. In stark juxtaposition, however, the Española Valley, which lies at the foot of "the hill," has a per capita income of $7,859. Eighty percent of its population graduates from high school, which gives it one of the highest dropout rates, at 20 percent, in the state. Furthermore, only 7.9 percent of its population have bachelors' degrees. Moreover, 23.5 percent of Española's families live below the poverty line and its population is 88 percent Hispano and Native American. The two economically and ethnically diverse areas are woven together and tied up with one another for their survival, but clearly some have prospered more than others. The military choices that Leslie Groves and Robert Oppenheimer made fifty years ago have left their legacy indelibly imprinted on the economic, cultural, social, and physical landscape of northern New Mexico.

Not only did the Cold War transform rural and supposedly empty landscapes, it also influenced the urban environment of the American West. The military buildup and technological advances of the Cold War drew many workers and their families, like mine, into the urban areas of the American West. For example, the Los Angeles Times in 1960 reported that one-third of the employees in the Los Angeles metropolitan area depended to some extent on the defense industry for their paychecks. This trend was even more pronounced in the suburban areas of Los Angeles, which were the real winners in the race to attain government contracts. By 1964, Orange County produced 90 percent of all advanced communication equipment for the United States, and a year earlier, aerospace-defense jobs accounted for 60 percent of all manufacturing jobs in the county. The result of all these military-related jobs was increased urbanization and suburbanization of the American West.

Furthermore, in postwar San Diego 78 percent of the city's manufacturing was related to national defense. Contractors such as Boeing Aircraft in Seattle transformed the Washington state economy by generating 73,000 jobs in 1958, at the peak of the company's construction of the B-52 bomber. Even a small town like Alamogordo, New Mexico, next to White Sands Missile Range and Holloman Air Force Base, grew by 220 percent during the 1950s. Overall, there was massive migration into the American West. Between 1945 and 1960 alone, the population increased by 13 million, from 32 to 45 million. It appeared as if no area lay beyond the reach of the Cold War's effects.

One of the most dramatic consequences of this growth can be seen along the Interstate 25 corridor between Colorado Springs and the Wyoming–Colorado border. This expanding metropolis reveals the impact of federal dollars and the military-industrial complex on the economy and urban environment, with all of its added problems of traffic congestion, air pollution, limited water resources, and uncontrolled sprawl. This I-25 corridor exemplifies a landscape overburdened by human use.

Denver and Colorado Springs saw remarkable growth in the decade between 1950 and 1960 (Denver grew by 52 percent and Colorado Springs by 93 percent). Denver's suburbanization was particularly dramatic, with suburbs like Arvada and Westminster (located next to Rocky Flats, which opened in 1952) growing by over 700 percent during that decade. Although growth throughout the rest of the Cold War era was not as dramatic, both suburbs continued to expand by at least one-fourth to one-third every decade. Farther afield, by 1980 the farming communities of Fort Collins and Greeley, north of Denver, had become urban by census bureau definitions. By the end of the Cold War, the entire Front Range from Cheyenne, Wyoming, south to Pueblo, Colorado, possessed an urban feel as the major cities reached out to touch one another and were strung together by the interstate.

The central location of the state, combined with its natural beauty and mild climate, attracted an unusually high number of facilities to the area. Colorado Springs alone lured the $200 million Air Force Academy, completed in 1958, and the army's Fort Carson Military Reservation. The city also houses the $150 million Combat Operations Center of the North American Air Defense Command, a "bombproof" shell within Cheyenne Mountain, that acts as the control center for directing defensive and offensive measures in the event of a nuclear attack. Consequently, Colorado Springs feels very much like a military or company town in which the federal government and its contractors dominate the workplace and living space of the community.

Farther north, Denver has also experienced the influence of the government's Cold War efforts. After the Soviet Union detonated its first atomic bomb in 1949, the federal government designated Denver as the alternative capital to Washington, D.C. in the event of a nuclear war. Consequently, the Denver Federal Center, on the west side of town, began to sprawl when agencies set up offices in the complex. Denver also remains home to such Cold War facilities as Rocky Flats, Lowry Air Force Base, the Rocky Mountain Arsenal, and defense contractor Martin Marietta. With over 33,000 federal employees by 1980, more than any other city except Washington, D.C., Denver ranked as the West's greatest federal nerve center. These economic forces, combined with the natural beauty of the area, have drawn hundreds of thousands to the Front Range and compelled them to stay.

The result has been a dramatic sprawl that extends beyond the immediate metro area of Denver and Colorado Springs. Each year of the Cold War saw Denver spread farther south to meet Colorado Springs's own sprawl and farther north to engulf towns like Westminster, Longmont, Loveland, and even Fort Collins. The environmental consequences have been potentially devastating. They have also been far-reaching. How much and how fast the Front Range of Colorado grows affects the rest of the state. Residents of Colorado's western slope, a relative loser in the bid for Cold War federal dollars, bitterly complain about the resources used by Denver and its environs. In particular, the Front Range's demand for Colorado River water always make them deeply suspicious. Dave Wattenberg, a state legislator from the western slope, says that it was not until he came to the capital that he found out the " 'Damn Denver Water Department' wasn't all one word." Even the San Luis Valley residents, 250 miles to the south, who sit on top of one of the largest aquifers in the West, fear losing the resource to the thirsty cities of Denver, Albuquerque, and even Los Angeles. As the Front Range's growth spirals out of control, questions arise as to how this growth rate can or should be sustained. How will traffic flow problems be resolved as the area continues to sprawl? Will Denver's and Los Angeles's "brown clouds" ever recede? Where will the water come from to wash the clothes, kids, and cars of this burgeoning population? Only now, when it is almost too late, have people and politicians on the Front Range come to realize the potential range of problems inherited from this postwar population boom.

How did all of these people get from their rural homes of the prewar era to their suburban landscapes today? The answer is highways. One indirect effect of the Cold War on the American western landscape has been the creation of the federal interstate highway system. It was not merely coincidence that President Dwight D. Eisenhower chose Lucius Clay to design and implement the country's highway system. In 1948 Clay had orchestrated the successful Berlin Airlift, one of the initial and most dramatic altercations of the Cold War. In the mind of the president, fighting the Cold War directly impacted the nation's civil defense system and the highways.

In 1956 President Eisenhower signed the Interstate Highway Act, institutionalizing the cross-continental system of travel that linked the West with the rest of America. The bill intended to finance 41,000 miles of limited-access, multi-lane highways, which would link all the major cities of the United States. In part, the government intended it as a civil defense measure in order to quickly move material and troops in the event of an invasion from a foreign government. The highways also supposedly provided a quick and usable escape route from the cities in the event of a nuclear attack. Planners naively envisioned an orderly procession of citizens calmly moving away from urban centers to the unpopulated hinterland. A plan for emergency mail service topped off the list of emergency procedures. Fortunately, the intended military uses proved unnecessary. The more far-reaching impact, however, and one that is still felt today, has been the real physical presence of the highways on the landscape.

The original appropriation of $27 billion allowed the federal government to transform the landscape in ways that probably had not been imagined. Massive earth-moving equipment, advancements in civil engineering, and relatively inexpensive materials, such as asphalt, allowed road builders to depart from the narrow confines of mountain passes and water-level routes. Now, highway engineers went through mountains with tunnels (Colorado's Eisenhower/ Johnson Tunnel is but one spectacular example, with almost nine million cars passing through it yearly), or simply moved mountains if they were in the way. Few natural topographic landforms would impede Americans' mobility.

Earlier in the nineteenth century, the power of the railroad to transform American business and home life overwhelmed commentators, who were impressed by the iron horse's ability to move goods and people across the landscape at such rapid speeds. The railroad allowed Americans to move farther faster. The highway system, however, exceeded all standards established by the railroads, and dominated the way Americans lived, organized their worlds, and traveled. Now Americans could move as fast as they wanted and where they wanted without having to rely on an institution to provide a service. The ability to transport oneself anywhere and at any time liberated Americans. This individualistic mode of transportation also transformed American communities. Small towns have died and others have been born because of the location of the highway. The highway system also transformed larger cities, as these federal monies gave cities an impetus to engulf and incorporate neighboring municipalities. Between 1950 and 1980, Houston expanded from 160 to 556 square miles, Phoenix from 17 to 324 square miles, and Oklahoma City from 51 to 603 square miles, each city all the while needing new roads and highway systems to move people efficiently. The highway system also produced an "exit" culture based on what Americans wanted when they got off of the highway for a break: a gas station, a fast-food distributor, and a clean bathroom, and preferably all in a one-stop location. Most Americans forgot about seeing local color or eating home cooking: it took too long and you might not get what you wanted to eat. A Big Mac is a Big Mac, no matter which exit you take.

Furthermore, locations where Interstates intersected—I-40 and I-25 in Albuquerque and I-70 and I-25 in Denver, to name but two—came to mark the crossroads of the nation. They further emphasized the "oasis" culture that has defined the American West. Long stretches of empty highway would periodically be broken up by the powerful lights of a city and the ability to make a ninety-degree turn and continue on your way efficiently. The highway system also provided infinite growth possibilities for urban areas, as trucking became a more efficient and cost-beneficial way for moving trade goods. Unconsciously, Americans have come to think about their place in the American West based on their access to highways, freeways, roads, and streets instead of thinking about their place in relation to natural geography such as rivers, mountains, or lakes. What began as a somewhat kooky defense measure has completely transformed the physical and mental landscape of westerners and their world.

The direct impact of the Cold War, because of the development of military installations and highways, has left the most visible marks on the American West. Nevertheless, the indirect effects of the Cold War and the culture of the postwar period have also influenced the use of land. People's demand to emerge from the scarce times of the Depression and the rationing of World War II pulled Americans into an unprecedented consumer culture that had never existed before in the United States. This was particularly acute in boom centers in the West. By 1980, for example, Houston was not only the national leader in population growth and employment growth, but also growth in retail sales and per capita income. This demand for durable goods, inexpensive fuel sources, and the perfect single-family home with a lawn became a part of the American Dream. Americans' search for this ideal created two consequences for the American West: exploitation of natural resources and suburbanization.

Because of the United States' emerging ties with the global economy and its increasing dependence on foreign oil, the post–World War II era saw this country engage in some of the most aggressive fuel exploration ever. In 1972 Texas alone produced 1.3 billion barrels of oil, and the state's petroleum industry employed 300,000 people. The energy crisis of the 1970s led to an intensive search for oil off the coast of California and in Alaska's interior. It also prompted such interesting experiments as searching for oil shale in order to extract the fossil fuel kerogen, which embedded itself in the limestone formations under western Colorado's, and parts of Utah's and Wyoming's landscape.

The western slope of Colorado, particularly towns such as Parachute and Rifle, saw another boom-and-bust period come and go in the 1970s with the oil shale experiment. Oil companies, with the help of subsidies from the federal government, moved in and promised jobs. Housing developments and communities such as Battlement Mesa grew to meet the potential demands of those flocking to the area. But, just as quickly as they came, the companies fled the area, leaving little behind but their abandoned sites and empty developments for those who had speculated on the power of such a nascent technology. Dee Martin, one local hopeful, summed it up best in Patricia Nelson Limerick's *Legacy of Conquest*: "Man, I had the American dream. A wife, 2½ kids and two cars. Now I have an empty pocket. We came in sunny side up this morning and the world turned upside down."

Oil shale was but one resource that held potential for solving the nation's energy shortage. Natural gas also seemed like a quick and easy fix for the problem. Project Plowshares, which set off small underground nuclear explosions in order to release natural gas from its hiding places in western Colorado, provides another example of the faith Americans held in nuclear technology. The high cost of fossil fuels led some states, California in particular, to experiment and use nuclear energy to meet the demands of the rapidly expanding urban economy. Nuclear energy seemed to be relatively clean, inexpensive in the long-run, and renewable. When anti-nuclear protestors, however, began to question the wisdom of locating reactors on geological faults, the industry was put on hold as scientists tried to engineer their way around the problem. Americans, and westerners in particular, have always been in love with cheap fuel and are not particular either: natural gas, oil, coal, or uranium all serve the purpose. What westerners, however, have not been so happy with are the consequences of their great love.

Oil spills off the coast of California, particularly the 1969 spill that contaminated the Santa Barbara Channel and the devastation caused by the Exxon tanker spill in Valdez, Alaska, underscore the risks westerners take everyday in their search for oil. Promoters of the Alaska pipeline quickly drew the public's attention to the increased per capita income lavished on Alaska's citizens and to the pictures of deer frolicking by the 4-foot-diameter pipeline. Yet, we still know little about the repercussions from bisecting an ecosystem with an eight-hundred-mile pipe and letting warm oil flow across the frozen tundra. In terms of impact on humans, the boom/bust cycle so typical to westerners again visited towns like Fairbanks, which endured the problems of overcrowding and limited facilities for the more than 20,000 workers and their families who came to work for the Aleyaska consortium of oil companies. Fairbanks's residents also had to pick up the pieces once the bust came and the jobs had moved elsewhere.

On the other hand, because of popular hostility to reactors, nuclear energy has provided even fewer viable solutions to the problems of western consumption. While a few reactors still supply western cities, most projects, like Diablo Canyon in California, have been closed in large part because of pressure from hostile public opinion. Instead, westerners, like other Americans, continue to rely on nonrenewable energy sources like coal and oil. Ironically, the real costs of extracting coal and oil, in terms of lives lost through mining accidents and related deaths, as well as the price we all pay each day as we breathe dirtier air, are arguably higher than the cost of reactors.

But the familiarity of mining coal and drilling for oil might make it less troubling to the western mind. The miner or oilman are quintessentially figures of western romance. Like the mountain man, rancher, and lumberjack, the wildcatter and miner fit in with the free-wheeling, buccaneer image of the westerner as speculator, living off the land, wandering from camp to canyon in search of natural bounty, and armed only with a mule and pickaxe. For suburban westerners, who have become accustomed to seeing the western landscape altered in this way, it may be easier to tolerate the depredations of the miner— the gouges in the earth, the mountains of toxic tailings, the eroded watersheds, and most of all, the hundreds of miners smothered by collapsing mines or black lung disease—than the silent, ominous presence of cooling towers. The reactors represent everything that the westerner allegedly rejects: immobile, centrally regulated structures that generate energy not from the local bounty of nature but rather from the cool artifice of technology.

Moreover, the effects of searching for coal and oil has had uneven results across the American West. The Four Corners area, with a mostly Native American and Mexican American population, is but one example of these disproportionate effects. What makes the area particularly vulnerable is the abundance of its rich natural resources that have provided coal, falling water, and uranium, depending on the state of technology and Americans' ability to extract the resource. In general, ethnic and poor communities have always borne the cost of living a miner's life through higher incidence of work-related deaths, emphysema, silicosis, and cancer. In particular, people on the Navajo and Hopi reservations have borne these costs and witnessed the erosion and devastating effects of Peabody Coal's strip mining of Black Mountain for coal. Uranium mining, the most recent endeavor on the reservation, has been no more friendly to those people who work in the mines or to the landscape itself. Westerners, mostly Native Americans, shoulder the cost of living in one of the most polluted areas in terms of air quality. The Navajo Coal plant near Page, Arizona, built, ironically, because David Brower and other environmentalists stopped the Grand Canyon dam project, spits out billows of dark air across the

Four Corners area. The plant cut back emissions only when tourists complained that the smog obstructed their view of the Grand Canyon. Furthermore, the Farmington–Four Corners coal-fired plants generate 22,000 megawatts of electricity, which mainly supplies Southern California. Together, the two complexes emitted such large amounts of steam and pollution that shuttle travelers noticed the pollution in the area as they orbited the earth.

The costs of environmental degradation, however, are not confined only to rural areas or to poor people. Residents of most western metropolises live everyday with the consequences of too many people making too much pollution. In Colorado Springs, residents look every day at "the Scar" on the side of one of the city's most visible mountains. The residue from the quarry is a testament to the boom in construction, which placed a large demand on the areas resources for creating cement. Residents of most urban areas, however, do not live with the costs of generating their electricity in remote locations like Nevada or Arizona. Whether for fuel, aesthetics, or convenience, westerners always seem willing to make a deal and absorb the costs—hopefully at someone else's direct expense.

Perhaps the most dramatic change that has occurred in the American West during the Cold War era has been the suburbanization of the landscape. World War II drew people away from their rural homes and into the burgeoning urban and suburban built environments of western, oasislike cities. The Cold War era saw an unprecedented increase in marriage and birth rates. People married younger, had more children, and searched for the ideal home safe from the outside world of Cold War politics and the threat of nuclear war. As Elaine Tyler May, in her book *Homeward Bound* points out, it was no accident that the "kitchen debates" between Vice President Richard Nixon and Soviet President Nikita Khrushchev became a focal point of Cold War politics. While Americans might have been willing to concede that the Communists could win in the space race, they remained unflagging in their faith that capitalism provided the best society for raising a healthy, happy, and socially and economically stable family.

This desire for the perfect life became embodied in the "ranch"-style home, which began dotting the suburban landscape from Orange County, California, to Levittown, Pennsylvania. Even the term *ranch* suggested an open, sprawling, western approach to living. No longer would women trudge up and down stairs as they went about their daily routines of cooking, clothes washing, cleaning, vacuuming, and chasing kids. Instead, the ranch home promised a world of easy living for the entire family, complete with large sidewalks and cul-de-sacs for children to play and a barbecue pit in the backyard so Dad could cook on the weekends. The consequences of this "good life" in suburbia have been played out on the environment of suburban sprawl. With this sprawl came increased demand for water, natural resources, and fuel, all of which Westerners too rapidly deplete.

Westerners see the tangible impact of the Cold War at almost every turn. What they may not realize is the mental adaptations they have made to accommodate this new environment. The Cold War influenced westerners' ideas about land, nature, and their relationship to it. They left their rural homes for the opportunities opened to them by cash-paying, blue- and white-collar jobs, urbanization, and suburbanization. This migration from rural to urban left "empty" places behind. What was now perceived as vacant and useless land could be turned over to other, more utilitarian, uses of rural space. The federal government, eager to continue its weapons programs to fight the Cold War, stepped into the void and converted thousands of square miles of this empty landscape into military installations, proving grounds, testing sights, and laboratories. It was, however, westerners' move to urban centers that made such land use by the federal government feasible and desirable.

Americans historically have deemed certain places as "empty" or "wasted" space. In the late eighteenth century, as the new nation formed, Americans labeled all the area west of the Mississippi empty and "reserved" it for Indians. Even as the American West filled during the nineteenth century, few European Americans were willing to venture into the desert: only with modern technology has the desert been deemed inhabitable and desirable. But this division between what Americans deem inhabited and uninhabited, rural and urban, empty and full, denies the interconnectedness of the world around us. These dichotomies also deny the profound effect that our connections to such seemingly remote places as WIPP, missile silos, or Los Alamos, can have on our lives and those of our children. Perhaps these dichotomies, and how we choose to view them, explain generational differences between baby-boomers and their parents. Children of the Cold War era who have lived with the legacy of the atomic age have been less willing to accept these dichotomies than have their parents. Rather, we see our connections to the larger world. I look at Rocky Flats and I cannot help but note my relationship to it and its relationship to the rest of the world. Cold War domestic and international politics have left me no choice.

BIBLIOGRAPHIC ESSAY

Recent general studies of the American West that have considered the twentieth-century history of the region include Patricia Nelson Limerick, *Legacy of Conquest: The Unbroken Past of the American West* (New York: W. W. Norton, 1987), and Richard White, *"It's Your Misfortune and None of My Own": A History of the American West* (Norman: University of

Oklahoma Press, 1991). Michael P. Malone and Richard W. Etulain, *The American West: A Twentieth-Century History* (Lincoln: University of Nebraska Press, 1989) provide a useful section on the economic consequences of the post–World War II buildup, and many of the examples in this essay come from their book. Richard Etulain and Gerald Nash, eds., *The Twentieth-Century West: Historical Interpretations* (Albuquerque: University of New Mexico Press, 1989) is also a helpful study of the era. Finally, Peter Wiley and Robert Gottlieb, *Empires in the Sun: The Rise of the New American West* (New York: Putnam, 1982) provide one of the most provocative looks at the relationship between eastern interests, the federal government, and westerners in the twentieth century.

Regarding the impact of World War II on the American West, see the following works by Gerald Nash: *The American West Transformed: The Impact of the Second World War* (Bloomington: Indiana University Press, 1985); *The American West in the Twentieth Century: A Short History of an Urban Oasis* (Englewood Cliffs: Prentice-Hall, 1973); *World War II and the West: Reshaping the Economy* (Lincoln: University of Nebraska Press, 1990), and "New Mexico Since 1940: An Overview" in *Contemporary New Mexico, 1940–1990*, ed. Richard Etulain (Albuquerque: University of New Mexico Press, 1994).

Historians have begun to look at the connections between the American West and the larger world market system throughout the nineteenth and twentieth centuries. In particular, see William Cronon, *Nature's Metropolis: Chicago and the Great West* (New York: W. W. Norton, 1991), who underscores the importance of thinking about how the West became economically and geographically tied to Chicago and consequently other eastern cities. See also, William Robbins, *Colony and Empire: The Capitalist Transformation of the American West* (Lawrence: University of Kansas Press, 1994).

Regarding the idea of deserts and their place in American society, see in particular Patricia Nelson Limerick, *Desert Passages: Encounters with the American Deserts* (Albuquerque: University of New Mexico Press, 1985); Wallace Stegner's biography of John Wesley Powell, *Beyond the Hundredth Meridian: John Wesley Powell and the Second Opening of the West* (Boston: Houghton Mifflin, 1954); and Edward Abbey, *Desert Solitaire: A Season in the Wilderness* (New York: Simon and Schuster, 1968).

One of the most exciting and new areas of scholarship has centered around the nuclear West. For a few examples of this work, see Phillip L. Fradkin, *Fallout: An American Nuclear Tragedy* (Tucson: University of Arizona Press, 1989); Peter Goin, *Nuclear Landscapes* (Baltimore: Johns Hopkins University Press, 1991); Tad Bartimus and Scott McCartney, *Trinity's Children: Living Along America's Nuclear Highway* (New York: Harcourt Brace Jovanovich, 1991); and Raye Carleson Ringholz, *Uranium Frenzy: Boom and Bust on the Colorado Plateau* (Albuquerque: University of New Mexico Press, 1991). For more personal accounts of people's experiences with the Cold War, see Terry Tempest Williams, *Refuge: An Unnatural History of Family and Place* (New York: Vintage Books, 1992), and Stewart L. Udall, *The Myths of August: A Personal Exploration of Our Tragic Cold War Affair with the Atom* (New York: Pantheon Books, 1994).

New Mexico has received more than its share of nuclear facilities, and Los Alamos National Laboratories are the most striking examples of this federal patronage. Regarding the history of the Pajarito Plateau and the coming of Los Alamos National Laboratories, see

Hal K. Rothman, *On Rims and Ridges: The Los Alamos Area Since 1880* (Lincoln: University of Nebraska Press, 1992), and Fern Lyon and Jacob Evans, *Los Alamos: The First Forty Years* (Los Alamos: Los Alamos Historical Society, 1984), which is a collection of primary source material that details the story of the labs' arrival and expansion.

New Mexico has also been a haven for artists and sick people looking for a rejuvenating climate. Regarding the art world see: Julie Schimmel and Robert R. White, *Bert Geer Phillips and the Taos Art Colony* (Albuquerque: University of New Mexico Press, 1994); Sherry Clayton Taggett and Ted Schwarz, *Paintbrushes and Pistols: How the Taos Artists Sold the West* (Santa Fe: John Muir Publications, 1990); and Charles C. Eldredge, *Art in New Mexico, 1900–1945: Paths to Taos and Santa Fe* (Washington, D.C.: National Museum of American Art, Smithsonian Institution, 1986). For a concise history of New Mexico's appeal to the sick, see Jake W. Spidle, *Doctors of Medicine in New Mexico: A History of Health and Medical Practice, 1886–1986* (Albuquerque: University of New Mexico, 1986).

The Denver metropolitan area has been another large beneficiary of Cold War dollars. For works relating to the Front Range in the post–World War II era, see Stephen J. Leonard and Thomas J. Noel, *Denver: Mining Camp to Metropolis* (Niwot: University Press of Colorado, 1990); Carl Abbott, Stephen J. Leonard, and David McComb, *Colorado: A History of the Centennial State* (Niwot: University Press of Colorado, 1982); Thomas T. Veblen, *The Colorado Front Range: A Century of Ecological Change* (Salt Lake City: University of Utah Press, 1991). For a more recent look at the impact of suburbanization on the area, see Michael E. Long, "Colorado's Front Range," in *National Geographic*, vol. 190 (November 1996), p. 80. For information on urban growth during the period in other areas, see Spencer Olin, "Globalization and the Politics of Locality: Orange County, California in the Cold War Era," *Western Historical Quarterly* 22 (May 1991): 143–62, and Robert B. Fairbanks and Kathleen Underwood, eds., *Essays On Sunbelt Cities and Recent Urban America* (College Station: Texas A & M Press, 1990).

Perhaps the most dramatic effects on the landscape have been created by the national highway system. Regarding the interstate system see Mark H. Rose, *Interstate: Express Highway Politics, 1939–1989* (Knoxville: University of Tennessee Press, 1990), and Phil Patton, *Open Road: A Celebration of the American Highway* (New York: Simon and Schuster, 1986). Although her book is about the early twentieth century, an interesting look at the impact of cars and mobility on American culture is Virginia Scharff, *Taking the Wheel: Women and the Coming of the Motor Age* (New York: Free Press, 1991).

Suburbs and commuting became a part of American life as a direct result of the interstate system. Regarding suburbanization see John M. Findley, *Magic Lands: Western Cityscapes and American Culture After 1940* (Berkeley: University of California Press, 1992); Kenneth T. Jackson, *Crabgrass Frontier: The Suburbanization of America* (New York: Oxford University Press, 1985); Carl Abbott, *The New Urban America: Growth and Politics in Sunbelt Cities* (Chapel Hill: University of North Carolina Press, 1987), and Carl Abbott, *The Metropolitan Frontier: Cities in the Modern American West* (Tucson: University of Arizona Press, 1993). Regarding the social impact of this suburbanization, see Elaine Tyler May, *Homeward Bound: American Families in the Cold War Era* (New York: Basic Books, 1988).

The search for available water resources has occupied westerners as they settle in the cities of the region. This rich literature includes such books as Marc Reisner, *Cadillac Desert: The American West and Its Disappearing Water* (New York: Penguin Books, 1993); Donald Worster, *Rivers of Empire: Water, Aridity, and the Growth of the American West* (New York: Pantheon Books, 1985); and Norris Hundley, Jr., *The Great Thirst: California and Water, 1770s–1990s* (Berkeley: University of California Press, 1992).

On the social costs of searching for fuel sources, see, for example, Mim Dixon, *What Happened to Fairbanks?* (Boulder: Westview Press, 1978), and John Meeham, *Atom and the Fault: Experts, Earthquake, and Nuclear Power* (Cambridge: MIT Press, 1984). Regarding the Four Corners area, in particular, see Arthur R. Gomez, *Quest for the Golden Circle: The Four Corners and the Metropolitan West, 1945–1970* (Albuquerque: University of New Mexico Press, 1994), and Donald Baars, *Navajo Country: A Geology and Natural History of the Four Corners Region* (Albuquerque: University of New Mexico Press, 1995). For particular information on the WIPP site in New Mexico see, Louis John Colombo, "Organizing in a 'National Sacrifice Area': The Radioactive Waste Campaign in New Mexico" (Ph.D. diss., University of Michigan, 1981); and *Waste Isolation Pilot Plan—WIPP* (Carlsbad, NM: U.S. Department of Energy, 1988).

For general information on missiles, see Samuel H. J. Day, ed., *Nuclear Heartland: A Guide to the 1,000 Missile Silos in the United States* (Madison: Nukewatch/The Progressive Foundation, 1988), and Thomas B. Cochran, Milton M. Hoenig, and William M. Arkin, *Nuclear Weapons Databook*, vol. 1: *U.S. Nuclear Forces and Capabilities* (Cambridge: Ballinger Publishing Company, 1984). Regarding nuclear weapons production and storage, see National Research Council, *The Nuclear Weapons Complex: Management for Health, Safety, and the Environment* (Washington, D.C.: National Academy Press, 1989); and Dana Coyle, et al., *Deadly Defense: Military Radioactive Landfills* (New York: Radioactive Watch Campaign, 1988).

CHAPTER TWO

MIGRANTS, IMMIGRANTS, AND REFUGEES

The Cold War and Population Growth in the American West

❧

KEVIN ALLEN LEONARD

As World War II ended, my grandfather, James E. Inman, returned from Europe to his home and family in Lombard, Illinois, a Chicago suburb. Although he may have experienced some anxiety about his future, he did not need to worry about a job. Prior to his induction into the Army, my grandfather had worked as a civil engineer for the Atchison, Topeka, and Santa Fe Railway for nearly twenty years. Even during the worst days of the Depression, he had been able to keep his job, although he worked reduced hours. After the war, he could anticipate returning to his comfortable position with the railroad.

Unlike my grandfather, however, many other World War II veterans could not look forward to good, secure jobs. As the nation demobilized, many Americans feared that the wartime boom would collapse and that depression would again engulf the country. People with a wide range of political beliefs argued that Congress needed to pass legislation to prevent the return of depression. This legislation, usually called "full-employment" legislation, committed the federal government to public works projects and other federal spending to maintain the low unemployment rate of the war years. Some people, most of them on the liberal end of the political spectrum, expected that demobilization would have an especially deleterious effect on members of racial and religious minority groups. They urged Congress to pass fair employment legislation, which would outlaw discrimination by employers and unions, as well as full employment legislation.

Congress did not pass fair employment legislation until 1964, but it passed a full-employment act in 1946. By 1950, however, the federal government had embarked on a program that rendered the full-employment law superfluous.

This program involved spending massive amounts of money (tens of billions of dollars in the 1950s; $300 billion by the late 1980s) every year to mobilize, maintain, and equip a standing army of at least 700,000 people, a navy of more than 500,000, an air force of more than 500,000, and a marine corps of around 200,000. The maintenance of this military might included the development and production of aircraft, ships, tanks, and weapons—nuclear, chemical, and "conventional."

This massive government spending on the military, a hallmark of the Cold War, had a direct impact on my grandfather and his family. The military's demand for uranium for its nuclear arsenal, coupled with the promise of nonmilitary uses for radioactive isotopes of the element, led some landowners in the West to develop uranium mines. In 1950 the Santa Fe railroad transferred James Inman to Prewitt, New Mexico, where it was digging such a mine. A year later, his wife Evelyn and his youngest child Ruth Ann (my mother) joined him in the West. The family established its home in Albuquerque. "I liked Albuquerque," my mother recalled, "but I didn't have all that wonderful a first year, because I didn't have that many friends." Eventually, she made friends with other young people and she was happy in New Mexico's largest city.

This essay begins with this story about my family because it is impossible for me to remove myself from the subject. The Cold War brought my family to the West, and I was born and grew up in the Cold War West. The essay begins with my family's story, too, because my family's experiences strike me as ordinary. In the West in which I grew up, I was surrounded by people who had moved to the West or within the West because of Cold War policies. The booming cities of much of the Cold War West were largely populated by families like mine, brought to the West by uranium mining, war production, or the military, and like María Montoya's, attracted from the rural valleys of the West to the urban centers of weapons and aircraft production.

Using my family and other individuals as examples, this essay will describe how the Cold War increased the population of the West. Like World War II, the Cold War brought millions of migrants, immigrants, and refugees to the western United States. The essay will argue that, unlike World War II, the Cold War tended to reinforce the existing segmentation within the western labor force. As White men secured high-paying technical and professional jobs, White women, African Americans, Mexican Americans, and immigrants from Latin America and Asia filled the low-wage jobs in the agricultural and service sectors of the western economy. Many of the immigrants who entered the United States were refugees fleeing from wars or from repressive regimes, most of them supported by U.S. administrations. The majority of these refugees settled in the West due to its proximity to their homelands and due to the existence of substantial Asian and Latina/Latino communities in the region. Cold War refugees of another kind—lesbians and gay men discharged by the U.S. military or by federal, state, or local governments in anti-gay purges—also settled in western cities in large numbers. Although Cold War military spending provided good jobs for many of the people who migrated to the West, many of those jobs evaporated when the Cold War ended after the collapse of the Berlin Wall in 1989. The end of the Cold War also seems to have contributed to increased racial and ethnic tensions in much of the West.

Any essay that purports to be about the West must define the boundaries of the region. In *"It's Your Misfortune and None of My Own,"* Richard White argued that history has defined the West. Western states are western, White pointed out, not because they possess some essential and timeless "western" characteristics, but because they have developed as western states. White states simply, "The American West is that contiguous section of the continent west of the Missouri River acquired by the United States, beginning with the Louisiana Purchase of 1803; continuing through the acquisition of Texas, the Oregon Territory, and the Mexican Cession in the 1840s; and ending with the 1854 Gadsden Purchase of the lands between the Gila River and the present Mexican boundary." White's definition coincides perfectly with my delineation of the boundaries of the West for this essay.

White's critique of an "essential" or "natural" West, however, seems to force scholars to defend their identification of certain trends or events as "western." It makes sense to discuss a "Cold War West," for example, only if we can show that there were distinctly western patterns of historical development during the Cold War. The rate of population growth in the West during the Cold War distinguished the region from other parts of the United States. According to U.S. census data, the seventeen contiguous western states, taken as a unit, saw their population increase by about 120 percent during the forty years of the Cold War. By contrast, the South's population increased by 75 percent during the same period, the Midwest's population grew by 36 percent, and the Northeast's population rose by 29 percent. At the beginning of the Cold War, fewer than one of every four residents of the United States lived in the West. Forty years later, one of every three U.S. residents lived in the West.

The West's population grew as a result of three important trends: the dramatic increase in the birth rate that followed World War II and lasted until 1964 (the "Baby Boom"); migration from the eastern, southern, and midwestern states; and immigration from outside the United States. The sustained increase in the birth rate during the first twenty years of the Cold War was more important than migration or immigration to the growth of most western states. This increase in the birth rate, however, was a national phenomenon.

With a few exceptions, the birth rate in the West was not significantly higher or lower than the birth rate in other parts of the country. The more important phenomena for the study of the Cold War West, then, are migration and immigration.

Most Americans who migrated to the West during the Cold War came in search of jobs. Federal spending during World War II had allowed a fairly small number of western corporations to build and expand military manufacturing plants. These firms competed successfully for a large portion of the federal military budget during the Cold War. Over the course of the Cold War, nearly one-tenth of the entire military budget went to firms headquartered in a single western state—California. This money contributed to the creation of hundreds of thousands of jobs in the West. As early as 1959, 940,000 people in California—nearly 20 percent of the state's nonagricultural employees—were employed either by the Department of Defense or by military contractors. The same year, 22 percent of Washington's nonagricultural employees were either employed by the DOD or by military contractors, and 17 percent of Arizona's nonagricultural employees were engaged in military work.

Pentagon contracts served to perpetuate their importance in the regional economy. The large corporations spawned smaller subcontractors and devoted billions of dollars to research and development, or "R and D." "R and D" money promoted the growth of a military manufacturing infrastructure in the West. The existence of this infrastructure enhanced the ability of corporations with plants in the West to secure additional contracts. In the first twenty years of the Cold War, 60,000 new jobs in the manufacture of durable goods were created in the state of Washington alone. In the same period, more than 240,000 of these jobs were created in Texas, and more than 570,000 such jobs were created in California.

The U.S. armed forces assisted western employers in their efforts to find employees. During the Cold War, the military ordered millions of its personnel to move to bases in the western states. John Tunney, for example, a New York City native and a graduate of Yale and the University of Virginia law school, was called to serve in the Air Force in 1960. The Air Force assigned him to the Advocate General's office at March Air Force Base near Riverside, California. Tunney was just one of more than eighteen million men and women who served in the U.S. armed forces between the eruption of the Korean War in 1950 and the demolition of the Berlin Wall in 1989. Although this number obviously included people from the West (especially from the populous states of California and Texas), it also included millions of people from the East, Midwest, and South who ended up being stationed at bases in the West. During most Cold War years, more military personnel were stationed in California than in any other state. Texas ranked second in the number of military personnel. In 1960, for example, 300,000 military personnel were on bases in California, and 160,000 were on bases in Texas. In both states, the number of military personnel far outnumbered the number of people employed by any other single entity.

Some of the people who were ordered to come to the West decided to remain in the region. When Tunney was discharged in 1963, for example, he decided to remain in Riverside and practice law. Tunney's recent arrival in the region did not prevent him from pursuing a career in politics. He was elected to the U.S. House of Representatives in 1964 and reelected in 1966 and 1968. In 1970 he won election to the U.S. Senate. Tunney's experiences were not typical of those of military personnel who were assigned to bases in the West. Most military personnel were enlisted personnel, not officers, and they took skilled jobs rather than professional positions when they were discharged.

Many of these military personnel, veterans, and other migrants found themselves living and working together in "urban fortresses," because weapons and aircraft manufacturers often situated their new plants near military bases. Military bases in Orange County, California—the Los Alamitos Naval Air Station, a Naval Weapons Station, and the Marine Corps air stations at Santa Ana and El Toro—helped to attract a number of manufacturers to the county. McDonnell-Douglas, Ford Aerospace, Hughes Aircraft, and General Dynamics operated plants in Orange County. Sailors, marines, and willing workers flooded into the county in the 1950s and 1960s. Anaheim, for example, grew by 1,045 percent in those two decades (from 14,556 to 166,701), and Fullerton, the site of the Hughes Aircraft plant, grew by more than 500 percent (from 13,958 to 85,826). According to one estimate for 1960, two-thirds of all manufacturing employment in Orange County was tied in one way or another to military contracts. By 1990, Anaheim's population had climbed to more than 266,000, and Fullerton's population had grown to 114,000.

A similar process occurred in the south San Francisco Bay Area. Lockheed moved part of its operations to Sunnyvale, near Moffett Field Naval Air Station, and Stanford University spawned a substantial number of high-technology firms. Sunnyvale's population soared from 9,829 in 1950 to 95,408 in 1970 (an increase of 870 percent); Mountain View's population rocketed from 6,563 in 1950 to 51,092 in 1970 (678 percent); and San Jose's population quadrupled, from 95,280 in 1950 to 445,779 in 1970. According to one estimate from the late 1960s, 70 percent of the new jobs in Santa Clara County depended in some way upon military and space-related money. By 1990, 117,000 people lived in Sunnyvale, 67,000 lived in Mountain View, and 782,000 lived in San Jose.

These patterns also affected cities outside California. For example, as military contractors opened plants in Tucson and as Davis-Monthan Air Force Base drew migrants to the city, its population grew from 45,454 in 1950 to 262,933 in 1970, an increase of 478 percent. By 1990, more than 400,000 people lived in Tucson. Fort Carson, an Air Force base, the Air Force Academy, the NORAD headquarters beneath Cheyenne Mountain, and plants operated by Digital Equipment, Honeywell, TRW Electronics, Raytheon, Hughes Aircraft, and Hewlett-Packard drew more than 200,000 new residents to Colorado Springs, whose population tripled between 1950 and 1970, and nearly doubled again between 1970 and 1990.

Although the military and military contractors created millions of jobs and brought millions of migrants to the West, the region's population growth was not even or uniform. My family's experiences underscore the complexity of the Cold War's impact on population growth in the West. My mother's family remained in New Mexico for only three years before the railroad sent her father back to Chicago. Although their stay in the West had been brief, it had a powerful impact on the Inmans. The move left them rootless. Before 1950, the family had lived in Lombard for more than fifteen years. After they returned to Illinois in 1953, the Inmans never lived in one place for more than a few years. First they lived in Park Forest, south of Chicago, where Ruth Ann graduated from high school. By the time Ruth Ann graduated from Illinois State Normal University in 1960, her parents had moved to Naperville, southwest of Chicago. By 1962, they had moved to Downers Grove.

While she was in college, Ruth Ann met Charles "Chuck" Leonard, a student at Illinois Wesleyan University whose life had also been disrupted by the Cold War. Leonard, a native of Rantoul, Illinois, had spent two years in the military before he met his future wife. In 1960 Ruth Ann Inman and Chuck Leonard married, and they established their home in Chuck's hometown. Chuck worked in his family's furniture store, and Ruth Ann taught first grade in a public school. In early 1961, Ruth Ann and Chuck moved to Onarga, a small town thirty miles north of Rantoul, where Chuck opened a branch of the furniture store. Chuck's mother, who managed the store in Rantoul, was dissatisfied with the performance of the Onarga store. By 1963, Ruth Ann and Chuck began to contemplate moving to the West. When the furniture store in Onarga closed in the fall of 1963, Ruth Ann, Chuck, and their one-year-old son left Illinois for Albuquerque. Two years later, James Inman retired and returned with Evelyn to Albuquerque, where they built a home.

In moving to New Mexico in 1963, my parents joined a stream of migrants to the Southwest. In the 1950s and 1960s, many residents of midwestern states left their homes for the milder climate of and the promise of good jobs in the "sunbelt West." More than 400,000 Iowans left that state in the first two decades of the Cold War. Some of these people undoubtedly moved to the metropolitan centers of Minneapolis and Chicago, but many others moved westward. Cold War migration patterns often continued earlier patterns. For example, during the 1950s and 1960s, nearly 900,000 people followed in the tracks of Depression and World War II migrants and left the three states of Arkansas, Oklahoma, and Louisiana. Although some of these people undoubtedly moved to Texas, that state's net population gain from migration was only 260,000. Some Arkansans, Oklahomans, and Louisianans stopped and stayed in New Mexico and Arizona, but thousands of others ended up in California.

In the first two decades of the Cold War, more than 2.8 million people left their homes in the South. The majority of southern African Americans and many White southerners who left the region went to the urban North, but many moved West, especially to Texas, Arizona, and California. Many of the people who moved into the "sunbelt West" came from other western states, such as Idaho, Montana, and Wyoming. In the first two decades of the Cold War, more than 80,000 people left Idaho, another 75,000 left Montana, and 60,000 left Wyoming.

This migration radically transformed the "sunbelt West." The states of California, Arizona, Nevada, Utah, Colorado, New Mexico, and Texas saw sustained (and sometimes spectacular) growth throughout the forty-plus years of the Cold War. From 1950 through 1990, Arizona's population increased nearly fivefold (389 percent), from less than 750,000 in 1950 to more than 3.6 million in 1990. California's population nearly tripled (181 percent), from 10.6 million in 1950 to 29.8 million in 1990. The population of Texas, the slowest-growing "sunbelt" state, more than doubled (120 percent), from 7.7 million in 1950 to 17.0 million in 1990.

Although it makes little sense to refer to Washington and Oregon as "sunbelt" states, since the majority of those states' residents reside in the cloudy and wet western valleys, growth patterns in both states resembled those of the sunbelt West. Washington's population doubled, from nearly 2.4 million in 1950 to more than 4.8 million in 1990, and Oregon's population grew by 87 percent, from 1.5 million in 1950 to 2.8 million in 1990. Although there were important differences among the "sunbelt" states and Oregon and Washington, it is possible to lump them together in order to contrast these states with the remainder of the western states. I will refer to these nine states as the "mild-winter West." Table 2.1 indicates how rapidly the population of the mild-winter western states increased between 1950 and 1990.

After five years in Albuquerque, my father decided that he could provide his growing family with a more comfortable life if he took a job as a route salesman for a candy company. This new job required my family to move north along

Table 2.1: Population Growth of "Mild-Winter" Western States, 1950–1990

State	1950	1960	1970	1980	1990	Percentage Change, 1950–1990
Nevada	160,083	285,278	488,738	800,508	1,201,833	651
Arizona	749,587	1,302,161	1,775,399	2,716,546	3,665,228	389
California	10,586,223	15,717,204	19,971,069	23,667,764	29,760,021	181
Utah	688,802	890,627	1,059,273	1,461,037	1,722,850	150
Colorado	1,325,089	1,753,947	2,209,596	2,889,735	3,294,394	149
New Mexico	681,187	951,023	1,017,055	1,303,302	1,515,069	122
Texas	7,711,194	9,579,677	11,198,655	14,225,513	16,986,510	120
Washington	2,378,963	2,853,214	3,413,244	4,132,353	4,866,692	105
Oregon	1,521,341	1,768,687	2,091,533	2,633,156	2,842,321	87

Interstate 25—"America's nuclear highway," according to Tad Bartimus and Scott McCartney—to Casper, Wyoming, where I received my primary and secondary education and where my parents still live. In moving to Wyoming, my family anticipated a larger trend. During the "energy boom" of the 1970s, the population of states such as Oklahoma and Wyoming grew at rates comparable to the growth rates of mild-winter western states.

Over the course of the Cold War, however, these states grew much more slowly than the mild-winter states. Whereas federal military-contract money poured into the mild-winter West, this money trickled into the "hard-winter West." In 1981, when California firms received military contracts worth $16.6 billion, Idaho firms received military contracts worth only $28 million. While the mild-winter West grew consistently during the Cold War, states in the hard-winter West sometimes saw their populations shrink. As Table 2.2 shows, during the 1960s, for example, South Dakota and North Dakota actually lost population, as did North Dakota and Wyoming in the 1980s. For the entire period, Idaho's population grew by only 71 percent, from less than 589,000 in 1950 to just over 1 million in 1990. Montana's population crept from 591,000 in 1950 to 799,000 in 1990, an increase of only 35 percent. At the opposite extreme from Nevada was North Dakota, whose population rose by only 3 percent, from 620,000 in 1950 to 639,000 in 1990.

The climate of economic growth in many mild-winter western cities attracted a diverse group of migrants to these urban areas. Many African Americans moved to western cities in the 1950s and 1960s. In 1961, for example, Maxine Waters, her husband, Edward, and their two children left St. Louis and

Table 2.2: Population Growth of "Hard-Winter" Western States

State	1950	1960	1970	1980	1990	Percentage Change, 1950–1990
North Dakota	619,636	632,446	617,792	652,717	638,800	3
South Dakota	652,740	680,514	666,257	690,768	696,004	7
Nebraska	1,325,510	1,411,330	1,485,333	1,569,825	1,578,385	19
Kansas	1,905,299	2,178,611	2,249,071	2,364,236	2,477,574	30
Montana	591,024	674,767	694,409	786,690	799,065	35
Oklahoma	2,233,351	2,328,284	2,559,463	3,025,487	3,145,585	41
Wyoming	290,529	330,066	332,416	469,557	453,588	56
Idaho	588,637	667,191	713,015	944,127	1,006,749	71

moved to Los Angeles. "Things were not going well" in St. Louis, Waters recalled. "California looked golden and we said, 'Let's go.'" As a result of the migration of people such as Maxine Waters and her family, the African American population of many western states increased rapidly. Table 2.3 indicates how dramatically the West's African American population increased.

As this table demonstrates, the African American population of both the mild-winter and hard-winter states increased significantly during the Cold War. In most of the western states, however, African Americans remained a small minority of the people. Only in five states—Texas, California, Oklahoma, Kansas, and Nevada—did African Americans constitute more than 5 percent of the population in 1990, and Texas was the only western state in which more than 10 percent of the residents were African Americans.

Although the promise of jobs in military industries may have attracted large numbers of African Americans to the urban centers of the mild-winter West, this promise often went unfulfilled. When she arrived in Los Angeles, for example, Maxine Waters did not find a better job than the one she had left in St. Louis. Instead, she worked in a garment factory. Her husband found a job in a printing plant. Eventually, however, Waters did find opportunities that had eluded her in Missouri. In 1966 she was hired as an assistant teacher in a Head Start program. From there, she went on to attend college, and she was elected to the California legislature in 1976. Los Angeles voters elected her to a seat in the U.S. House of Representatives in 1990.

Waters's experiences suggest some of the ironies of the Cold War economic boom in the West. The job that most helped Waters to break out of poverty was funded by the U.S. Department of Health, Education, and Welfare, not

Table 2.3: Increase in African American Population of Western States, 1950–1990

State	1950	1960	1970	1980	1990	Percentage Change, 1950–1990
Nevada	4,302	13,484	27,762	50,791	78,771	1,731
North Dakota	257	777	2,494	2,568	3,524	1,271
Colorado	20,177	39,997	66,411	101,702	133,146	560
Washington	30,691	48,738	71,308	105,544	149,801	388
California	462,172	883,861	1,400,143	1,819,282	2,208,801	378
South Dakota	727	1,114	1,627	2,144	3,258	348
Arizona	25,974	43,404	53,344	75,034	110,524	326
Utah	2,729	4,148	6,617	9,225	11,576	324
Oregon	11,529	18,133	26,308	37,059	46,178	301
New Mexico	8,408	17,063	19,555	24,042	30,210	259
Idaho	1,050	1,502	2,130	2,716	3,370	221
Nebraska	19,234	29,262	39,911	48,389	57,404	198
Texas	977,458	1,187,125	1,399,005	1,710,250	2,021,632	107
Kansas	73,158	91,445	106,977	126,127	143,076	96
Montana	1,232	1,467	1,995	1,786	2,381	93
Oklahoma	145,503	153,084	171,892	204,658	233,801	61
Wyoming	2,557	2,483	2,568	3,364	3,606	41

the Department of Defense. This suggests that a different federal policy could have provided better jobs for all residents of the United States. Because politicians did not portray the Cold War as a national emergency comparable to World War II, however, state and federal governments did little to discourage discrimination against prospective employees on the basis of race or ethnicity. During World War II, the President's Committee on Fair Employment Practice (FEPC), despite its weakness, attempted to prevent military contractors from discriminating against ethnic minorities. A similar federal agency did not exist during the first fifteen years of the Cold War.

Even after Congress outlawed employment discrimination in the 1960s, African American workers confronted inequality within the U.S. industrial infrastructure. In the aerospace divisions of military contractors, as many as 50 percent of the jobs were technical, salaried positions filled by highly educated and well-trained individuals. Inferior schools in African American communities prevented many African Americans from receiving the necessary education and training for these jobs. Although Waters was able to parlay her

Table 2.4: Increase in American Indian Population of Western States, 1950–1990

State	1950	1960	1970	1980	1990	Percentage Change, 1950–1990
Texas	2,736	5,750	17,957	50,296	65,877	2308
Colorado	1,567	4,288	8,836	20,682	27,776	1673
California	19,947	39,014	91,018	227,757	242,164	1114
Kansas	2,381	5,069	8,672	17,829	21,965	823
Oregon	5,820	8,026	13,510	29,783	38,496	561
Washington	13,816	21,076	33,386	61,233	81,483	490
Utah	4,201	6,961	11,273	19,994	24,283	478
Oklahoma	53,769	64,689	98,468	171,092	252,420	369
Nevada	5,025	6,681	7,933	14,256	19,637	291
Idaho	3,800	5,231	6,687	10,405	13,780	263
New Mexico	41,901	56,255	72,788	106,585	134,355	221
Nebraska	3,954	5,545	6,624	9,059	12,410	214
Arizona	65,671	83,387	95,812	154,175	203,527	210
Wyoming	3,237	4,020	4,980	8,192	9,479	193
Montana	16,606	21,181	27,130	37,623	47,678	187
North Dakota	10,766	11,736	14,369	19,905	25,917	141
South Dakota	23,344	25,794	32,365	45,525	50,575	117

education and her abilities into a career in politics, then, many other African Americans remained mired in poverty.

Cold War spending in the United States tended to allow White, male U.S. citizens to move from low-paying jobs in the service sector into higher-paying jobs in the industrial sector of the western economy. At the same time, the economic boom of the Cold War years also promoted the proliferation of low-wage jobs in the service sector. White women and African American men and women took many of these jobs, but not enough African Americans and European Americans moved to the West to fill all the jobs at the low wages that employers were willing to pay. Euro- and African Americans were joined in western manufacturing centers by American Indians and Mexican Americans.

The promise of good jobs attracted American Indians to cities such as Los Angeles, Oakland, and Seattle, but the federal government's policies of termination and relocation also encouraged many Indians to leave reservations. Washington's American Indian population increased from under 14,000 in

1950 to 81,000 in 1990. California's Native American population soared from under 20,000 in 1950 to 242,000 in 1990.

The dramatic growth of the Mexican American population in the West matched the impressive increase in the African American and American Indian populations. In 1950, the census counted slightly more than two million people with "Spanish surnames" in the West, almost all of them in the states of Texas, California, New Mexico, Arizona, and Colorado. This category included both immigrant aliens and U.S. citizens. By 1990, the census counted more than twelve million people of Mexican ancestry in the West. Some of the growth of the Mexican-origin population in the West clearly resulted from natural increase—more births than deaths—but the bulk of the population increase can be attributed to massive immigration from Mexico. Between 1950 and 1960, more than 319,000 Mexicans moved to the United States. During the 1960s, more than 443,000 Mexicans came to live and work in the United States. Between 1970 and 1980, more than 580,000 Mexican immigrants came to the United States, and, in the 1980s, nearly one million Mexicans moved north.

Like U.S. citizens who moved to the West from other regions, most Mexicans came to the West with hopes of finding good jobs. "It's very hard, the life in Mexico," Vidal Olivares, an immigrant, said. "We hardly had the money to eat. I had to leave my wife. We were newlyweds, we had been together only about ten months, and when I left she was pregnant. I wanted to get together the money for her and for my baby that was to be born."

Immigrants from Mexico outnumbered immigrants from any other nation during the forty years of the Cold War, but immigrants from virtually every nation came to the West during the period. Before 1965, Canadians moved to the United States in numbers nearly equal to those of Mexican immigrants. Large numbers of people from Germany and Great Britain also came to the United States. After Congress reshaped the nation's immigration laws in 1965, hundreds of thousands of immigrants from Asia joined immigrants from Mexico in the mild-winter West.

So many jobs existed in the United States, and so many people from around the world desperately wanted those jobs, that millions of people who could not or who chose not to comply with U.S. immigration laws entered the country. According to an estimate produced for the U.S. Senate Judiciary Committee, in 1975 nearly six million people worked in a vast underground economy in the United States. These workers—often pejoratively labeled "illegal aliens" and "undocumented workers"—received no protection from minimum-wage, occupational safety, or workers' compensation legislation. About half of these six million people lived and worked in the western United States. By 1990, according to some scholars, the underground economy had expanded to encompass about ten million workers, despite the fact that 1.2 million long-term residents had received permanent resident status under the amnesty provisions of the Immigration Reform and Control Act of 1986. The labor force of the underground economy came from many different nations, but approximately two-thirds were from Mexico.

Like African American newcomers, immigrants from Latin America confronted the rigid segmentation of the western labor market. Few immigrants had the necessary education to work as engineers or technicians for high-technology firms. Most worked as semiskilled or unskilled laborers in the manufacturing or service sectors of the economy. Graciela Mendoza Peña Valencia, for example, worked in a cannery and as a housekeeper for Anglo-American families in El Paso before she moved to California to work as a migrant farm laborer. Valencia's experiences typify the effects of this segmentation on Mexican immigrants. Many immigrants moved frequently in order to find jobs. Tens of thousands of Cold War immigrants from Mexico moved from the mild-winter West to cities and towns throughout the United States, and significant numbers returned to Mexico.

Many immigrants, especially those who arrived after 1975, were refugees fleeing the destruction and chaos of their homelands caused in part by the Cold War. The Cold War exacted a heavy toll on countries in Asia and Central America. Refugees from these regions often settled in the West because of its proximity to their homelands and because many large Asian American and Latina/Latino communities existed in western cities.

The flow of Cold War refugees began when the Cold War began but increased dramatically in the late 1950s and 1960s. As early as the 1950s, many well-educated, middle-class Filipinos found their aspirations frustrated by economic problems and the power of their nation's political and social elite. As a former colony of the United States, the Philippines had strong economic ties to the United States and an educational system modeled after public education in this nation. Many frustrated Filipinos sought greater opportunity by moving to the United States. Luz Latus, who came to the United States as an exchange student in 1959, remembered that "it seemed like everybody, all my friends and even the teachers in the school, wanted to come here. We were always having farewell parties for people who were leaving for the United States." Only 17,000 Filipinos had entered the United States during the 1950s, but in the 1960s nearly 100,000 Filipinos migrated to the United States.

When President Ferdinand Marcos declared martial law in the Philippines in 1972, many more Filipinos began to consider leaving. The Cold War affected U.S. responses to conditions in the Philippines. The U.S. government feared the possibility of a left-leaning regime in the Philippines and sought to protect

its investment in military bases in the island nation. Three Republican administrations and one Democratic administration embraced Marcos's authoritarian government. During the first decade of Marcos's iron-handed rule, 360,000
Filipinos came to the United States. Edgar Gamboa, who came to the United
States in 1974, said that his father "wanted me to leave because he was concerned that my student activism would eventually get me in trouble." His
father, Gamboa recalled, told him, "You have to fight your battles, but more
importantly, you have to know which battles to fight. If you stayed here and
kept demonstrating against the government, you'll end up in prison, just like
your friend Fred, and you won't be able to achieve your goals."

As a resistance movement gained momentum and Marcos's regime responded with greater violence and repression, the movement of refugees continued. The revolution of 1986 did not stem the flow of refugees to the United
States. Continued political and economic instability led many Filipinos to continue to seek asylum in the United States. More than 430,000 Filipinos moved
to the United States during the 1980s. Although Filipino refugees have come
from all social classes, a substantial percentage have been professionals, such as
doctors, dentists, lawyers, pharmacists, and nurses. Some sources estimate that
as many as one-quarter of Filipino immigrants to the United States have been
professionals. Although people of Filipino ancestry in the United States lived
in every U.S. state by 1990, the majority remained on the Pacific Coast. Half of
the 1.4 million Filipinos in the nation in 1990 lived in California.

A chain of events similar to that in the Philippines led to substantial Cold
War migration from South Korea. The number of Koreans who came to the
United States during the 1950s and 1960s was small. Fewer than 36,000 Koreans migrated to this country in the 1960s, and at least a third of that number
were women who had married American military personnel. Conditions in
South Korea, however, grew more intolerable as the Cold War continued. The
South Korean government used much of the nation's resources to maintain a
military force that could prevent or repel an attack from North Korea, and it
responded violently to criticism, especially from university students. The U.S.
government supported the ruling regime in South Korea, despite that regime's
repressive stance towards its own citizens. By the 1970s, many Koreans had
made the decision to leave. Nearly 240,000 Koreans moved to the United
States in that decade. This massive migration of Koreans to the United States
continued through 1989, as more than 300,000 Koreans came to this country
in the 1980s. Like immigrants from the Philippines, Korean immigrants often
tended to be highly educated professionals. Like Filipinos, they also tended to
remain on the Pacific Coast, although substantial numbers did join friends and

relatives in New York City. Nearly a third of the 800,000 people of Korean ancestry in the United States in 1990 lived in California.

The U.S. war in Southeast Asia also contributed to the movement of Cold War refugees to the United States. Since the fall of Saigon in 1975, more than 530,000 Vietnamese refugees have come to the United States. About 120,000 Cambodians and more than 150,000 Laotians also fled the aftermath of the war by coming to the United States. The federal government encouraged Southeast Asian refugees to distribute themselves across the nation, and church groups helped many people to move to small towns in the East, South, and Midwest. Many families, however, decided to move to the Pacific Coast states. The moves often resulted from children's desire to be around more Vietnamese people. In 1990, more than half of all Vietnamese immigrants lived in the West. The majority of these immigrants lived in California (especially in Orange County, Los Angeles, San Jose, San Diego, and San Francisco), but significant Vietnamese, Cambodian, Laotian, and Hmong communities also developed in Seattle, Portland, Phoenix, Dallas, and Houston. Like their counterparts from Korea and the Philippines, many of the first wave of Vietnamese refugees were professionals. Few of these professionals, however, have been able to practice their professions in the United States. More recent arrivals, such as the "boat people" from Vietnam who arrived in the 1980s and most of the Cambodians, Laotians, and Hmongs, have included more peasants and workers.

Asia was not the only continent from which Cold War refugees streamed to the western United States. The histories of several Central American republics have been marked by conflicts between a small ruling elite—often descendants of Spanish colonizers—and large numbers of peasants and workers—many of them indigenous peoples. After World War II, radical political parties gained strength in a number of countries. The opponents of these parties attached the "Communist" label to radicals and reformers of any stripe and appealed to the United States. Drawing on a policy toward Latin America still influenced by the Monroe Doctrine, the United States used its influence in Central America to stifle the growth of "Communist" parties in the 1950s. Internal problems and U.S. policy had long-term, disastrous consequences for the region. As U.S.-supported regimes clamped down on opposition parties, these parties sometimes resorted to armed struggle. As civil war erupted in several nations, many people fled their homelands.

More refugees came to the United States from El Salvador than from any other Latin American nation. According to data compiled by the U.S. government, 15,000 Salvadorans came to the United States between 1961 and 1970. That number more than doubled in the 1970s, to more than 34,000. In the

1980s, however, as civil war gripped their homeland, more than 134,000 Salvadorans fled to the United States. Unofficial estimates, however, dwarfed those of the federal government. Some observers claimed that 300,000 Salvadorans lived in Los Angeles alone by 1983. Many Salvadorans' experiences in the United States ran parallel to those of so-called illegal immigrants from other Latin American countries. The Reagan administration refused to consider Salvadorans refugees; many people tried to live underground to avoid the Immigration and Naturalization Service. They worked as cooks, house cleaners, gardeners, and day laborers. Instability and repression in Guatemala led more than 55,000 Guatemalans (according to U.S. government data) to come to the United States in the 1980s. Most of these refugees entered the United States from Mexico and remained in the western states. In 1990, for example, more than half of the Salvadorans admitted intended to live in Los Angeles, while another eighth intended to live in Houston.

This movement of African Americans, immigrants, and refugees from Latin America and Asia dramatically transformed the mild-winter West. Not only did the region's population grow rapidly during the Cold War years, but it also grew rapidly more diverse. In 1950, for example, the census indicated that nearly 94 percent of California's residents identified themselves as "White." Forty years later, only 70 percent of the state's residents identified themselves as "White"; 7.4 percent of the state's residents identified themselves as "Black," and 9.5 percent put themselves in the category of "Asian, Pacific Islander." More than a quarter of California's residents identified themselves as "of Hispanic origin." (People "of Hispanic origin" may identify themselves with any "race.") In the next most diverse western state, Texas, more than 87 percent of the state's residents had identified themselves as "White" in the 1950 census. By 1990, that percentage had fallen to 75.2. Twelve percent of Texans called themselves "Black," and more than a quarter of the state's residents said that they were "of Hispanic origin."

Although some of this increase in the diversity of the West's population might have occurred in absence of the Cold War, much of it would not have. Refugees from the Philippines, Korea, southeast Asia, and Central America all came to the United States in part because of U.S. foreign policy influenced by the Cold War. This is one of the great ironies of the Cold War: as the United States lent support to authoritarian regimes around the world, the citizens of nations ruled by those regimes often sought relief by coming to the United States.

The Cold War and U.S. Cold War policy affected the development of many different communities within the United States. Many of the large ethnic communities in the West owe their existence in part to the Cold War. So, too, do the lesbian and gay communities in many cities. After Danny Flaherty was expelled from Northern Illinois University in 1965 for being gay, he moved to California. In 1966 Flaherty was drafted; he spent two years in the U.S. Army and served in Vietnam. Flaherty spent his final months in the Army stationed at the Presidio in San Francisco. When he was discharged, he remained in San Francisco. As Randy Shilts reported in *Conduct Unbecoming: Gays and Lesbians in the U.S. Military*, Flaherty knew that "he could never return to Spring Valley. He understood who he was now and he realized there was no place for him in Illinois."

Danny Flaherty was lucky. He survived investigations into homosexual activity in the Army and received an honorable discharge. Many of the lesbians and gay men who moved to western cities, however, were not so lucky. Although soldiers had been drummed out of the Continental Army for homosexual activity even before the United States achieved its independence from Great Britain, the military did not identify a class of people as "homosexuals" and declare such people unfit for military service until 1942. During World War II and the Korean and Vietnam wars, however, military officials needed all the men and women who could serve, and they did not strictly enforce the ban on lesbians and gay men. In the more "peaceful" years of the Cold War, however, the demand for military personnel declined and military officials enforced the ban more enthusiastically. Officers could even win commendations and promotions for exposing "homosexual rings." According to Navy records, that branch of the service alone discharged an average of 1,100 sailors a year for homosexuality between 1950 and 1965. Throughout the early 1980s, the number of military discharges for homosexuality remained at levels comparable to those of the 1950s, when many politicians had equated homosexuals with "Communists." The number of people discharged by the military for homosexuality does not include the tens or hundreds of thousands of people like Danny Flaherty who managed to conceal their homosexuality and receive honorable discharges.

The lesbians and gay men who were discharged for homosexuality, and those who survived the military's investigations into their personal affairs without being discharged, often decided not to return to their hometowns, especially if they were from small or medium-sized towns or cities in which their sexual orientation might become public knowledge. Like lesbians and gay men who had "come out" during World War II, they sought the anonymity of large cities, and many decided to remain in or return to cities in which they had been stationed. Consequently, the lesbian and gay communities in cities such as Los Angeles, San Francisco, and San Diego grew rapidly as a result of the Cold War.

Lesbian and gay veterans were joined by people who were driven out of government jobs by anti-gay measures instituted in the 1950s that remained in effect until the 1970s. In April 1953, President Dwight D. Eisenhower issued Executive Order 10450. This order, designed to protect the U.S. government from espionage by its own employees, declared "sexual perverts" to be security risks and denied them access to federal jobs. Many state and local governments adopted similar measures, and many lesbians and gay men, denied access to twelve million government jobs, migrated to large cities in which they would have anonymity and access to good jobs. According to journalist Randy Shilts, "The massive purges of gays from the military and government during the McCarthy era increased the number of gay refugees in the Bay Area. A full contingent of former State Department employees moved en masse to nearby Sausalito, say gay old-timers, after anti-gay hysteria swept the foreign service." By the 1970s, some observers estimated that 200,000 of San Francisco's 700,000 residents were gay men and that at least another 50,000 were lesbians. Even larger lesbian and gay communities emerged in Los Angeles, the West's largest city, and sizeable communities surfaced in Houston, Dallas, Denver, San Diego, Portland, and Seattle. Visible, if smaller lesbian and gay communities developed in smaller cities such as Sacramento, Salt Lake City, and Albuquerque.

The Cold War clearly contributed to the dramatic population growth of the western United States after World War II. The U.S. armed forces brought millions of people into the mild-winter West, and a significant percentage of these soldiers, sailors, and marines decided to remain in the region. Contracts for weapons, aircraft, and other military hardware created millions of new jobs for skilled workers. These jobs drew millions of people to the mild-winter West. The militarization of the mild-winter western economy, a process that began before and during World War II, attracted professionals, such as engineers and research scientists, and skilled workers to these states. These people came from all over the United States. The militarization of the economy also created a number of good jobs for people like my parents, who sold homes, insurance, furniture, and even candy to the people who moved into the region to take war production jobs.

Jobs attracted people to the mild-winter West during the Cold War, but U.S. foreign policy also encouraged some people to come to these states. The U.S. government waged two major wars and several smaller wars during the forty-year period. People who allied themselves with the United States in these wars often felt they had no choice but to come here when U.S. troops withdrew.

The U.S. government also supported many authoritarian regimes because they opposed Communism. Hundreds of thousands of dissidents decided to leave countries such as the Philippines and South Korea, and hundreds of thousands more fled violence in countries such as Vietnam, Cambodia, Laos,

El Salvador, and Guatemala. These refugees often ended up in the western United States because the West was closer to their homelands than other parts of the United States and because substantial Asian, Asian American, and Spanish-speaking communities existed in many mild-winter western states.

Many of the early refugees came from middle-class backgrounds. But most of the refugees who came to the mild-winter West in the late 1970s and 1980s joined the flow of poorer U.S. citizens, many of them African Americans, such as Maxine Waters, who moved to the mild-winter West and found only low-wage jobs in the region's farm fields, food processing plants, garment factories, and restaurants. These refugees and U.S. citizens alike were casualties of the Cold War, which perpetuated class, race, and ethnic divisions within western society. In the mild-winter West, suburbs grew up to house some of the most affluent people in the United States. Not far from these suburbs lay ghettoes and *barrios* in which some of the poorest and most exploited people in the nation lived. The suburbs, the ghettoes, and the *barrios* all grew at astonishing rates during the Cold War.

The Cold War clearly transformed the mild-winter West, but its effect on the hard-winter western states was less pronounced. Except during the "energy boom" of the 1970s, when the development of coal and uranium mines and oil exploration drew hundreds of thousands of people into states such as Oklahoma and Wyoming, the hard-winter western states attracted few migrants, immigrants, or refugees. Through most of the Cold War, people actually left the hard-winter states and migrated to the mild-winter states.

Like the atomic bombs that the U.S. armed forces exploded above the western landscape, federal policies during the Cold War have dropped fallout on western society. When pundits and politicians declared victory in the Cold War in 1989, federal lawmakers decided that they could cut the military budget. Although these budget cuts were not draconian, they did send shock waves through the mild-winter western economy. The recession of the early 1990s in California demonstrated how dependent the mild-winter West had become on Washington's military spending. The anger of many westerners, however, was not directed at federal policies that had made much of the West dependent on military spending. Instead, many residents of the mild-winter West blamed the recession on immigrants, refugees, and ethnic minorities—people who had come to the West as a result of the Cold War but who had not benefited directly from Cold War spending.

The post–Cold War recession had little effect on Wyoming, where my parents remain. Three of their four children left Wyoming during the Cold War to pursue educational or vocational opportunities outside the Equality State. (The fourth is now gone, too.) Although my parents have not suffered from the persistent discrimination and exploitation faced by African Americans, Mexican Americans, and many immigrants from Latin America and Asia, they, too, are casualties of Cold War policy. Although they are not miserable in Wyoming, they have been stranded in Casper by the Cold War. They could not afford to purchase a home if they were to move to the mild-winter West. They do not have the education or the skills that would allow them to obtain high-wage jobs. My parents benefited to some degree from the military spending that at times hypercharged the western economy, but, ultimately, like the West itself, perhaps they were left poorer by the country's failure to develop an economic policy that would have promised greater prosperity and security for all of its people.

BIBLIOGRAPHIC ESSAY

Historians have not looked carefully at the movement of migrants, immigrants, and refugees into the western United States during the Cold War. In "The People of the West since 1890," in *The Twentieth Century West: Historical Interpretations*, ed. Gerald D. Nash and Richard W. Etulain (Albuquerque: University of New Mexico Press, 1989), Walter Nugent argued that the Cold War West could be divided into four regions: "(1) the interior northwest, including much of Joel Garreau's 'empty quarter': Montana, Wyoming, Idaho, Utah, and Colorado; (2) the desert states of New Mexico, Arizona, and Nevada; (3) the Pacific Northwest of Washington and Oregon; (4) the offshore states of Alaska and Hawaii; (5) California, with 52 to 57 percent of the entire region's people after 1950." My interpretation emphasizes the similarities among the population growth rates of the "mild-winter" western states and the critical differences between those states and the remaining western states. My essay's interpretation of demographic change in the West relies heavily on data collected by the U.S. Department of Commerce, Bureau of the Census, and presented in decennial reports and in the annual Statistical Abstract of the United States.

A number of scholars have explored the Cold War's impact on the U.S. economy, although few have attempted to draw connections between economic growth and migration to the West. Among the books and articles that I have found most useful are James L. Clayton, "The Impact of the Cold War on the Economies of California and Utah, 1946–1965," *Pacific Historical Review* 36 (November 1967): 449–53; James L. Clayton, comp. and ed., *The Economic Impact of the Cold War: Sources and Readings* (New York: Harcourt, Brace & World, 1970); David Horowitz, ed., *Corporations and the Cold War* (New York: Monthly Review Press, 1969); and Seymour Melman, ed., *The War Economy of the United States: Readings on Military Industry and Economy* (New York: St. Martin's Press, 1971). For an interesting discussion of the relationship between military spending and urban politics, see Roger W. Lotchin, *Fortress California, 1910–1961: From Warfare to Welfare* (New York: Oxford University Press, 1992). Historians have largely ignored the migration of African Americans to the West after World War II, although Mike Davis discusses the consequences of labor-force segmentation in *City of Quartz: Excavating the Future in Los Angeles* (London:

Verso, 1990). Donald L. Fixico treats the federal government's efforts to force American Indians to leave reservations in *Termination and Relocation: Federal Indian Policy, 1945–1960* (Albuquerque: University of New Mexico Press, 1986).

Sociologists and demographers have examined immigration to the United States during the Cold War years, but only a handful of historians have written about this important trend. For an early interpretation of "illegal" migration from Mexico, see Julian Samora, *Los Mojados: The Wetback Story* (South Bend, IN: University of Notre Dame Press, 1971). A number of different perspectives on immigration from Mexico are presented in Arthur F. Corwin, ed., *Immigrants—and Immigrants: Perspectives on Mexican Labor Migration to the United States* (Westport, CT: Greenwood Press, 1978). Some valuable information is contained in Thomas Kessner and Betty Boyd Caroli, *Today's Immigrants: Their Stories* (New York: Oxford University Press, 1982); Ronald Takaki, *Strangers from a Different Shore: A History of Asian Americans* (New York: Penguin Books, 1990); and Herbert Barringer, Robert W. Gardner, and Michael J. Levin, *Asians and Pacific Islanders in the United States* (New York: Russell Sage Foundation, 1993).

Information about John Tunney and Maxine Waters is available in *Current Biography*. Graciela Mendoza Peña Valencia's story is in June Namias, *First Generation: In the Words of Twentieth-Century American Immigrants*, rev. ed. (Urbana: University of Illinois Press, 1992). Vidal Olivares tells his story in Marilyn P. Davis, *Mexican Voices, American Dreams: An Oral History of Mexican Immigration to the United States* (New York: Henry Holt and Company, 1990). The words of Luz Latus and Edgar Gamboa are in Yen Le Espiritu, *Filipino American Lives* (Philadelphia: Temple University Press, 1995).

On the Cold War's impact on the rise of lesbian and gay communities in the West, especially in San Francisco, see Allan Bérubé, *Coming Out under Fire: The History of Gay Men and Women in World War Two* (New York: Free Press, 1990); Frances FitzGerald, *Cities on a Hill: A Journey through Contemporary American Cultures* (New York: Simon and Schuster, 1986); and two books by Randy Shilts, *The Mayor of Castro Street: The Life and Times of Harvey Milk* (New York: St. Martin's Press, 1982), and *Conduct Unbecoming: Gays and Lesbians in the U.S. Military* (New York: St. Martin's Press, 1993).

CHAPTER THREE

CONTAINMENT AND EMANCIPATION
Race, Class, and Gender in the Cold War West

❧

A. YVETTE HUGINNIE

When one thinks of the Cold War, words such as "conformity," "suppression," and "containment" immediately come to mind. Indeed, the narrowing of politically and socially acceptable behaviors and options was the predominant tendency within the United States. Domestically, the Cold War was a conservative effort to restructure U.S. society by containing the progressive transformations in gender, race, and class relations wrought during the Great Depression and World War II. At the same time, however, a contrary tendency existed—that of emancipation. Some groups continued their struggles to end long-standing discrimination despite the repression of the times. The Black Civil Rights Movement is the most notable national example of this emancipatory impulse. Although much smaller in scale than that of containment, the liberatory impulse nonetheless is a crucial characteristic of the period. Oftentimes, these two tendencies were dialectically connected: for both African Americans and Asian Americans, the exigencies and rhetoric of Cold War politics circumscribed the range of acceptable political voices, and yet, at the same time, facilitated an improvement in racial relations; for gays and lesbians, the repressive conservative politics of containment scarred individual lives while simultaneously helping to define new communities, identities, and spaces. In these and other instances, oppression and resistance dialectically intersected, that is, they were closely interrelated. Furthermore, it is crucial to remember that the very meaning or experience of containment and emancipation varied among individuals and groups. Given the hierarchical nature of U.S. race, class, and gender relations, the liberation of one group oftentimes came at the expense or the containment of another.

While the entire nation experienced the Cold War, each U.S. region expressed its own variations. Specific regional characteristics were due both to prior regional race, gender, and class relations as well as to the interaction of Cold War events and policies. For the West, significant prior conditions included large numbers of peoples of Asian, Mexican, and Native American descent whose presence and histories gave a more varied and complicated contour to race relations—beyond Black and White—than in any other area of the country. The multifarious nature of the western racial landscape in turn shaped regional class and gender relations. Another regional feature was the West's long-standing relationship to the federal government, a central theme in western American history. The Cold War accelerated and broadened the federal government's influences and the West's dependency upon federal monies. National and international issues came to hold more influence over regional social relations. While the Cold War lasted for forty-five years, this essay will concentrate on the early Cold War period, from 1945 to 1965. These years of pronounced foreign and domestic Cold War policy gave lasting shape and tempo to the rest of the period.

Throughout the early Cold War period, social relations were in flux. One of the central shifts in U.S. and western racial relations was the ending of sanctioned political discrimination against racialized (non-White) groups. This came about due to internal and external pressures. Racialized peoples and progressive Whites within the United States continued long-standing campaigns to end discrimination, at times utilizing Cold War rhetoric to highlight injustices. Meanwhile, the U.S. government faced international criticism— from the Soviet Union and China, European allies, and emerging independent nations in Asia, Latin America, and Africa—that challenged the notion of the U.S. as the leader of the "free world" given its treatment of non-Whites. Given these internal and external pressures, the ending of de jure discrimination became a Cold War imperative. In the West, Asian Americans were in the spotlight of this transformation, whereas nationally it was African Americans. One transformation in western race relations, therefore, was the decline of de jure discrimination against Asians and Asian Americans.

Anti-Asian practices and sentiments had been a distinguishing characteristic of western race and social relations for nearly a century. These attitudes and practices were reflected in California's Alien Land Law, the Chinese Exclusion Act, low immigration quotas for Asians, as well as extralegal prohibitions and de facto segregation that limited Asian Americans' access to jobs and neighborhoods throughout the West. The Cold War was a turning point, in that the regional anti-Asian attitudes and barriers, which had culminated in the internment of people of Japanese descent during WWII, declined. Sanctioned political discrimination was struck down, and the status of and attitudes toward Asian Americans improved; their ameliorated situations were related closely to Cold War politics.

The United States' anti-Communist stand forced it to alleviate most anti-Asian de jure discrimination. For instance, U.S. concern with maintaining and strengthening U.S. military alliances with India and the Philippines led the federal government to enact in 1946 the Luce-Cellar bill that granted naturalization rights to Asian Indians and Filipinos. Yet the United States continued to limit all Asian groups to low immigration quotas, a pattern established in 1943 with the revocation of the Chinese Exclusion Act. Similarly, other Cold War events also proved to be consequential for Asian Americans. Reacting to the rise of Communist China in 1949 and the beginning of the Korean War in 1950, and fueled by its desire to contain Communism, the United States opened up Chinese immigration to allow the five thousand Chinese students then studying in the United States to become permanent residents and also to accept other political refugees from China. This limited expansion of Chinese immigration precipitated a significant shift in the class and ethnic makeup of the Chinese American population in the West, as the students and political refugees were from elite backgrounds, highly educated, and Mandarin, and thus had significant class, cultural, and linguistic differences from the Cantonese laborers who had immigrated during the nineteenth century. Cold War politics thus led to increased numbers of Chinese Americans while at the same time producing a greater diversity among them.

Cold War military action in Korea similarly affected U.S. laws that discriminated against Koreans and Japanese. The United States rebuilt war-torn Japan, reconstructing it as a vital ally in the plan to maintain U.S. military power in the Pacific and to expand U.S. economic markets. The shift of Japan from enemy to ally was reflected in improved relations at home. The 1952 McCarran–Walter Act struck down more anti-Asian provisions, thus allowing Koreans and Japanese immigrants to naturalize; ironically, this was the same act that threatened suspected subversives with internment. Across the West and the nation, there was less stigmatization of Japanese Americans; overall, White Americans approved of Japanese re-entrance into U.S. society after internment, even in many western communities that had pressed for internment. In 1956 California repealed its alien land laws, which had been used to curb Asian Americans' economic advancement. A final example of the improved status of Japanese and other Asian Americans was the admission of Hawai'i to statehood in 1959. In the congressional debate, Cold War imperatives—for example, that U.S. military bases central to continued influence in the Pacific and Asia were located in Hawai'i—won out over anti-Asian sentiments. Since most Asian

Americans lived in Hawai'i, that state quickly became a political stronghold for them. Cold War efforts to contain Communism abroad led to increased liberation in the United States for other peoples of Asian descent. In these instances, containment and emancipatory impulses intersected.

As anti-Asian sentiments and politics declined and substantial numbers of Asian Americans experienced upward mobility, discriminatory treatment of African Americans and Mexican Americans worsened. This represented a second shift in western racial relations. The population of both of these groups had increased significantly during the World War II period as they moved out of their subregions, the American South and the American Southwest, respectively. Anti-Mexican and anti-Black sentiments and politics were not new in the West, but their increasing prominence in western society was. Moreover, the movement from an anti-Asian toward an anti-Black emphasis shifted western racial relations toward the national profile. Although the end of de jure discrimination during the early Cold War period also benefited Mexican Americans and African Americans, in the West their practical conditions and treatment worsened. The poor treatment and attitudes they faced—wage and housing discrimination, de facto segregation in housing and schooling—were related to their overwhelmingly working-class position. Ironically, the success of Asian Americans' struggles to defeat politically sanctioned discrimination was in part due to African Americans' and Mexican Americans' efforts to do the same. In the reconfiguration of western race relations during the early Cold War, the liberation of some accompanied the containment of others.

A third transformation in western social and racial relations grew out of the desegregation of the U.S. armed forces in 1947. Pressed by internal and external criticism, President Truman mandated the end of formal discrimination in the armed forces. This order precipitated a greater range of racial interaction in the West, as opposed to elsewhere in the United States, given the region's diverse population. During World War II, Filipino, Japanese American, and African American men had been denied the right to serve, restricted to noncombat units, or assigned to segregated combat units. Desegregation ended the commonplace actions and assumptions that reserved fighting for one's country as a White man's duty and privilege. Desegregation, therefore, portended significant consequences for racialized understandings of masculinity. The Korean War—a war often overlooked—was the first armed conflict in which a non-segregated, multiracial U.S. armed force was used.

The full implications of the desegregation of the U.S. armed forces have yet to be discerned; much more research is needed. Ultimately, desegregation involved not only the men and women who served in the military but also their families and communities. Participation in the military and then the G.I. Bill enabled some racialized individuals to get footholds into the middle class. Moreover, the experiences of racialized service personnel in the West led to increased interracial interaction. Military buildup in western areas during World War II and the Cold War combined with desegregation to produce a small but significant movement of African American and other racialized peoples into small towns in the Rocky Mountains, the Great Plains, and other isolated western areas. For the most part, the experiences of these service personnel and their families, as well as the responses of White locals, has yet to be recorded. At the same time, the social costs of isolation from co-racial communities, and isolation within predominantly White institutions and areas, also needs exploration.

Although most formal prohibitions against racialized groups ended during this period, poor protection of their rights persisted, as did discriminatory attitudes and practices. Overall, the Cold War did not upset the economic imbalance in the West among racialized groups and Whites; the former remained overwhelmingly poor and working class. The general impetus of the early Cold War period was toward the maintenance of social inequalities and hierarchies, despite the decline of politically sanctioned discrimination. Ultimately, those who were not able to obtain middle-class lives faced even more formidable obstacles. In the place of formal prohibitions, a "cold war" ensued that used economic and class relations to demarcate and enforce social divisions. The emphasis upon economics may have been new, but the intent was not.

Part of the backdrop behind this new stress upon economics was the reshaping of the regional economy. The early Cold War period was a watershed in the western economy and job-market structure, as the region became a center for manufacturing and electronic industries and for high-technology research and production. These developments were most clearly seen in suburban areas in California, but many other locales, such as Seattle, Portland, Denver, Phoenix, and Albuquerque, also experienced this transformation. Much of this remaking of the western economy was directly due to Cold War expenditures, as the federal government pumped more than $150 billion into existing and new aerospace, electronic, and related industries in the West. Most of these new industries were located in new suburban areas, outside older urban centers. Furthermore, the character of economic expansion signified internal regional power relations and the class bias of Cold War policies. Public monies were used to finance research, and that research was then funneled into private companies. The practices of using public monies to support private companies is but one instance of the Cold War's pro-business bias.

Another example of this strong bias is the attack on organized labor and the Left. The 1947 Taft–Hartley Act, the purge of Communists from unions, the expulsion of Communist-led unions, the 1946 Federal Employee Loyalty Act, hearings before the House Committee on Un-American Activities, and the 1952 McCarran–Walter Act illustrate the constraining tendency of Cold War domestic policy. The Taft–Hartley Act, for example, narrowed the range of fair practices by labor and criminalized unfair practices by labor. At the same time, the legislation made comparable acts by employers only civil offenses. For many working-class peoples, the hard-won gains of the 1930s and the World War II period began to slip away due to anti-Communist and anti-labor repression, as well as the continued maldistribution of income (the top 10 percent of the U.S. population netted 40 percent of the national income). Regionally, the proliferation of anti-union right-to-work laws in western states further established barriers to working-class activism. In the West, working-class peoples who attempted to organize themselves came under harsh attack; for instance, Chicano and Mexicano labor leaders and Chinese leftists faced repression and deportation. The growing anti-union attitude in the West attracted to the region new industries in search of cheap and tractable labor forces. In response to repression and cooptation, organized labor moved away from addressing wider social issues, to policing its membership and to narrow business unionism.

Further scholarship on unions, leftists, and Communists is a key to understanding the contours of western power relations during the early Cold War. We need to know more about how the politics of anti-Communism and anti-unionism played out and its meaning and significance among diverse western communities. In particular, the histories of African American, Asian American, and Mexican American leftists in the West begs for more study. These individuals were pivotal in establishing organizations and bettering workers' access to jobs or higher wages. For instance, Chinese leftists in San Francisco worked with Whites outside of Chinatown and with the White Left in order to improve the chances of Chinese getting jobs. At the same time, however, they suffered repression both from within Chinese American communities and from the federal government because of their political beliefs. In another case, in order to avoid red-baiting attacks, the Los Angeles chapter of the National Association for the Advancement of Colored People (NAACP) disassociated itself from African American leftists and modified its demands; such pressures and accommodations increasingly tilted Black Civil Rights activism away from economic issues, limiting it to the political arena. Researchers must dig beyond contemporaries' erasure of the role of leftists in their community, whether this be due to internal divisions, Cold War suppression, or efforts to Americanize or assimilate.

The direct beneficiaries of the containment of organized labor and the Left were business elites. Such oppressive policies reinforced class dominance, enabling elites to assert themselves as public leaders and as the supposed impartial directors of society's interests. Cold War policies not only liberated business from the skepticism that its poor management of the economy had earned it during the Depression, but actually directly augmented the power and prestige of business. The Cold War gave renewed strength to business or pro-development power blocs in the West by spurring the resurgence of business leadership in local, regional, and national politics. These blocs took on greater ascendance and used their power and position to squelch critics. In Los Angeles, for example, business elites used Cold War red-baiting attacks and rhetoric to oppose the building of public housing in the downtown. In this and other instances, the Cold War fortified the dominant class hierarchy in the West.

This containment of organized labor and the Left thus had consequences for the larger society. Of particular importance was the removal of leftist, progressive, and labor advocates as legitimate voices in the larger debate on public policy. For instance, when most of the United States' World War II and Cold War allies were establishing broad social policy for their citizens for which labor and leftist groups were among the leading voices—for example, national health care in Canada, England, France, and Germany—there were no comparable efforts in the United States. By silencing alternative voices, the Cold War both nourished the misconception that the United States was a classless society, while at the same time adding to the arsenal of elite and monied interests. A further examination of how Cold War policies helped to bolster elite dominance might lead to a requestioning of the larger Cold War, in particular the degree that elite class interests drove U.S. domestic and foreign policy and how this bias was rationalized to the public.

The continuation of long-standing gender and racial hierarchies despite changes within the western economy is another example of the constraining nature of Cold War domestic policy. White men continued to hold the majority of white-collar and high-paying blue-collar jobs. They were the group in the best position to take advantage of these new job openings: trade unions were male-dominated and tended to exclude non-Whites and White women, so White men were positioned at the top of the job and training ladder. The G.I. Bill gave veterans—who were overwhelmingly White due to wartime military discrimination during World War II—access to the education needed for many of the new jobs. Furthermore, with the end of the wartime labor shortages, both White male employers and workers could exercise their prejudices to keep non-White men and women and White women out of the better-paying jobs.

Despite White men's continued dominance, there were two notable shifts in the western labor market. First, the regional growth in manufacturing jobs expanded the range of paid labor for White women. While they still faced sex-based discrimination and were often limited to the low end of manufacturing jobs, which offered fewer avenues for advancement, a greater range of manufacturing and clerical sectors were available to them as compared to the pre-1930s western labor market. The other significant shift was the entrance of Asian and Asian American men with training in engineering and science into Cold War–related industries and research centers. As a result, there was an expansion of the middle- and upper-middle-class community of Chinese- and other Asian Americans which, unlike other racialized middle-class groups, had extensive contact with the White middle class. This advance was not without its roadblocks. Asian Americans still earned less money than their White counterparts and they could not obtain supervisory positions over Whites, even though Japanese Americans tended to have more education than Whites. Other western racialized groups experienced a slight increase in the numbers of professionals, but they remained segregated within their co-racial communities.

While the western job hierarchy in limited ways opened up for many White women and highly educated Asians and Asian Americans, other racialized groups fared less well. During the early Cold War period, Native Americans, African Americans, and Mexican Americans disproportionately lost wartime jobs as companies and unions gave priority to returning White servicemen. These groups and working-class Asian Americans struggled to gain access to training and good-paying production jobs. Racialized women had the fewest opportunities. The manufacturing and clerical jobs open to White women remained closed to them; these women therefore remained overrepresented in low-paying domestic and service work. While some jobs were available within racialized communities—for example, Chinese American women obtained some clerical and manufacturing jobs in San Francisco's Chinatown—only with the application of pressure by community groups, such as the National Association for the Advancement of Colored People and the Asociación Nacional México-Americana, did a few White employers open up a limited range of jobs to racialized women. Most racialized men fared better than co-racial women in terms of both wages and access to jobs. A few had gained lasting footholds into these new industries during the war. During the 1950s, others had limited success in breaking down exclusionist trade-union policies and gained limited entry into trade and manufacturing jobs.

Meanwhile, many Mexican American and some Asian American men, women, and children remained locked into seasonal agricultural work. The vast majority of racialized groups, especially African Americans, Mexican Americans, and urbanized Native Americans, remained overrepresented in low-wage, nonunionized sectors. With limited economic opportunities, inflation driving up the cost of housing and basic necessities, the lack of access to good schooling for their children, and isolation in urban areas during the suburbanization of the regional economy, these groups were pushed behind. The ending of politically sanctioned discrimination only let through, or up, the few who were in the position to take advantage of it and who were willing to make the social and cultural accommodations demanded. For the vast majority of racialized groups, the abolishment of de jure segregation did little in the face of economic and political repression as they faced greater resistance from local, regional, and national elites who sought to curb the advances made by working-class peoples during the war.

While elites still dominated western power relations, the early Cold War period did experience a massive expansion of the middle class. Generally heralded as a liberatory shift, this change was riddled with repressive impulses that further increased class and racial inequities in the West. More than just an expansion of the middle class, this was a realignment of the social geography of race and class relations. For the middle class, especially the White middle class, Cold War policies offered new homes, education, high consumption patterns, the continuation of racialized hierarchies and de facto segregation, and an illusion of calm and peace in a society that was becoming more unequal.

The federal government played a crucial role in this realignment of the western social geography. Federal monies underlay the construction of highways—part of a Cold War military evacuation plan—that connected suburban developments to older industrial and urban centers. Federal monies underwrote suburban housing developments and the G.I. Bill, all part of Cold War domestic policy that made the social mobility and movement out of cities possible. These very same housing projects—postwar welfare for White middle-class people—included covenants that specifically excluded African Americans and sometimes Mexican Americans. Thus, federal tax monies—paid by all working peoples—were used to redraw racial, geographical, and class boundaries that helped to define the middle class—in particular, the White middle class. Moreover, it was in the suburbs, near these housing projects, that the new higher paying jobs were located.

Much has already been written about the modern White middle class: single family homes in suburban communities where nuclear families had their green lawns, cars, and many other consumer items. These consumerist patterns were central to both the middle class and the post–World War II economy. As many scholars have noted, the ability to participate in the new consumer culture was largely due to the extension of credit and women's paid employment. Another crucial underpinning of consumerism, however, often has been overlooked. The dramatic expansion of the western middle class—with its suburban lifestyle, consumption patterns, and rising standard of living—was dependent upon low-wage agricultural, manufacturing, and service sector work by others, oftentimes racialized groups. The federal importation of Mexican nationals is a good example: initially a wartime measure, the Bracero program was extended until 1964; between 1948 and 1964, the federal government and western growers brought in 4.5 million Mexicans to do low-wage agricultural work. The workers grew and harvested—at very low wages—the strawberries, cantaloupes, and lettuce that graced the tables of the expanded modern consumer middle class.

While the vast majority of those moving into the new suburbs were White, in some western areas and especially in California, Asian Americans also participated in this shift. Among them were many Chinese political refugees. These newcomers moved into middle-class, predominantly White suburbs and had only limited contact with Chinatown businesses and residents. Although not always welcomed in the predominantly White areas, Asian Americans were not excluded by covenants. More studies need to be done about this 1950s and 1960s generation of racialized peoples who sought integration and sometimes assimilation. Did integration—a process in which individuals broke out of the containment of de facto and de jure segregation—have the effect of robbing racialized communities of their middle class? What were the social costs of this mobility? How did these individual families navigate the terrain of culture, class, and race? Did they maintain cultural and other ties, for example, to churches, family meetings, cultural centers, and holiday celebrations in their old neighborhoods?

The overall realignment of western social geography is evidenced in cities like Houston, Tucson, and Los Angeles. These urban locations became more Black and Mexican and poor, as some affluent Asian Americans and Asian immigrants joined the many upwardly mobile Whites in the move to the suburbs, which is also where new higher-paying jobs were located. In Houston, Blacks were segregated from both Whites and Mexicans, and Black women faced the greatest housing discrimination, as female-headed households were turned away more often. Further research is needed to study the relationship among different racialized groups, social mobility, and the separation from supposed undesirable groups. For instance, after internment many Japanese Americans did not return to their old neighborhoods, in part because Blacks and Mexicans now predominated in them. Through the Japanese Relocation Program, many instead moved away from centers with large numbers of other Japanese Americans and into new, predominantly White suburban areas. For Asian Americans, White ethnic groups, racialized members of the Armed services, and others, did moving up the western racial and class hierarchy perpetuate some old patterns of marginalization while challenging others?

In contrast to the "cold war" of race relations and the intensification of class differences, the realm of gender and sexuality was a "hot war." Domestic policy during the early Cold War period focused attention upon gender and sexuality, making them supposed measures of either normalcy or deviance. The increased importance of these arenas was in itself a culmination of a shift that had started during the turn of the century, in that the formerly "private" realms of sexuality and gender increasingly occupied more public space and policy. The Depression and World War II had brought further transformations: for example, the delay of heterosexual marriage due to poor economic conditions and later the war; an increase in premarital sexual activity and out-of-wedlock pregnancies; creation of same-sex communities on both the war front and home front; women gaining access to "men's" jobs during wartime. Cold War domestic policy sought to restrain World War II–era developments and to substitute conservative notions of sexuality, masculinity, and femininity. These issues increasingly became part of public policy and public debate, as gender and sexuality joined race and class as markers of "otherness."

One of the predominant areas of research on sexuality and gender during the Cold War is the family. We know that Cold War domestic ideology emphasized a nuclear family with prescribed gender roles for men and women—wage-worker and household head for men, and mother and wife for women. Scholars have called attention to the fact that this White middle-class nuclear family ideal was, in fact, itself a new phenomenon and that within this structure there were variations and tensions. Among Californian Italian Americans, for instance, the organization of families varied within an individual's adult life. A host of personal, emotional, social, and economic influences—marriages, family strains, job losses—directly affected Italian Americans' ability to participate in the larger transformation of the White American family. This scholarship, it should be noted, is overwhelmingly focused on the White middle-class nuclear family and thus largely overlooks the existence of diverse western populations and social groups.

To expand this field of study to the West, new questions concerning sexuality and gender, and their intersections with race and class relations, need to be studied. For instance, if this icon of family rested upon professional employment for the man, how was family configured for those groups without that level of social status and economic means? How did Cold War domestic family ideology work for non-White and non-middle-class families? Was there pressure, internal or external, upon non-White and non-middle-class groups to replicate the gender and sexual patterns of the White heterosexual middle class? How did expectations regarding family and gender roles function, for example, within Mexican migrant labor families? Did their marginalization from the U.S. dominant norm reinforce traditional patterns within their families? What did local and state child labor laws and enforcement, particularly in agricultural areas, say about different notions of childhood and family for racialized and working-class groups? How did the politics of family play out in struggles against ethnic or racial discrimination? Was emulating this normative model instrumental for upward mobility? How were mainstream White anxieties regarding southern Californian zoot suiters related to Cold War domestic policy on the family and notions of juveniles? This field is ripe for further investigation. A closer look at four situations will illustrate both increased state intervention in the realm of gender, family, and sexuality and how these issues played a greater role in Western social relations of this period.

First, assimilation into newly emerging gender and family patterns may account for the rapid assimilation into the dominant U.S. society of many Japanese Americans during the early Cold War period. Prior to World War II, mainland Japanese and Japanese Americans in the West tended to live in predominantly Japanese neighborhoods, speak Japanese at home, and live in Issei-dominated (Japan-born) patriarchal families. By the early Cold War period, many of these distinguishing gender and familial patterns had been eliminated. The World War II internment experience shattered the Issei-dominated family structure, and postwar federal relocation policy sought to disperse many Japanese Americans away from the West Coast and into the Mountain West. The lessening of anti-Japanese sentiments may have been due more to Japanese Americans' increased assimilation into the dominant mainstream White society than to increased acceptance of Japanese American culture.

Second, during the Cold War the Native American family faced renewed state intervention. The special statutory and constitutional relationship between the federal government and Native American tribes made them particularly susceptible to state interference. Previously, under New Deal Indian policy, Natives had been encouraged to reconstitute tribal associations. Under the Cold War policy named Termination, the Bureau of Indian Affairs sought to release the federal government from its legal responsibilities to Native Americans. Termination entailed four prongs: the end of federal obligations; the breakup of tribal governments and common land holdings; urban relocation; and the reorganization of Native family patterns. As part of the latter, the policy attempted to end Native American communal and multigenerational familial patterns. Increased rhetoric regarding the inferiority of the Native family led to a policy in which many Native children were taken off reservations, often without tribal or parental consent, and adopted into White families—a replaying of historic notions and practices of rearing Native children in White culture as a means of "saving the Indian." Such assaults upon Native American tribal life and family eventually led to increased pan-Indian political activism, starting during the mid–1960s, which brought an end to termination.

Third, campaigns against gays and lesbians in the military and in government also point to the escalation of gender and sexuality as a basis for "otherness." By portraying homosexuality as a menacing specter, Cold War domestic ideology sought to contain homosexuality and suppress increasingly visible gay and lesbian bars and communities that appeared in major cities throughout the West during the Depression and World War II. Cold War policies drove individuals from jobs, dishonorably discharged military personnel known or suspected of being homosexuals, and violated the constitutional right to privacy of tens of thousands of Americans. An irony of the high-profile persecution of gays and lesbians is that it helped to "mark"—define and advertise—that very identity. This increased notoriety and visibility helped to end the isolation of individuals with same-sex desires and helped to put Los Angeles and San Francisco on the map as West Coast centers for gays and lesbians. The repression spurred resistance by some outspoken gays and lesbians, such as those who formed the Mattachine Society in Los Angeles in 1950 and the Daughters of Bilitis in San Francisco in 1955. Both of these organizations struggled for and gained limited civil rights for gays and lesbians while advocating assimilationist, middle-class respectability—in contrast to other gays and lesbians who embraced more countercultural practices and visions.

Finally, Cold War era repressive emphasis upon family inadvertently played a liberatory role for some groups. For Chinese Americans, for instance, the increased public-policy emphasis on the family led to an expansion of Chinese immigration. During the early Cold War period, Chinese Americans successfully pressed the government to include them in the family reunification and war brides immigration programs. With its high-profile removal of anti-Asian laws, the federal government had little option other than to allow Chinese and other Asian groups to participate in these programs. As a result, more Asian immigrants entered under family reunification and war bride provisions than under the still-low Asian immigration quotas. With the immigration of wives and daughters, the sex ratios in Chinese American communities became more balanced, losing their overwhelmingly male population profile established in the nineteenth century.

These examples point to the richness and complexity of research to be done in the field of gender and sexuality in the Cold War West. Gender and sexuality intersected with race and class in the web of social hierarchies in the West. At times, the attempt to maintain social hierarchies and to impose conservative notions of gender and sexuality created fissures through which marginalized groups carved space for themselves. Further work is needed in order to understand how and why heightened conflict around sexuality and gender in U.S. society swelled at the same time as de jure discrimination based on race and nationality gave way. How did issues such as family and sexuality become tools for conservative forces? How did gender, family, and sexuality become the language to express and maintain other kinds of social hierarchies?

The conservative and emancipatory struggles over western race, class, and gender relations during the early Cold War period could be likened to an earthquake, produced by tectonic plates rubbing against each other as they slowly jostled for position. From that friction, a thin, long crack opened up, ending some long-standing bases of stratification and discrimination, along which a number of previously marginalized groups and individuals broke through. Although shaken, the structures on the surface remained standing and intact, and new means of shoring them up appeared. Two large tremors closed this early Cold War period, while also indicating that there was continued instability and pressure building up beneath the surface. The first of these seismic events was the passage of three decisive pieces of legislation: the Civil Rights Act of 1964, the Voting Rights Act of 1965, and the Immigration Act of 1965. The second event was the civil disturbances in Watts (Los Angeles) in 1964. While the former were important achievements, for far too many people the potential of newly acquired political rights was contained by shifts in the economy and the larger society. The 1964 civil disturbances in Watts expressed the frustrations of many who had been marginalized by the new economic and social order. The struggles between forces of containment and those of liberation not only characterized the early Cold War period but established signposts for the subsequent periods.

Indeed, the key issues of a second Cold War period, which lasted from 1965 to 1974, the year Richard Nixon resigned from the presidency, in large part grew out of the changes and conflicts wrought during the first. The best example of these continuities is the flowering of movements at this time that challenged traditional conservative societal hierarchies, for example, Black Power, the Chicano Liberation Movement, the Women's Movement, and Gay Liberation. These efforts broadened political debate beyond formal political rights to include cultural struggles and the politics of identity. At the same time, however, these movements ultimately failed to dislodge the dominant class structures that continued to restrain the advancement of most racialized peoples. Increased structural inequalities—a 20 percent drop in real wages since 1973—combined with anti-liberatory conservative actions (sometimes violent, such as FBI repression of activists and the murder of Civil Rights leaders) combined to stall these progressive movements.

The dramatic effect that the United States' involvement in the Vietnam War had on the domestic scene, however, led to important changes. One effect of the war in Southeast Asia was to shift the definition of masculinity. In this period, many young, White, middle-class men redefined their masculinity in ways that did not include military service for one's country, thus moving away from older notions of White masculinity. (The alteration is personified in President Bill Clinton, who did not serve in Vietnam, and Vice President Al Gore, who did.) This change, combined with inequitable draft policies that gave exemptions to men in college, resulted in a disproportionate number of working-class White men, African Americans, and Chicano men being drafted. Whereas the Korean War had been the first time that fighting for one's country had not been primarily reserved for White men, the war in Vietnam placed the dangerous burden of frontline duty on the country's most disenfranchised men. The consequences of this shifting understanding of White masculinity and the recomposition of the U.S. armed forces were far reaching. One indicator is the decline in privileges, prestige, and benefits associated with military service as the color of the U.S. soldier changed.

A third Cold War period began in 1974. It is characterized by powerful conservative responses to social diversity and liberation and to growing economic constraints for most people. This period is marked, moreover, by the return of bellicose conservative rhetoric and policy, much akin to that of the 1950s, that viewed complex social relations through a simplistic individualistic lens. By the mid–1970s, New Right politics—rooted in conservative politics that had gained strength in rural and suburban areas of the West during the 1960s—had emerged as a dominant national influence.

Increased inequities in the western social structure dramatically affected people's lives in the Cold War West. Conservative fiscal and social policies, such as California's Proposition 13, redistributed wealth upward and restructured local and state-level tax bases such that adequate housing, quality education, and well-paying jobs became scarcer commodities, especially in urban areas. On the national level, the increased stratification of society was also clear. Between 1977 and 1990, the gap between rich and poor widened, as income for the wealthiest 20 percent of society rose by 33 percent while at the same time the income for one of out every three working Americans fell below the poverty line. Meanwhile, conservative fiscal and social policies were rationalized with renewed calls to fight Communism abroad and the adoption of a bellicose conservative policy at home. Racialized groups, gays and lesbians, and immigrants were "scapegoated" in the New Right's domestic fiscal and economic policies. The Immigration Reform and Control Act of 1986, for instance, was just one volley in an effort of the Right to blame economic problems on immigrants and nondocumented peoples.

While I have suggested a beginning date for this third period—1974—deciding on a terminal date for it and the Cold War is more problematic. The year 1989, which is commonly used, emphasizes political shifts in Europe—the fall of the Berlin Wall, the end of Soviet domination in Eastern Europe. But this date ignores the persistence of Cold War issues in Asia, such as the continued existence of two Koreas, two Chinas, and U.S. troops in Asia. The continuation of the Cold War in Asia, incidentally, is a fact to which western American historians should be more attentive, given both the diverse Asian populations in the West as well as the relationship between the Far West and Pacific Rim countries. If the economic aspects of the Cold War rather than the political changes are emphasized, however—that is, if one sees the Cold War as largely an effort to extend U.S.-dominated capitalism around the world—then the reintroduction of capitalist market economics into Communist China and Vietnam suggests another way to mark the end of the Cold War. Or, if we focus on the domestic scene, then the scapegoating of immigrants, the poor, and gays and lesbians in the late-1980s and the 1990s suggests that the Cold War, as a conservative effort to shape U.S. society, is not over.

Each of these three periods—from 1945 to 1965, from 1965 to 1974, and from 1974 on—embodies struggles between constraining and liberatory forces in the western and larger U.S. society. If one were to look back at the entire Cold War period, it is clear that the first tendency, containment, was the most successful. True, there had been remarkable movement in the extension of full political rights to previously marginalized racialized groups and to gays and lesbians. But the enforcement of these rights and the transformation of cultural and social patterns have lagged far behind. Usually, it has been the few more wealthy, educated, and mainstream among marginalized groups who have been able to take advantage of these opportunities. These exceptions do not camouflage the fact that containment has been a dominant tendency throughout the period. A similar interrelationship between liberatory and conservative efforts, and the ultimate triumph of the latter, can be seen in the experiences of White women as well. Only those of well-to-do backgrounds were socially and politically able to move up, and only so far before encountering glass ceilings. Ultimately, the Cold War shaped the western social structure along exclusionary lines, all the while maintaining a deceptive western ethos of independence and mobility. Even the highly praised expansion of the modern middle class was constructed along these conservative lines.

That conservative forces triumphed over liberatory ones and, moreover, that they were able to shape and derail progressive efforts, are points suggested in this final example. On April 28, 1989, Colonel and Chief Nurse of the Washington State National Guard Margarethe Cammermeyer said the words "I am a lesbian" in response to routine questions asked by agents of the Defense Investigative Service. Those words prompted the Army and National Guard to discharge her. Cammermeyer's subsequent legal battle, and those of other out gay and lesbian people, to remain part of the armed services hurtled the issue of gays and lesbians in the military to the forefront of national attention. Interestingly, this debate came at the same time that the Cold War between the United States and the Soviet Union was drawing to a close.

The legal, political, and social contentions raised by Cammermeyer are indicative of larger, long-term changes and strivings within U.S. society about gender, race, and class relations. Many of the extraordinary changes and the limitations issued forth during the Cold War are symbolized in Cammermeyer's story. First, her ability to have a career is a result of public and private revolutions concerning appropriate roles for males and females. Second, the facts that as a White, middle-class woman Cammermeyer pursued her career for twenty-eight years in the military and that she defines herself foremost as an Army person in the service of her country are both indicative of the extent to which the national psyche has been "militarized"—that is, they show that militarism has been mainstreamed and integrated into multifarious sectors of the civilian economy and society. Third, Cammermeyer's insistence that gays and lesbians "are no different" points to a conservative transformation within the primarily middle-class and White Gay Liberation movement; the earlier flowering and expression of the movement in the late-1960s had emphasized its difference from the mainstream heterosexual world, whereas by the late 1980s the movement stressed similarities. Fourth, the Army's discharge of Cammermeyer illustrates the Cold War escalation of gender and sexuality as a basis for "otherness." Finally, both Cammermeyer's private and public choices, and the Cold War, are intricately tied to region, specifically the American West. Cammermeyer lived in Seattle, but moved to San Francisco to further her military career. While there, she met out lesbians and began to come out herself. Her partner is based in Los Angeles. On the one hand, those are superficial associations with region, as surely there are similar stories along the eastern seaboard and elsewhere. Yet, the West is significant as being a site for a large, out, gay and lesbian population in the San Francisco Bay area, and the West experienced the greatest growth of public and private military spending during the Cold War. So, while the specifics of Cammermeyer's story are not unique to the West, the region's extensive militarization and connection to San Francisco as the nation's gay capital tie these issues and her story to the region.

Cammermeyer thus symbolizes the triumph of containment, in general, and more specifically its cooptation of emancipatory efforts. The very fact that a principal struggle among gay and lesbian groups during the late 1980s and early

1990s was to enable gays and lesbians to serve openly in the military is in itself a sign of the rightward shift—the triumph of containment—upon the regional and national social and political landscape. Cammermeyer's struggles point out how, throughout the Cold War, containment and emancipation were inextricably linked, but the former has been victorious ultimately in its conservative structuring of western U.S. society.

BIBLIOGRAPHIC ESSAY

Racial, class, and gender relations overlap both in people's lives and in the historiography of the Cold War West; therefore, readers seeking to pursue any one issue should cross-reference among the following categories.

For works on racialized groups, see Sarah Deutsch, "Landscape of Enclaves: Race Relations in the West, 1865–1990," in *Under an Open Sky: Rethinking America's Western Past,* ed. William Cronon, George Miles, and Jay Gitlin (New York: W. W. Norton, 1992); Sucheng Chan, Douglas Henry Daniels, Mario T. García, and Terry P. Wilson, eds., *Peoples of Color in the American West* (Lexington, MA: D. C. Heath, 1994); *Making Face, Making Soul = Haciendo Caras: Creative and Critical Perspectives by Feminists of Color* / edited by Gloria Anzaldúa. San Francisco: *Aunt Lute Foundation Books,* c1990).

Works on Native Americans include Mary Crow Dog, *Lakota Women* (New York: Harper Perennial Books, 1991); Alvin M. Josephy, Jr., *Red Power: The American Indians' Fight for Freedom* (New York: American Heritage Press, 1971); Donald Fixico, *Termination and Relocation: Federal Indian Policy, 1945–1960* (Albuquerque: University of New Mexico Press, 1986); Donald L. Parman, *Indians and the American West in the Twentieth Century* (Bloomington: Indiana University Press, 1994); Elaine M. Neils, *Reservation to City: Indian Migration and Federal Relocation* (Chicago: Department of Geography, University of Chicago, 1971); Kenneth R. Philip, *Indian Self-Rule: First-Hand Accounts of Indian–White Relations from Roosevelt to Reagan* (Salt Lake City: Howe Bros., 1986); Stephen E. Cornell, *The Return of the Native: American Indian Political Resurgence* (New York: Oxford University Press, 1988).

Writings on African Americans include Albert S. Broussard, *Black San Francisco: The Struggle for Racial Equality in the West, 1900–1954* (Lawrence: University Press of Kansas, 1993); Lawrence P. Cruochett, Lonnie G. Bunch III, and Martha Kendall Winnacher, *The History of the East Bay Afro-American Community, 1851–1977* (Oakland: Northern California Center for Afro-American History and Life, 1989); Mary L. Dudziack, "Desegregation as a Cold War Imperative," *Stanford Law Review* 41 (November 1988): 61–120; Jay David and Elaine Crane, eds., *The Black Soldier: From the American Revolution to Vietnam* (New York: William Morrow and Co., 1971); Quintard Taylor, "Blacks and Asians in a White City: Japanese-Americans and African-Americans in Seattle, 1890–1940," *Western Historical Quarterly* 22 (November 1991): 401–29; Quintard Taylor, *The Forging of a Black Community: Seattle's Central District, from 1870 through the Civil Rights Era* (Seattle: University of Washington Press, 1994).

For works on Asian Americans, see Ronald Takaki, *Strangers from a Different Shore: A History of Asian Americans* (New York: Penguin Books, 1990); Sucheng Chan, *Asian Americans: An Interpretive History* (Boston: Twayne Publishers, 1991); Ruthanne Lum McCunn, *Chinese American Portraits: Personal Histories, 1828–1988* (San Francisco: Chronicle Books, 1988); Judy Yung, *Unbound Feet: A Social History of Chinese Women in San Francisco* (Berkeley: University of California Press, 1995); Edwin B. Almirol, *Ethnic Identity and Social Negotiation: A Study of a Filipino Community in California* (New York: AMS Press, 1985).

For scholarly works on Mexican Americans, see Mario Barrera, *Race and Class in the Southwest: A Theory of Racial Inequality* (Notre Dame: University of Notre Dame Press, 1979); Matt S. Meier and Feliciano Rivera, *The Chicanos: A History of Mexican Americans* (New York: Hill and Wang, 1972); Arnoldo De León, *Mexican Americans in Texas: A Brief History* (Arlington Heights, IL: Harlan Davidson, 1993); Mario T. García, *Mexican Americans: Leadership, Ideology, and Identity, 1930–1960* (New Haven: Yale University Press, 1989); David Gutiérrez, *Walls and Mirrors: Mexican Americans, Mexican Immigrants, and the Politics of Ethnicity* (Berkeley: University of California Press, 1995); Juan Gómez-Quiñones, *Chicano Politics: Reality and Promise, 1940–1990* (Albuquerque: University of New Mexico Press, 1990).

Scholarly writings on the western economy often speak to class relations. For analysis of western economic growth following World War II, see Gerald D. Nash, *The American West in the Twentieth Century: A Short History of an Urban Oasis* (Englewood Cliffs, NJ: Prentice-Hall, 1973), and Bradford Luckingham, "The American Southwest: An Urban View," *Western Historical Quarterly* 15 (July 1984): 261–80.

For the interaction between Cold War politics and labor issues, see George N. Green, "Anti-Labor Politics in Texas, 1941–1957," and Monsignor Charles O. Rice, "The Tragic Purge of 1948: A Personal Recollection," both in *American Labor in the Southwest: The First One Hundred Years*, ed. James C. Foster (Tucson: University Press of Arizona, 1982); Richard M. Bernard and Bradley R. Rice, eds., *Sunbelt Cities: Politics and Growth Since World War II* (Austin: University of Texas Press, 1983); Luis Leobardo Arroyo, "Chicano Participation in Organized Labor: The CIO in Los Angeles, 1938–1950," *Aztlán* 6 (1975): 277–301; David Montejano, *Anglos and Mexicans in the Making of Texas, 1836–1986* (Austin: University of Texas Press, 1987); Juan Ramon García, *Operation Wetback: The Mass Deportation of Mexican Undocumented Workers in 1954* (Westport, CT: Greenwood Press, 1980).

For writings on women and wage labor, see Lourdes Arguelles, "Undocumented Female Labor in the United States Southwest: An Essay on Migration, Consciousness, Oppression and Struggle," in *Between Borders: Essays on Mexicana/Chicana History*, ed. Adelaida R. Del Castillo (Encino, CA: Floricanto Press, 1990); Evelyn Nakano Glenn, *Issei, Nisei, War Bride: Three Generations of Japanese American Women in Domestic Service* (Philadelphia: Temple University Press, 1986); Rosalinda Méndez González, "Distinctions in Western Women's Experience: Ethnicity, Class, and Social Change," in *The Women's West*, ed. Susan Armitage and Elizabeth Jameson, (Norman: University of Oklahoma Press, 1987); Patricia Zavella, *Women's Work and Chicano Families: Cannery Workers of the Santa Clasa Valley* (Ithaca, NY: Cornell University Press, 1987).

For readings on leftists of color in the West, see Him Mark Lai's "To Bring Forth a New

China, To Build a Better America: The Chinese Marxist Left in America to the 1960s," and "A Voice of Reason: Life and Times of Gilbert Woo, Chinese American Journalist," both in *Chinese America: History and Perspectives* (1992): 3–82 and 83–124, respectively; Karl G. Yoneda, *Ganbatte: Sixty-Year Struggle of a Kiei Worker* (Los Angeles: Asian American Studies Center at the University of California, Los Angeles, 1983); and Mario T. García, *Memories of Chicano History: The Life and Narrative of Bert Corona* (Berkeley: University of California Press, 1994).

Works on the family include Elaine Tyler May's *Homeward Bound: American Families in the Cold War Era* (New York: Basic Books, 1988); Juan L. Gonzales, Jr., *Racial and Ethnic Families in America* (Dubuque, IA: Kendall/Hunt Publishing Co., 1992); and Micaela di Leonardo, "The Myth of the Urban Village: Women, Work, and Family Among Italian-Americans in Twentieth Century California," in *The Women's West*, ed. Susan Armitage and Elizabeth Jameson (Norman: University of Oklahoma Press, 1987).

For works on gender and sexual relations or gays and lesbians, see John D'Emilio and Estelle Freedman, *Intimate Matters: A History of Sexuality in America* (New York: Harper & Row, 1988), and Allan Bérubé, *Coming Out Under Fire: The History of Gay Men and Women in World War II* (New York: Macmillan, 1990); Susan Stryker and Jim Van Buskirk, *Gay by the Bay: A History of Queer Cultures in the San Francisco Bay Area* (San Francisco: Chronicle Books, 1996); Katie Gilmartin, "The Very House of Difference: Intersections of Identities in the Life Histories of Colorado Lesbians, 1940–1965," (Ph.D. diss., Yale University, 1995 and forthcoming from the Columbia University Press); John D'Emilio, *Sexual Politics, Sexual Communities: The Making of a Homosexual Minority in the United States, 1940–1970* (Chicago: University of Chicago Press, 1983); Randy Shilts, *Mayor of Castro Street: The Life and Times of Harvey Milk* (New York: St. Martin's Press, 1982); Stuart Timmons, *The Trouble with Harry Hay: Founder of the Modern Gay Movement* (Boston: Alyson, 1990); and Walter L. Williams, *The Spirit and the Flesh: Sexual Diversity in American Indian Culture* (Boston: Beacon Press, 1986).

For works on the intersection of the politics of masculinity and femininity and the Cold War, see Cynthia Enloe, *Does Khaki Become You? The Militarization of Women's Lives* (Boston: South End Press, 1983); and Susan Jeffords, *The Remasculinization of America: Gender and the Vietnam War* (Bloomington: University of Indiana Press, 1989).

CHAPTER FOUR

THE GREAT CANTONMENT
Cold War Cities in the American West

❧

RIC DIAS

The modern trans-Mississippi American West is overwhelmingly urban. A higher percentage of residents in the American West live in urban areas than do people in any other part of the United States. Westerners themselves might be surprised to learn that 80 percent of all western residents live in metropolitan areas that have a population in excess of 60,000, while 10 percent live in communities from 2,500 to 60,000 in size. This fact seems to contradict the popular mythology of the West's landscape consisting solely of wide open spaces, its inhabitants living in small towns and isolated ranches. As we approach the twenty-first century, the lone cowboy or rancher on the range remains an indelible image of western life recognized around the globe, yet this deep-seated imagery masks the reality of the West's urban past and present. Western cities have always played a critical role in the region's settlement.

The last fifty years have seen western cities explode in size and influence (just 43 percent of westerners were urban dwellers in 1940), making for one of the most fascinating population shifts in U.S. urban history. After forty years of migration westward, more than one in four Americans today lives in a western city. With the advent of the Cold War in the late 1940s, the factors that had driven western city building up to that time intensified, catalyzed by a greater and persistent federal presence. For the first time in American history, the government maintained a huge number of functioning installations in spite of the absence of a declared war. The Pentagon operated approximately three hundred military bases and installations west of the Mississippi during the Cold War. This powerful and pervasive martial presence helped mold burgeoning western cities, contributing to the urban West's spectacular growth (the total metropolitan population of the West rocketed from 11.8 million in 1940 to 63 million in 1990). This essay will explore the influence of military installations on the urbanization of the West, and how they helped create the region's unique cityscapes during the Cold War.

LONG-TERM TRENDS IN WESTERN URBANIZATION

In his famous essay, "The Significance of the Frontier in American History," delivered at the World's Columbian Exposition in Chicago on July 12, 1893, Frederick Jackson Turner argued that exposure of immigrants to life on the American frontier provided the seminal experience for creating our singular national institutions and values. The consequences of "savagery and civiliza-tion" meeting on the frontier set Americans apart from other peoples. While contemporary historians have pointed out significant omissions and errors in Turner's essay, two aspects of his work merit attention here. Turner reminds us that western settlement patterns are closely tied to the topography of the land, foliage, mineral deposits, and the relative abundance of open space. Second, Turner depicts the new man created in the West (he ignored women in this process) as one who possessed a strong sense of individualism, thereby under-scoring the disdain westerners had for heavy-handed government control (Tur-ner did not mention the dependence westerners had on government money and protection). The modern western city is a product of environmental fac-tors and the choices its residents made for how it should look and function.

The mental picture most people have of the West as a land of desolate open space has some factual basis. Turner, for example, emphasized the "wild" and "uninhabited" nature of the West. Western observers have noted the relative lack of rainfall west of Mississippi (notwithstanding the significant exceptions, such as the rain belt along the Pacific Coast). The Great Plains receive 10–20 inches per year, approximately half the annual amount registered in the Mis-sissippi Valley. The Southwest and parts of the Northwest have expansive arid regions. The West's aridity has forced residents to congregate together and to exploit water resources, often aided by massive government support. Geogra-phy has helped determine why no other region of the United States is both so full of open space and so urban.

With its high ratio of open land to population, the western environment has encouraged city builders to push outward more enthusiastically than upward. Americans have always displayed a strong desire to own their homes, but the dense urbanization of the eastern United States during the industrial revolu-tion of the nineteenth century excluded many residents from participating in widespread land ownership. In the new cities sprouting in the West, however, the majority of residents still could become landowners. In this country's insatiable push to the Pacific, cities formed the forward edge of the juggernaut. Urban areas contained land offices, banks, stores, and military outposts—all the institutional underpinnings of an expansionist modern society. Reflecting Americans' incessant movement and affection for growth, these early western cities were largely unplanned and assumed a ragged and piecemeal layout.

With time, western cities cleaned up their appearance, but they continued to look different than their eastern counterparts. Western urban residents noted and approved of the differences between eastern and western cities. In the early twentieth century, leading figures in city planning, such as Walden Sweet, Clarence Dykstra, and Frank Clark, popularized a "western viewpoint" on city building, laying out spacious and low-density urban areas. These men wanted to build cities that facilitated home ownership. Los Angeles emerged as the epitome of the rambling western city, a distinction that it still holds. The West's generous amount of land has shaped the choice of home-building styles. As a result, Spanish colonial, bungalow, and ranch-style homes have become conspicuously popular in the West. In their architecture Western homes tend to have larger windows to appreciate the outdoors, patios and porches to bring the environment into the living space, and dominant horizontal lines. Suburbs and single-family dwelling units have long dominated western cityscapes. While eastern cities also contain suburbs and single-family dwellings, interesting regional differences remain. Western cityscapes are characterized by a preponderance of low-profile, often single-story houses. Tall buildings and two-story houses do rise from western cities, but most of the western skyline is noteworthy for its low uniformity. Older, eastern cities seem taller and more congested by comparison. Peaked roofs and double-story construction dominate eastern metropolitan areas. Even apartments and federal housing projects in the West often eschew the height reached by similar dwellings in the East.

This western urban strategy of building outward became manageable for larger cities with the popularization of two technological achievements in this century: the automobile and the highway. The car made great strides in public acceptance in the 1920s and 1930s, displacing public transportation systems across the West (until their more recent comeback). Auto makers and tire manufacturers did not conspire to force westerners to dump trolleys and buses against their will; people preferred the freedom of movement offered by the auto. The overwhelming desire of westerners to drive their own vehicles on smooth-moving freeways allowed rapid movement in the growing cities of the West. Turner believed that the frontier closed in 1890, but quite possibly he would have seen in the car-dominated cities of the modern West the persistence of frontier individualism. Yet, the greater freedom of movement afforded by technology did not result in all western residents enjoying unimpeded access within cities. Mike Davis and John Findlay have pointed out how effective decentralized western cities have been in keeping different ethnic, racial, and class groups virtually isolated from each other. Building outward, a process the automobile greatly facilitated, should not be confused with social fluidity. Behind its uniform appearance, the western city has internal structure and demarcated borders.

Beyond the effects of the environment and technology in shaping western cities, the federal government has exerted a special influence. In the nineteenth century, Anglo-Americans looked to the state to eradicate and manage Native Americans, disperse land, and make internal improvements (e.g., railroad construction and water projects). In the twentieth century, the federal government remains the largest single landowner in the West, and it continues to exert tremendous control. During the New Deal of the 1930s, the government stepped up involvement in western development. Washington funneled billions of dollars to the West in the New Deal, and used the Departments of Interior and Agriculture to plan the region's economic development. The Federal Housing Administration and the Veterans Administration bolstered home ownership nationwide. The completion of huge federal water projects like Hoover Dam (and later Grand Coulee, and Bonneville Dams) made water and electricity available to areas previously limited in development due to the harsh environment. The New Deal energized the modern West's "take-off."

As the nation turned from fighting the Great Depression to fighting the Axis powers, federal support for the West experienced a dramatic increase. Indeed, the impact of the Second World War, as Gerald Nash has shown, was phenomenal. Over $100 billion dollars flowed west as the country prepared for and then fought World War II. To prosecute the two-front war, Washington spent over $4 billion on construction and maintenance of western bases between 1940 and 1945. The West possessed military installations before 1940, but America's participation in the war transformed these installations into giants. Over 7 million people moved west between 1940 and 1945, virtually all of them to the burgeoning western cities on the Pacific Coast to work in installations and defense-related factories. Suddenly, these affected communities found new foci for development, jobs, and political power.

Had World War II ended with the Soviet Union and the United States as allies, the bases, depots, hospitals, and training camps would surely have closed, just as they had after 1918, with the end of the Great War. The government would have mustered out the troops and maintained only a skeleton military force, dictated by Americans' traditional distaste for maintaining large standing armies. Many in labor, business, and government feared a repeat of the "reconversion depression" that followed the 1918 armistice because of defense industry cutbacks. That reconversion to a peacetime economy, however, never really materialized after 1945. As tension between Moscow and Washington escalated, a state of virtual warfare quickly emerged.

THE COLD WAR HEATS UP WESTERN URBANIZATION

Americans discovered that the struggle against the Communists would last longer than that against the Axis powers. The government called for constant vigilance against the "Red Menace," and the nation maintained a state of alertness that frequently lapsed into paranoia. Defense spending slowed briefly in the late 1940s, but it quickly rose again to between $35 to $50 billion per year during the 1950s, bankrolling a formidable fighting force. Located adjacent to cities, defense plants and military installations brought the Cold War close to home. The cities of Hanford, Washington, and Los Alamos, New Mexico, shared an obvious connection to the nation's nuclear defense strategy. But hundreds of western cities felt the Cold War's impact on urbanization even if they lacked atomic laboratories or missile silos. With broadly placed missile silos, Strategic Air Command (SAC) bases, and fighter squadrons stationed near American cities, the Pentagon fought the Cold War in Americans' backyards. In short, the Cold War institutionalized the state of war and induced the cantonment of the American West.

While some states felt the federal government's war on world Communism more than others, every western state, to a greater or lesser degree, participated in the effort. Accurate numbers for the impact on each state are difficult to arrive at because of the oscillatory nature of military budgets, the transitory nature of provocative international incidents, and the movement of forces and production between sites, but some western states clearly played a larger military role than did others. In Oregon and Wyoming, the number of people employed in defense industries or stationed at military bases stayed small, under 5,000 apiece, and the total number of bases and installations in each states remained under ten. At the other extreme, California and Texas corralled the most sites, possessing between them approximately 150 at one point. At their peak, California installations employed upwards of 125,000 to 150,000 civilians, while those in Texas employed some 70,000. The West's most populous states had the greatest martial presence.

To fight the Cold War, the government depended heavily on existing installations and added new ones as needed. Immediately following the end of

World War II, the government began closing bases deemed as surplus, but international tensions temporarily reversed this action. The greatest flurry of reactivation came during the heightened anxiety of the Korean Conflict of 1950–53. Approximately twenty bases were reopened in the West alone. Despite these Cold War tensions, economic considerations nevertheless forced the Pentagon to consolidate resources and close more installations than it opened. Western bases remained open, however, because the United States fought its most significant overseas Cold War conflicts, Korea and Vietnam, in the Pacific theater. And because of the activity on nearby bases, Western cities became, in effect, staging grounds for war. The Pentagon constructed installations of various types during the Cold War, and most of them, over two dozen in all, lay west of the Mississippi. A prime example of the military's great interest in the West can be seen in the growth of the Strategic Air Command. Of the twenty-five SAC bases (as of 1982) in the United States, seventeen are located west of the Mississippi. The environment also made the region attractive. The West's huge plateaus, salt beds, and deserts offered open spaces and year-round clear skies. If the Cold War ever became hot, it would be fought primarily in the skies with long-range bombers, missiles, and satellites. Thus, it was crucial to test and carry out war preparedness measures in fair weather and open spaces. During World War II, Army Air Corps planners recognized the connection between fair weather and the military utility of an airfield. New bases were built with this fact in mind. Historian Carl Abbott quotes one general of the 1940s, "It can be stated that the difficulty of continuous flying training is in direct proportion to the distance north of approximately the 37th parallel." Virtually every major western city south of this line acquired a new or expanded air base during World War II. During the Cold War, these "sunshine belt" bases continued in operation.

The trans-Mississippi West particularly appealed to Pentagon planners. The availability of public and sparsely populated land was the main draw. The federal government has always been the largest landowner in the West, and having access to large amounts of land expedited construction. As of the 1980s, the federal government held 30 percent or more of all land in ten western states (in descending order they are: Nevada, Idaho, Utah, Wyoming, Oregon, California, Arizona, Colorado, New Mexico, and Washington). Nevada tops the list at 85 percent. Bases built on western lands, which were scattered over a wide, thinly populated area, could be expanded without the danger of running up against impacted urban areas. For example, in the 1990s, Texas is over 80 percent urban and has about fifty-four people per square mile, contrasted with 371 people per square mile in New York.

Desire for open space did not mean that the Pentagon always looked for isolated locations. The military did not favor the West because it could escape human settlement. While military planners sought remote locations for a few installations of a sensitive or dangerous nature (such as White Sands Missile Range in the New Mexican desert and Dugway Proving Grounds in Utah), most military bases adjoined cities of varying sizes. The ten largest military bases west of the Mississippi (Pendleton, North Island, Carson, Pearl Harbor, Long Beach, Kirtland, Sill, Bliss, and Lewis) were either contiguous to or within an easy drive of western cities. Today, each of these sites has more than 20,000 civilian and military employees, not counting dependents. In fact, proximity to urban centers was an important factor in the success of installations because of their dependence on civilians for labor and provisions. Civilians with special skills, such as scientists, engineers, and mathematicians, are more easily recruited from cities than from the hinterlands or from the military's labor pool. Similarly, products like food and building materials are often more easily obtained from local sources. Most civilians probably have little notion of the military's dependence on nonmilitary personnel. Two large complexes in California (with figures from the early 1990s) are instructive. The Marine Corps' Camp Pendleton in California houses some 35,000 active-duty personnel and employs 3,700 civilians, while the China Lake Naval Base has 1,000 active-duty and 5,200 civilian employees, which constitutes a civilian-to-military ratio of 5:1.

Although it may appear that the government steamrolled into the West and imposed its martial presence during the Cold War, in reality westerners largely accepted the installations, embraced them, and even queued up for more. Regional politicians and area boosters have generally fallen over themselves to steer military projects to their areas, often bringing themselves into conflict with other like-minded communities. Because of the sizeable revenue that can flow into a city from a nearby military site, many communities have become dependent on installations for their livelihood, leading to a situation historian Roger Lotchin calls "a kind of military welfarism." Some westerners have bristled at efforts by Washington to regulate land use (as seen in the "sagebrush rebellion" of the 1970s and 1980s), but few have objected to the construction or expansion of Washington's military sites. As Gregory Fontenot has suggested, the relationship between city and base was viewed as symbiotic, not parasitic.

Western communities have organized groups to promote growth and have curried support from Washington. Richard White has called these powerful booster groups "growth networks," a term that reflects the varied community elements that constitute them. Representing interests from finance, real estate, business, and politics, growth networks have taken advantage of Washington's commitment to arm the region during the Cold War. These groups have tried to bring some focus and planning to the influx of money, industry, and population into the region. Some growth networks have tried to invigorate traditional downtown areas. Others have tried to spur growth in newer, peripheral zones. Either way, growth networks have looked to federal money to underwrite economic expansion in their localities (although they often chaffed at the regulation that accompanied federal funding). The idea was that federal projects would be less affected by economic peaks and valleys than projects funded by private-sector sources.

San Antonio, Texas, is one of the outstanding examples of the close relationship between base and city in the Cold War. In the early 1980s the dollar inflow for the military payroll flowing into San Antonio was staggering. San Antonio and Bexar County are home to some 40,000 active-duty people. The region boasts of four Air Force bases, an Army fort and hospital, the Fifth Army headquarters, plus a handful of Navy and Marine Corps units. Not to be overlooked, the county is also home to 35,000 retired personnel (who often locate near bases to use health care and shopping privileges). The yearly military payroll totals over $1.5 billion. County officials estimate that for every military dollar spent, over $2.50 is generated in business. The early 1980s were tough for western states such as Texas whose economies were heavily based in energy. But because of the river of federal money flowing into San Antonio, the community could rest easier knowing that every year over $8 million dollars would arrive to help pay for the education of military dependents. The president of the San Antonio Economic Development Foundation supported the military presence and told *US News and World Report* in 1982 that "the military cushions us against recession."

Gregory Fontenot's study of Junction City, Kansas, and Fort Riley demonstrates the orchestration between local business interests, politicians, and the military. Since the 1860s, city fathers in Junction City realized that the city's economic fate depended upon the fort. Therefore, good relations with Fort Riley became a standing priority. World War II greatly enlarged the fort, and local boosters wished to continue its tremendous impact on the community through the Cold War. Junction City has taken a personal approach to dealing with the military bureaucracy. Local leaders have made it a point to invite officers to local parties and events. Special organizations, such as the Fort Riley Fund and the Fort Riley Ambassadors, have been formed to bring together members of the community and the base. Local politicians, Republicans and Democrats alike, have "locked arms when the welfare and future of Ft. Riley was at stake" and have taken advantage of relationships forged with people stationed at Fort Riley who then moved to assignments in Washington. Since 1972, Junction City has maintained a full-time representative in the nation's capital.

Junction City's aggressive strategy of soliciting the government's approval has been quite successful. In the face of recurring threats from Washington to cut back or move forces elsewhere, Fort Riley has remained large. As of the early 1990s, Fort Riley houses some 15,700 active-duty personnel and 31,000 dependents, as well as employing 4,200 civilians. The total wages paid out at Fort Riley total $400 million every year. On two occasions since 1945, Junction City boosters have steered the First Infantry Division to Fort Riley when Washington had wanted to send it elsewhere. The city's growth network has been greatly responsible for the rise in population in Junction City, which has grown from being a hamlet in 1940 to a town of 20,000 in 1980. To close an installation is not a decision that originates in communities; it starts with the military command. Still, Junction City has proven the effectiveness of local action.

Not all westerners welcomed the lasting changes brought by military installations during the Cold War. Farmers around Fort Riley formed the most vocal group to oppose base expansion in the 1960s. They resented orders to sell land coming from a distant government authority (as Turner might have predicted), against whom there was little or no hope for appeal. Ultimately, these five hundred residents lost their bid to halt expansion, swamped by the enthusiastic embrace of military bases typical of urban westerners during the Cold War. In other communities, some residents objected to the large numbers of unfamiliar people moving into their hitherto intimate and sometimes exclusive communities, and to the growing stress placed on municipal services. Others objected to the diversification of their communities. Military bases bring hundreds or thousands of people, many with different colored skin and unfamiliar accents. Carl Abbott describes most western communities through the early 1940s as fairly quiet, insulated, and interested in maintaining the status quo. Growth networks had to silence traditional politicians who balked at change. Denver Mayor Ben Stapleton represents this old guard of western politicians who were determined to stop unwanted social changes threatened by the Cold War. Old business interests in downtown Denver backed Stapleton and his politics of favoritism, as he made change a campaign issue in the 1940s. Stapleton railed against the recent swarm of defense-related arrivals into Denver. Stapleton had been mayor since 1923 with only a brief interruption, but his unwillingness to embrace the newcomers and charge forward with rapid growth finally cost him his job. In 1947, pro-growth candidate James Q. Newton took the mayoral election and signaled the dawn of a new era for Denver. Newton swept into office with a power base of recent arrivals and small business people, fresh sources of capital, and a staff of outside advisors. Still, Denver politics, like politics in the rest of the West, did not change overnight.

While military installations have enjoyed enthusiastic approval by boosters because they were perceived as being revenue catalysts, the reality of economic boom from bases has actually been more complicated. San Antonio's rather steady and high returns from its military installations have not been reproduced equally throughout the West. Darwin Daicoff has compiled data from a number of studies examining the local impact of installations. The magnitude of local impact varies tremendously, depending on an installation's size and function, its percentage of civilian employees, and its on-site facilities. For example, shipyards employ mostly civilians (large numbers of them), while SAC bases have far less call for civilians. The housing and shopping opportunities an installation provides for personnel also dramatically alters its local monetary impact. If proponents for a base claim that a new base's payroll will amount to $10 million per year, most of that money might never see its way off the base. Married personnel who live on-base tend to spend about 60 percent of their income on base, on food and housing, leaving 40 percent for the community. On the other hand, installations staffed predominantly by single men (like missile silos or test ranges) might find that 70 percent of the salaries are spent on recreation and entertainment in the community. When news of the opening or expansion of an installation hit the local press, property rates around the site soared. This was especially true for rentals and lower-cost housing units. Construction workers and military personnel quickly soaked up available housing around the installation. With sizeable growth, the government was often asked to fill the housing void. Stopgap federal housing, however, was often substandard in construction, and over the long term tended to become dilapidated. House trailers became common around military installations to meet the needs for low-cost housing. These accommodations gave transitory military families affordable shelter, but they quickly deteriorated, which resulted in depressed property values surrounding the base. Daicoff did not report that real-estate values rose over the long term in cities tied to expanding installations. Civilian employees, being less transitory than military personnel, tended to buy nicer homes in burgeoning suburbs around an installation. And the retail trades enjoyed an even more significant boost from bases over time than did the real-estate market. Daicoff pointed out that new housing around installations usually included shopping centers. This combination contributed to the multi-centered character of western cities.

Closures and cutbacks, however, are also part of the life-cycle of installations, an aspect not usually trumpeted by proponents. San Antonio and Junction City are examples of cities that so far have survived the recent base closures. Since 1945, San Antonio has grown and diversified its economy. Today it is tied to, but not solely dependent on, the military for economic health. Junction City, on the other hand, is very vulnerable. If one of San Antonio's bases closed, the impact would ripple through the area, and then the community would likely recover. If Fort Riley folded, Junction City would hemorrhage severely. The small Kansas community has attracted other employers, but it is still dangerously dependent on that single installation. Daicoff pointed out that while diversified areas can usually benefit in the long run from a base closure, the same is not always true with smaller, less economically diversified cities. Even if a base closure results in long-term benefit for a city by providing new business opportunities through privatization, it can pull smaller communities through an economic roller coaster. Several waves of military cutbacks during the Cold War have deactivated bases and shattered small communities across the nation.

Because of their potential for growth and their need for space, labor, and resources, military facilities have encouraged the decentralization or multi-centralization of cities. They have, in other words, acted as magnets for economic activity. Albuquerque, New Mexico, provides a striking example of the effect a growing military base can have on the creation of a modern western cityscape. In 1940, one year after the government had built Fort Kirtland outside of town, Albuquerque's population stood at 35,449. The town had relied heavily on the railroad to sustain growth up to that time. With trucks coming into greater use, however, long-term prospects for that industry after the war did not appear promising. Albuquerque's leaders put their hopes on the military instead. Cold War military expenditures on Kirtland reinforced Washington's presence in Albuquerque (nicknamed "Federal City"). By 1950, the city's population had more than doubled to 96,815, and it doubled again to 201,189 by 1960. Even the slower growth in population that took place after 1960 is impressive (in 1970 Albuquerque's population was 244,501, and in 1980 it was 332,239). By the 1980s, Kirtland boasted some 6,000 active-duty personnel with 7,000 dependents, 15,000 civilian employees, and a yearly payroll of approximately $175 million. Spatially, the city spread across the desert during the Cold War as the base grew. In 1940, the fledgling Fort Kirtland was served by a city of Albuquerque covering approximately eleven square miles. When the Second World War ended, the city occupied about sixteen square miles. By 1973, it had burgeoned to seventy-three square miles, and in the 1990s it approaches one hundred square miles.

Albuquerque represents one modestly sized western city that grew where ostensibly no city should have grown in the first place. It overcame the physical limitations of existing in the desert by exploiting water resources. The low land values in the desert encouraged the building of single-family dwellings. The military took advantage of the favorable environmental conditions and supportive community and built a major installation with broad civic support. Vendors moved to be near their bustling martial customer, setting up a host of nearby supporting businesses. Employees looked for an easy commute and found suburbs sprouting outside of town to accommodate them. Ultimately, these suburbs became capable of supplying most of the needs of their residents for goods, services, and jobs, lessening the relative appeal and power of downtown. Suburbs offered residents a chance to own their own homes with more green space than existed in the city center. With proximity to shopping centers and jobs, Albuquerque residents, like millions of westerners, chose to live in suburbs.

Critics have castigated modern city building as being driven by profligate growth, and have saved their most intense criticism for western cities. William Whyte characterized the far-flung communities constituting greater Los Angeles as "vast smog-filled deserts that are neither city, suburb nor country." In western political struggles, residents against aggressive growth strategies label their opponents as promoting "sprawl," while pro-growth advocates claim to bring prosperity and jobs. The term *sprawl*, however, implies less structure than actually exists in the West's low density, multi-centered urban areas.

A key to understanding the western city that emerged during the Cold War era may be found in the layout of western military installations—although there is no single blueprint for the layout of the military base. Transportation arteries are key to the smooth running of any city or installation. Installations are particularly clear in allowing movement of people and material between the specialized nuclei on the base and the surrounding urban areas. Aerial photographs of bases reveal that their structures are built around streets, lots, and other means of vehicular access. Little on a base lacks direct access to a car or truck. Military installations are as car-friendly as any western city. The configuration of buildings, roads, and any special features of an installation depends on a host of factors. If it is an air base, then the dominant features will include a control tower, runways, and hangars. But even among air bases the design varies because of environmental considerations such as prevailing winds, bodies of water, and existing urban areas. The bulk of the buildings at military sites tend to be built rather low to the ground with generous space left between the structures. Multi-story hospitals and control towers break the base skyline rather than characterize it. It is rare for a base to have a centralized core of tall, important buildings that form a nucleus, or "downtown." (Randolph Air Force Base, outside of San Antonio, is one of the possible exceptions.) Instead, buildings of similar function are usually grouped together, forming a multi-centered arrangement. Similarly, housing units are grouped together into a discrete residential zone or zones, sometimes into married, single, officer, and enlisted-personnel areas. With few exceptions, buildings display a bland institutional sameness. The point here is that the description of the typical military base could be applied to any city in the modern American West.

With the end of the Cold War, America's military will no doubt continue to downsize, a process well underway, and the number of the country's military installations will steadily decrease. In the mid–1980s, America had some two million people under arms and over 730 military installations operating nationwide. There is talk in the mid–1990s of reducing the size of the armed forces by 25 percent, but voices of restraint in Congress might curtail cuts this deep. Cities around the nation will certainly lobby to insure that their installations are not put on the chopping block.

The other side of base closures is that some businesses are hoping to turn the old facilities into new economic opportunities. This is the scenario for March Air Force Base in Southern California. March is situated several miles from the city of Riverside, a city of 250,000 people. During the Cold War, a collection of buildings adjacent to the March Air Station coalesced into the low-density community of Moreno Valley. Today, the greater Moreno Valley area (castigated by many in neighboring communities for its "sprawl") boasts a population zooming toward 100,000, and the city virtually surrounds March. There is no downtown in Moreno Valley, but instead several malls that serve residents. Like so many "post-suburban" areas, Moreno Valley has shed its dependence on larger urban areas and has acquired more political and economic clout. Local growth networks fought to keep March operating at full capacity, but it now appears that a drastic scaling-back will occur. Rather than dwelling on defeat, a local paper called the base a "Field of Dreams," citing its jet-capable 13,000-foot airstrip, its rail service, its eight hundred buildings, and its 7,000 acres of land. The March Joint Powers Commission is laying the groundwork for the reuse of the base and is weighing ideas for privatization. But there are obstacles. Like many former bases, March is pocked with contamination. March has forty-three contaminated sites, and the clean-up cost is estimated to be in excess of $110 million. Homeowners from around the base have organized to call for a ban of jet aircraft from the field, complaining that the noise reduces their property values. In spite of these problems, March will probably find business residents, and Moreno Valley will continue its heady growth as long as people continue to find affordable housing and proximity to services and jobs near the former base.

Looking ahead, a likely legacy of the Cold War on western urbanization will be the persistence of low, expansive, automobile-dominated, multi-centered cities. The federal imperative to urbanize the West has helped create a unique set of cityscapes. As the military consolidates in the post–Cold War era, the privatized sites will exert their influence on urbanization, drawing influence and encouraging new foci for power and influence. The impact of the cantonment of the West will be felt for a long time to come.

BIBLIOGRAPHIC ESSAY

Within the larger field of urban history, there has emerged a growing and vital subfield devoted to the study of western city building. The most prolific contributor to twentieth-century western urban history is Carl Abbott. Two books important to writing this essay were Abbott's *The New Urban America: Growth and Politics in Sunbelt Cities* (Chapel Hill: University of North Carolina Press, 1981), and *The Metropolitan Frontier: Cities in the Modern American West* (Tucson: University of Arizona Press, 1993). See also his *Portland: Planning, Politics, and Growth in a Twentieth-Century City* (Lincoln: University of Nebraska Press, 1983). Also useful in writing this essay was Mike Davis's *City of Quartz: Excavating the Future in Los Angeles* (New York: Verso, 1990), a lively and provocative social history of Los Angeles, and John Findlay's *Magic Lands: Western Cityscapes and American Culture after 1940* (Berkeley and Los Angeles: University of California Press, 1992). All three authors—Abbott, Davis, and Findlay—address urban planning in depth and stress the tendency of modern western cities to adopt multi-centered, low-density, and low-rise layouts with internal divisions that segregated residents along racial, ethnic, and class lines. Excellent essays on recent trends in western city building can be found in Rob Kling, Spencer Olin, and Mark Poster, eds., *Post Suburban California: The Transformation of Orange County Since World War II* (Berkeley: University of California Press, 1991).

Gerald D. Nash has edited a helpful collection of essays that addresses regional urbanization, and several of these discuss the role played by the military. See Nash's *The Urban West* (Manhattan, KS: Sunflower University Press, 1979). The chapters most relevant here are by Roger Lotchin, "The Metropolitan–Military Complex in Comparative Perspective: San Francisco, Los Angeles, and San Diego, 1919–1941"; Mark S. Foster, "The Western Response to Urban Transportation: A Tale of Three Cities, 1900–1945"; and Howard Rabinowitz, "Growth Trends in the Albuquerque SMSA, 1940–1978." Nash has also produced a body of thoroughly researched work on the West in the twentieth century. He interprets World War II as the defining event in the "maturation" of the American West. See Gerald Nash, *The American West in the Twentieth Century: A Short History of an Urban Oasis* (Englewood Cliffs: Prentice-Hall, 1973); *The American West Transformed: The Impact of the Second World War* (Bloomington: Indiana University Press, 1985); *World War II and the West: Reshaping the Economy* (Lincoln: University of Nebraska Press, 1990); and "Planning for the Postwar City: The Urban West in World War II," *Arizona and the West* 27 (July 1985): 99–112. For a review of Frederick Jackson Turner's work and recent trends in western history, see Wilbur Jacob's *On Turner's Trail: 100 Years of Writing Western History* (Lawrence: University of Kansas Press,

1994). An essential background study to western urbanization is William Cronon's *Nature's Metropolis: Chicago and the Great West* (New York: W. W. Norton, 1991).

Roger Lotchin is the leading figure in studying the relationship between base and city. See Roger Lotchin, ed., *The Martial Metropolis: U.S. Cities in War and Peace 1900–1970* (New York: Praeger, 1984). In this collection, Gregory Fontenot's piece, "Junction City–Fort Riley: A Case of Symbiosis," was of particular importance to this essay. Also see Lotchin's *Fortress California, 1910–1960: From Warfare to Welfare* (New York: Oxford University Press, 1992). Ann Markusen has produced a large corpus of work that examines the impact of military installations on their environment. For example, see Ann Markusen and Joel Yudken, *Dismantling the Cold War Economy* (New York: Basic Books, 1992). Gerald Breese edited a text that deals with the influence of installations (military bases and defense factories) on several communities, none of which are located in the West. See Gerald Breese, ed., *The Impact of Large Installations on Nearby Areas: Accelerated Urban Growth* (Beverly Hills: Sage Publications, 1965). See also Paul A. C. Koistinen, *The Military-Industrial Complex: An Historical Perspective* (New York: Praeger, 1979). Darwin Daicoff provided essential data for this essay in a chapter in Bernard Udis, ed., *The Community Impact of Military Installations and the Economic Consequences of Reducing Military Spending* (Lexington: D. C. Heath & Co., 1973). Also, Darwin Daicoff edited *Economic Impact of Military Base Closings* (Washington, D.C.: U.S. Arms Control and Disarmament Agency, 1970). Most literature on bases deals with closure, for example, John Lynch, *Local Economic Development After Military Base Closure* (New York: Praeger, 1970).

Directories of military bases provided much of the raw data for this essay. William R. Evinger, ed., *Directory of Military Bases in the U.S.* (Phoenix: Oryx Press, 1991), proved particularly thorough. Robert Mueller has produced a very useful reference book, *Air Force Bases: Active Air Force Bases Within the United States* (Washington D.C.: Office of Air Force History, 1989). Each of the U.S. military's branches maintains a historical unit. Vincent Demma of the U.S. Army, Richard Hallion of the U.S. Air Force, Danny J. Crawford of the U.S. Marine Corps, and F. G. Leeder of the U.S. Navy provided generous information. The *Riverside (California) Press Enterprise*, March 20–21, 1994, reported on March Air Force Base during its recent downsizing.

CHAPTER FIVE

THE LEGACY OF CONTAINMENT
The Military–Industrial Complex and the New American West

❦

MICHAEL WELSH

Reflecting upon the changes brought to the American West by five decades of postwar military spending, the *Denver Post* in the summer of 1995 published a series of articles entitled "The Atomic Legacy." Reporter Jim Carrier wrote no fewer than fifteen stories about the revolution in public and private life visited upon an area that had depended upon federal largesse since the earliest days of the republic. "In a region once isolated," said the *Post's* Carrier, "the bomb and its aftermath produced enormous wealth, waste, growth, cultural upheaval and scientific and global awakening." Some $4 trillion in federal monies were spent, the Post noted, between 1949 and 1989, to make the West "the front line for the Cold War." At the close of his series, Carrier then asked rhetorically, "Why did we build the Bomb, if not to use [it]?" The concerned reader, said Carrier, could only turn for answers to the solitude of the same deserts where J. Robert Oppenheimer and the Los Alamos scientists had detonated the world's first atomic device on July 16, 1945.

Upon closer examination, Carrier's lament is less cryptic than it seems. The quest for security, whether diplomatic, military, political, or economic, can lead societies and individuals down a divided path of prosperity and destruction the results of which cannot be divined for decades. Now that the titanic ideological struggle between the erstwhile Soviet Union and the United States has subsided, the more mundane features of post-1945 history are coming into view. For the American West, the investment made first by the federal government in World War II, and then in the succeeding four decades of the "Cold War," has transformed the landscape that Jim Carrier discovered as he explored one aspect of the postwar economy: atomic "fallout" and its repercussions.

87

One of the first scholars to speak to the significance of military spending in the American West was Gerald D. Nash, professor emeritus of history at the University of New Mexico. In a series of articles and books on the region in the twentieth century, Nash outlined what he called the "pacesetter" thesis: that the American West in the first half of the century stood in the shadow of the more wealthy and powerful East, only to explode financially and demographically after the Second World War as the originator of many trends and patterns of public and private behavior. In *The American West Transformed: The Impact of the Second World War* (1985); *World War II and the West: Reshaping the Economy* (1990), and his seminal work, *The American West in the Twentieth Century* (1973), Nash defined the West as more than merely Frederick Jackson Turner's individualistic, romantic frontier. Highly urban from its inception (two of three westerners in 1890 resided in a town of 2,500 or more), the region relied heavily upon technology, science, engineering, investment, and immigration to builds its infrastructure. What distinguished the federal presence in the years from 1941 to 1945, and for two generations thereafter, was the scale and scope of public spending in a part of America that could not support itself alone.

Because scholars have yet to examine fully the implications of the military economy nationwide, it has been difficult to determine just how vast and pervasive was the expenditure of public monies in the seventeen states that comprise the American West (from the Dakotas to Texas, from Kansas to California, and to Alaska and Hawai'i). James L. Clayton, editor of *The Economic Impact of the Cold War: Sources and Readings* (1970), believed that the same conditions that brought ten million servicemen and women, and three million more defense workers to the West from 1941 to 1945, appealed to the nation's military strategists as they prepared for the long twilight conflict of values with the Soviet Union. "Cheap land, isolated testing areas, good weather," said the preeminent economist of the military–industrial complex in the West, "a pro-business tax structure, a productive but tractable labor force, and relatively good schools seem to have been the most important location factors." Richard White, author of *"It's Your Misfortune and None of My Own": A New History of the American West* (1991), noted with some amusement that "for military planners all the old liabilities of the West suddenly became virtues." Even the "previously embarrassing surplus of electricity from the Columbia [River]," said White, "became a godsend for the manufacture of aluminum, the major construction material in the airplanes that the military so greatly needed."

The "godsend" that White described resulted from the failure of the social-welfare philosophy of Franklin D. Roosevelt's New Deal to resolve the chronic problems of unemployment in the West and nationwide. When FDR took office in 1933, some 25 percent of America's adult workforce was unemployed. After six years and $60 billion of what conservative critics called "wasteful" spending, unemployment still hovered around 20 percent and a conservative Congress had terminated what it considered the more egregious examples of New Deal abuse. Then war with Germany and Japan brought all able-bodied men and women either into uniform or the workplace, so that by 1945 the rate of unemployment stood at a miniscule 1 percent.

Fearful that the furlough of sixteen million troops, coupled with the loss of factory work upon cessation of wartime contracts (as had happened in 1919 after World War I) would return the nation to the depths of the Depression, the Roosevelt administration advocated more public spending to ease the transition to a peacetime economy. Two measures, in particular, passed Congress in December 1944 that would redefine the West and the nation in the postwar era: the Flood Control Act and the G.I. Bill. The former called upon the West's federal water resource agencies (the U.S. Bureau of Reclamation and the U.S. Army Corps of Engineers), to draft plans for the construction of hundreds of dams and reservoirs that would employ veterans and civilians alike. These public works would also provide such ancillary multipurpose benefits as hydroelectric power, flood protection, irrigation, recreation, and municipal and industrial storage. The latter legislation provided for government assistance to veterans in health care, education, job training, and housing. In both cases, the immediate beneficiaries were not merely soldiers, but citizens who found in public spending a future that the free market could not readily guarantee.

Scholars of the past decade, especially those interested in the environment, have excoriated the excesses of postwar western water development. They have noted with disdain the seemingly thoughtless manner in which these projects altered the natural and human landscape. Yet these students of the environment rarely link these projects to a larger universe of federal efforts to preserve the financial prosperity that World War II had restored after a decade of Depression. Into this arena, then, came word in 1949 that the Soviets had detonated their own atomic device, using plans stolen from the Los Alamos scientific laboratory in remote northern New Mexico. This, as much as anything, shifted the emphasis of the Truman administration from social-welfare programs (the "Fair Deal") to the expansion of what President Dwight D. Eisenhower would lament in his 1961 farewell address as the "military–industrial complex"—the economic and political partnership between weapons manufacturers, politicians, and the nation's armed forces that, in the words of the former Supreme Allied Commander, "would pose costly defense programs as simple solutions" to national security crises.

The triangulation of the G.I. Bill, public works infrastructure projects, and the Cold War allowed the nation's economy to expand in ways that Franklin Roosevelt's Keynesian economic advisors in the 1930s could only have imagined. By 1955, the United States produced 50 percent of all the world's goods and services (this with less than 8 percent of the world's population). American automobiles, consumer products, food and fiber, and technology all changed the face of the globe, creating what diplomatic scholars have referred to as the "Pax Americana" (a comparison to the ancient Roman domination of the Mediterranean world). Yet the linchpin of this prosperity was national security, whether in the actual weaponry and force structure that the United States projected around the world, or whether in the manufacturing and service economy that arose to provide the means of protecting democracy against the hated Communism associated with such countries as the Soviet Union, China, and their client states.

Many students of the Cold War divide the era into two parts: 1945–1960 and 1960–1990. The former was marked by a rapid increase in military capacity and the dispersal of American forces to provide what U.S. State Department official George S. Kennan described as the policy of "containment." This included such foreign engagements as the Berlin airlift (1948), the conflict in Korea (1950–1953), and sparring between America and the Soviet Union in the Middle East, Eastern Europe, and Indochina. Then, the stakes rose in the early 1960s, as the United States committed over half a million troops to the defense of South Vietnam. Following that tragic confrontation were more efforts by both sides in the "war of words" to control oil in the Persian Gulf, and eventually the return of American military prowess under the massive defense rearmament of President Ronald Reagan (1981–89). Only when the agricultural economist-president of the Soviet Union, Mikhail Gorbachev, decided in 1985 to cede defeat to the United States did the nation and the American West learn the full cost of fighting for freedom worldwide.

Most striking for the first generation of postwar military spending in the West are the statistics for population growth. Phoenix, in 1940 a small city of 60,000, grew in two decades to 500,000, and Arizona itself quadrupled in size from 1945 to 1960. California more than doubled in population in the same time period, growing from 9 to 19 million people. The Pacific Northwest, anchored by the shipyards of Portland and the Boeing aircraft plants of Seattle, expanded by 40 percent in the first generation after World War II, and the Rocky Mountain states, led by Denver and Albuquerque (the latter advancing from 35,000 to 200,000), increased some 16 percent. All of this stood in comparison to a national population growth rate of 13 percent, and the only region of the West not to prosper demographically was the Great Plains, which saw slight declines from the Dakotas to Oklahoma.

Many factors merged in the heated atmosphere of the early Cold War to stimulate this growth. The expansion of highways, aided and abetted by the Interstate Highway Act (1956), linked all portions of the isolated West more closely to the burgeoning urban centers from Seattle to San Diego, and from Houston to Grand Forks. Air conditioning, unknown to masses of Americans prior to the Second World War, permitted residents of the desert Southwest to ignore the grimness of western summers. Neil Morgan, journalist and author of the influential *Westward Tilt: The American West Today* (1963), recognized a new type of person drawn to this redesigned West. "The heroes of the new West," said Morgan after surveying the region just prior to the war in Vietnam, "are men not of the past, but of the future." Using a term (*new West*) that a later generation would claim as its own, Morgan observed a region "dominated by the young, and best understood by them, just as the changing terms of science and industry are grasped most readily by the young."

What Morgan chronicled was the proliferation of well-educated scientists, engineers, and businessmen, encouraged to inhabit the new network of suburbs and small towns by G.I. Bill training and housing, federal highways, and employment in the defense industries of California and the West Coast. "More than half of California's economic growth between 1947 and 1957," he concluded, "was attributable to [the] defense industry." The West belonged, as America always had, to the young and the restless, funded in great measure by the U.S. Treasury. "Throughout the West," wrote Morgan, "science and industry tend to travel in tandem." Yet, he could also find historical connections to the western fantasies of long ago: "To the science-oriented youth of the 1960s, the West indeed may seem as much a land of outsized heroes as to the schoolboy of another generation who found his heroes in the West of Zane Grey."

That hopeful generation, whom David Beers would lament three decades later in his 1993 *Harper's Magazine* article, "The Death of Blue-Sky California," was explained best by James Clayton at the defining moment of Cold War western expansion: the late 1960s. Clayton, who taught economics at the University of Utah, addressed the philosophical and statistical realities of the Cold War economy in both the region and nation. One could not escape the lessons of World War II, said Clayton, such as the $2 billion spent in four years to develop and detonate the atomic bomb. From the nuclear communities of Los Alamos, New Mexico, and Hanford, Washington, to the small physics department of the University of New Mexico, money poured into research and development that would whet the postwar appetite of cities and towns throughout the West.

What Clayton found most intriguing in the years 1945–1965 was the West's transcendence of the old industrial order (what later economists would call the "industrial crescent" from Baltimore to Minneapolis). California, which in World War II had ranked third in defense spending (behind New York and Missouri), assumed the nation's lead in military contracting by the peak of the Vietnam era. More impressive was the upward spike of Texas, whose ascent from eleventh place in 1945 to second place a generation later could be linked to the political power of House Speaker Sam Rayburn in the 1950s and to his protégé, Lyndon B. Johnson, who served throughout the 1950s and '60s as Senate Majority Leader, Vice President, and President. Yet, equally surprising was Clayton's discovery that ten of the bottom twenty states in defense spending in 1966 were the western neighbors of the Lone Star and Golden States. California had 17 percent of all defense employees nationwide that year, and the ten western states at the bottom combined for less than 3 percent of American defense employment.

Perhaps most telling was the statistic for research and development, the "intellectual" phase of defense spending. The Golden State in the mid–1960s claimed 69 percent of all such funding from the fledgling National Aeronautics and Space Administration (NASA), and 39 percent of the research contracts let by the Atomic Energy Commission (AEC), the precursor to the Department of Energy (DOE). Because of its status as the "birthplace" of the atomic age, New Mexico in 1964 had 20.4 percent of all AEC research and development monies, divided among the Albuquerque facilities at Sandia Labs and Kirtland Air Force Base, and the Los Alamos compound made famous in World War II. New Mexico thus symbolized the power of western defense investment, in that the Land of Enchantment's overall economic performance in the years from 1945 to 1995 was never strong, ranking anywhere from a peak of thirty-third to a low of forty-seventh in per capita income, even though it ranked from tenth to first in defense spending annually. Only Massachusetts, because of its major universities, and Missouri, with defense contractors surrounding St. Louis, managed to perform at levels more consistent with the West during the Cold War.

If Clayton needed evidence of the connection between western expansion and federal capital, he found it in statistics for economic retrenchment caused by closure of military bases and other defense installations as the Vietnam conflict persisted. Yet, funding for NASA (especially the Apollo moon program), and for rockets (with such mythological names as "Nike," "Zeus," and "Thor") in the 1950s and 1960s, shifted ever further westward. "Although less than one-sixth of the nation" lived in the West, said Clayton in 1967, "in recent years one-fourth of all Department of Defense military and civilian personnel, one-third of all military prime contract awards, and two-thirds of all missile awards have been let to business firms and other organizations located there." In particular, NASA expenditures in the West from 1961 to 1965 (the start of President John F. Kennedy's space program) "amounted to $5,317 million or 48 percent of the total national expenditures of that rapidly growing administration."

Walter McDougall, author of . . . *the Heavens and the Earth: A Political History of the Space Age* (1985), wrote that JFK and his advisors believed that the New Frontier should follow a dual track of peaceful space research and advanced weapons testing. "The Apollo moon program," said McDougall, "was at that time the greatest open-ended peacetime commitment by Congress in history," while "the Kennedy missile program was the greatest peacetime military buildup." Like space itself, the West, said McDougall, offered Kennedy's staff the continuity from success in World War II and the Cold War: "Limitless space, limitless opportunity, limitless challenge." Thus it was no surprise that the decade of the 1960s in the West witnessed the rise of Silicon Valley, near San Jose, known for its research and computer companies, and the growth of Orange County south of Los Angeles, the beneficiary of $50 billion spent by the federal government in Southern California in the 1950s on defense and space research.

As definitive as was the expansion of California under federal investment, Clayton compared the Golden State to his own home of Utah. There, he realized an even more dramatic consequence of public dollars linked to the Cold War. "From 1930," said the Salt Lake City professor, "Utah consistently had a lower per capita personal income than the nation and several other western states." Yet from 1950 to 1966, "Utah's non-agricultural employment rate doubled the national average, and thereafter to 1962 it was four times the national average." These statistics Clayton attributed to the Beehive State's geographical location equidistant from Seattle, San Francisco, Los Angeles, and San Diego. In addition, Utah had "an excellent climate for storage purposes and good transportation facilities for distribution to the remainder of the West." While in World War II the state benefited primarily from storage of chemical weapons (Tooele and Dugway), steel production (the Geneva Iron Works near Provo), or from Hill Air Force Base and the Ogden Ordnance Depot, "beginning in 1957, the emphasis on missile and rocket fuels [prompted by the Soviet launch of the satellite Sputnik] began to create a new defense industry in Utah." Six years later, the state "was receiving $408 million in defense contracts, an absolute gain of 1,700 percent since the Korean war, and the largest gain recorded by any state."

What Clayton proved in his comparison of California and Utah to the national effort in the Cold War was that without defense spending, California's "manufacturing growth probably would have been about one-third, other things being equal, and her net in-migration [averaging 6,000 per month at its height] about one-half of its present level." In the case of Utah, "for the past 55 years [1910–1965] defense expenditures alone have made it possible for [the state] to attract outside residents in significant numbers." Unspoken was the fact that defense contracts for Morton-Thiokol at Brigham City, and other investments, allowed Utah and its dominant Mormon Church to grow strong internationally, and to become a major force in retail, trade, computers, and tourism. It was thus fitting that Clayton closed his 1967 study of the western military–industrial complex by noting: "Defense spending will loom as the single most important economic and demographic factor in the history of the Far [West] during the past two decades."

Also unspoken in Clayton's work, and in most other treatments of the West written in these years, was the "dark side" of federally induced growth. Coinciding with the radicalism spawned by the postwar "baby boom," the civil rights movement, and war in Vietnam, many people in the West and nationwide disliked the militarization of the economy and the control that science and technology had over humans and their environment. The second generation of Cold War activity, then, would witness ever greater programs, again relying upon the infrastructure of the West, and harsher criticism from disaffected citizens. Gerald Nash, writing in "The West and the Military–Industrial Complex" (*Montana, The Magazine of Western History* [1990]), noted that the post-Vietnam shift in weapons production, plus the need to store nuclear wastes more carefully, drew the ire of protesters throughout the region. "It would be difficult," said Nash, "to understand the growth of western cities without accounting for the military establishment." Yet, "the long-range consequences of the [West's] relationship seemed far more ominous [by 1990] than they had been in the past, raising questions of benefit-cost analysis, of public health, of long-term economic growth, of moral issues, and perhaps of sheer survival."

Inferred in Nash's argument was the web of second-generation defense/space expenditures crafted in the years after Vietnam, especially those championed by California's Ronald Reagan. Determined to revitalize the American economy (caught in the late-1970s in a web of spiraling inflation and stagnant growth), President Reagan declared war on the social-welfare programs of the more-optimistic 1960s that Lyndon Johnson had dubbed the Great Society. Ann Markusen and Joel Yudkin, authors of *Dismantling the Cold War Economy* (1993), believed that "in retrospect, the Reagan defense buildup [$2 trillion from 1981 to 1989] turned out to be a tremendous stimulus for the economy in the 1980s," obscuring the deterioration in the rest of the American industrial base. Markusen and Yudkin, an economist and engineer, respectively, saw this as a "quiet industrial policy" that encouraged more sophisticated defense research and weapons procurement. Much of this good fortune showered down on Reagan's adopted home, with Silicon Valley receiving more defense dollars per capita than any other area of the country. Yet "back in the heartland," said Markusen and Yudkin, "saddled with aging plants and a shutout of government support, traditionally strong American industries like steel, autos, machining, and consumer electronics languished, making them attractive targets for government-supported industries in Europe and Japan."

The 1980s meant much to the "new West" because NASA and the Department of Defense moved in the post-Vietnam era to upgrade conventional weapons, decommission nuclear stockpiles, and to make space even more accessible. This brought into sharp focus for Markusen and Yudkin a concept that they called the "Gunbelt": a crescent from Alaska south to Los Angeles/San Diego, then running eastward through the Southwest and Texas to the Southeast of Georgia and Florida. This arc of states benefiting from the latest round of military and space initiatives then looped northward through Virginia and Maryland (neighbors to Washington, D.C.), and then on to Massachusetts and Connecticut (with their proximity to Boston and New York City, respectively). A striking case study of Gunbelt growth was Colorado Springs, which in 1940 had but 40,000 people. "The 'Springs,'" said Markusen and Yudkin in 1993, "is one of the most successful military–industrial communities in the nation." If one considers such facilities as Fort Carson, the U.S. Air Force Academy, the North American Air Defense Command (NORAD) at Cheyenne Mountain, Peterson and Falcon Air Force Bases, and the phenomenon of thousands of military retirees, they argued, then "the Pentagon accounts for half of the Colorado Springs' $4 billion economy."

Not surprisingly for Markusen and Yudkin, political power had emerged within this crescent (which bore a striking resemblance to the Spanish Borderlands described in the 1920s by the historian Herbert E. Bolton, for its shared access to the Atlantic and Pacific Coasts, its temperate climate, and its appeal to colonizing nations like Spain, France, and England). The Gunbelt, they argued, made Los Angeles "the undisputed capital of cold war design and production." The "spectacular rise" of the City of Angels "to surpass Chicago as the nation's number-two city is symbolic of this lopsided, cold war-propelled development pattern." In addition, "postwar presidents, all of whom hailed from the Gunbelt with the exception of the never-elected Gerald Ford [who, in turn, retired to the Colorado mountains and Palm Springs desert], ensured that their local constituencies got good chunks of the defense pie." Echoing the words written in 1969 by Richard Nixon's favorite political commentator, Kevin Phillips, Markusen and Yudkin found that "the Gunbelt has altered the geopolitics of the nation and accounts in large part for the extraordinary shift in voting power and congressional representation to the West and the South."

As evidence of the second-generation growth of the Cold War West, Markusen and Yudkin cited a 1983 study that gave the Pacific states 175 percent of the national average of Reagan-era defense research and development monies. In contrast, the East North Central states (the Great Lakes and New York) garnered but 14 percent of the national average. Missile contracts in the 1980s for the Pacific Coast were three times the national average. Not surprisingly, California had surged even further by the early 1980s in nuclear weapons research and manufacture, "accounting for 13 percent of prime contracts in 1962, but 57 percent of all such contracts by 1982." Los Angeles, Orange, and San Diego counties had collected more than $23 billion in "prime procurement contracts" in the year 1984 alone (at a time when the entire defense budget was some $300 billion). Los Angeles County that year ranked first nationally in prime Defense Department contracts ($13.7 billion), more than double the second-ranked county (St. Louis). Of the top nine counties in defense spending at the close of Reagan's first administration, three were in California: Los Angeles, Santa Clara (Silicon Valley), and San Diego.

By the 1980s, military and space monies had transformed more than just southern California. Markusen and Yudkin noted that "despite a net loss of industrial jobs nationally from 1972 to 1986, California, Washington, and the rest of the defense-oriented mountain states experienced growth in excess of 30 percent." This came at the expense of "most of the older heartland states," which "endured losses in excess of 20 percent." A "revolving-door" syndrome had also guaranteed continued funding for weapons and space in the West, as "technical and professional military personnel exiting the service [could] often be more easily recruited at the site of their last assignment, where many have invested in housing because they like the location." Amenities like good weather, open space, recreational potential, and lower relative costs of living attracted these defense/space employees, as they had the postwar generation. Also helping secure the place of the West in this economic growth, said Markusen and Yudkin, was the use of the "cost-plus" contracting method, whereby "many normal locational constraints were eliminated" as contractors could "locate more or less where they pleased within the continental United States."

All of this munificence, Markusen and Yudkin argued, came under challenge in the early 1990s with the decline of the Cold War internationally. "Jobs in California's aerospace instruments fell by 11 percent in 1989 alone," they reported, with further shrinkages to come in the 1990s. In addition, the Reagan administration agreed to reduce the number of military installations around the country. "What defense cutbacks represent," Markusen and Yudkin suggested in 1993, "especially in light of the Gulf War, is a major shakeout and restructuring of the military market." Speaking primarily of defense installations, they speculated that "military bases near air or seaports from which ground units can be speedily deployed will be favored over those in more remote locations." Also critical would be the cost of doing business in an age when conservative politicians called for shrinking the size of the federal government. This led to a host of mergers among the nation's defense contractors, the loss of thousands of military and civilian jobs, and the need for all aspects of the nation's military–industrial complex to undergo what Markusen and Yudkin called the search for "a coordinated and highly visible alternative to the military-based economy."

With the imperatives of the Cold War quickly receding in the public consciousness, scholars, journalists, and commentators in the 1990s conducted exercises examining the legacy of containment similar to that of the *Denver Post's* Jim Carrier's. David Beers had grown up in Silicon Valley in the 1960s, a child of an aerospace engineer and the quintessential suburban California family. Contemplating in 1993 the meaning of his and his parents' lives under the shadow of the Cold War, Beers noted that "everyone now seems to agree that the fate of the nation rests on how efficiently we compete at the global level in producing new kinds of consumer goods." It had become obvious to the *Harper's* contributor that "aerospace and California were made not just for but by each other." This symbiosis had occurred in 1945 because "what California needed at that precarious moment was a space age, preferably one that was militarized."

From this commitment to advanced technology and engineering in the cause of national security, said Beers, came the concept of "blue-sky" science, a reference to the belief that enough money and talent could be unleashed in the nation's laboratories and universities to create "an atom bomb, a space station, the most beautiful missile." In so doing, said Beers, "the nation's very will would be invested, a monolith of our best minds put to it and given a deadline." As evidence of the power of such thinking to sweep nationwide, Beers wrote that "by 1963 the missiles and space business with 700,000 employees, was vying with the auto industry as the country's top employer." Then, "at the close of the Sixties, weapons spending slowed, coinciding with a cyclical slump in commercial-jet sales." These in turn prompted "mass aerospace layoffs, particularly in California." In the White House was another son of the Golden State, Richard Nixon, whose commitment to ending the war in Vietnam and reducing the social-welfare programs of the 1960s, hampered any federal commitment to restoring the boom of the Cold War economy. Thus, Ronald Reagan's call to restore the American Dream, thought Beers, would of necessity one day lead to yet another round of defense layoffs and questioning of the wisdom of "blue-sky" science.

As the United States and the West move inexorably toward the third millennium, it behooves scholars to consider the Cold War in light of the larger forces, regionally and nationally, that have defined American economic behavior. Ironically, the military frontier has echoes of Frederick Jackson Turner's much-maligned thesis about the surge of settlement from East to West. The same hopes and dreams that drove Europeans from their homes centuries ago, and which still animate citizens of Mexico, Central America, and Asia, also touched the hearts of engineers, scientists, and developers of western growth in the years 1945–1995. By ignoring the place of the military-industrial complex in the larger scheme of the western economy, one falls victim to the arguments posited in a special August 1994 issue of the *Pacific Historical Review*. Edited by Roger Lotchin, himself a scholar of military spending in the West, most notably in is book, *Fortress California, 1910—1961: From Warfare to Welfare* (1992), the authors of the special issue challenged the sweeping generalizations made by Gerald Nash about the West as both a colonial dependency of the East, and as a "pacesetter" in the postwar economy.

Paul Rhode, in "The Nash Thesis Revisited: An Economic Historian's View," suggested that the New Mexico historian had overstated his case for the power of World War II to shape the future of the West and the nation. Rhode, an economist at the University of North Carolina, disliked, as did Lotchin, Nash's belief that prior to 1940 the region represented a "backward" (Nash had used the term "Third World") economy. Rhode conceded that the Second World War did indeed influence the California economy in many ways. Yet he and Lotchin refused to accept the significance of the events of 1941 to the West that Nash had declared two decades earlier. "By 1940," said Rhode, California "possessed an internal dynamic of development and . . . the wartime expansion was the result of this economic dynamism, not its cause." Lotchin, writing in the same special issue about "California Cities and the Hurricane of Change: World War II in the San Francisco, Los Angeles, and San Diego Metropolitan Areas," considered the Golden State "mature, modern, and very growth-conscious." After all, said Lotchin, "when a state is born in a Gold Rush, it is not easy to find anything else in its history which is quite so unprecedented."

Because Lotchin and Rhode seemed more determined to refute the specific assertion of Gerald Nash that World War II made the West a national "pacesetter," they did not analyze in similar fashion the consequences of two generations of the military–industrial complex, either in the Golden State or the West as a whole. Lotchin himself noted that "of the major metropolitan counties in [California], twelve made their largest absolute gains during the era of Dwight D. Eisenhower [1953–1961] instead of during World War II." Further proof for Lotchin of Nash's limitations was the statement: "In the one decade of the sixties, Orange County grew by 706,000, more than the World War II total of Alameda, Contra Costa, San Francisco, Solano, and Sonoma counties put together!" Even Los Angeles, starting from a much higher population base than other California counties in the first Cold War generation, said Lotchin, had "absolute growth . . . alone in the 1950s . . . more than three times the advance of the same five counties in the 1940s." These statistics, said Lotchin, revealed that California's "demography increased, but in a rather unexceptional way." "The global conflict," he further asserted, "had an ambiguous, contradictory, and perhaps ultimately ironic effect," what he called "largely conservative, rather than unprecedented, effects at home."

The *Pacific Historical Review* issue appeared at yet another moment of truth for the economy of the American West. Just as with the Gold Rush, no one could predict the consequences of the decline of the Soviet Union on the vast network of military installations, defense contractors, and employees scattered across the region and nation. Lotchin's own statistics revealed that the more critical phase of modern western growth may not have come from his and Rhode's suggested continuity from prewar years, or even Gerald Nash's World War II. Instead, the culprit may have been the stunning investment made by taxpayers in the five decades since J. Robert Oppenheimer stared out into the Tularosa basin of southern New Mexico and quoted the *Bhagavad Gita*: "I am become death, the shatterer of worlds." More study needs to be done on the seductive power of technology, the comfort level generated by the outpouring of public capital since 1945, and the ways that the West has reinvented itself to accommodate the blessings and curses of the Cold War economy.

Until then, the legacy of containment will continue to be defined as the polarity between the appeal of "blue-sky" science and the condemnation made by William Appleman Williams, a diplomatic historian and 1944 graduate in electrical engineering from the U.S. Naval Academy. Williams, credited in the 1960s with forming the "New Left" school of historians, wrote in the November 1955 issue of the *Pacific Historical Review* about "The Frontier Thesis and American Foreign Policy." Contending that the arms race pursuant to World War II had dire consequences for a nation still believing in its innocence, Williams concluded:

The United States had finally caught up with History. Americans were no longer unique. Henceforward they, too, would share the fate of all mankind. For the frontier was now on the rim of hell, and the inferno was radioactive.

BIBLIOGRAPHICAL ESSAY

For a subject as vast and intricate as the military–industrial complex in the American West, there are no general sources that one can consult in single-volume format. Thus, one begins with the basic texts written within the past generation. Of these, Gerald D. Nash has prepared the most comprehensive analyses of both World War II and its aftermath. These works include: *The American West in the Twentieth Century: A Short History of an Urban Oasis* (Englewood Cliffs: Prentice-Hall, 1973), *The American West Transformed: The Impact of the Second World War* (Bloomington: Indiana University Press, 1985); and *World War II and the West: Reshaping the Economy* (Lincoln: University of Nebraska Press, 1990). Nash also has written "The West and the Military—Industrial Complex," which appeared in *Montana, The Magazine of Western History* 40 (winter 1990): 72–75.

Recent general treatments of the West include sections on the post–World War II era. Among these are Michael P. Malone and Richard W. Etulain, *The American West: A Twentieth-Century History* (Lincoln: University of Nebraska Press, 1989), and Richard White, *"It's Your Misfortune and None of My Own:" A New History of the American West* (Norman: University of Oklahoma Press, 1991). An early, but still useful reading of contemporary regional change and the Cold War is Neil Morgan, *Westward Tilt: The American West Today* (New York: Random House, 1963).

The theme of the atomic West has drawn the majority of interest in the past decade, given the golden anniversary in 1995 of the Trinity Site explosion. Popular treatments of the topic include Tad Bartimus and Scott McCartney, *Trinity's Children: Living Along America's Nuclear Highway* (New York: Harcourt Brace Jovanovich, 1991); Phillip L. Fradkin, *Fallout: An American Nuclear Tragedy* (Tucson: University of Arizona Press, 1989); and the series of stories written by Jim Carrier of the *Denver Post* in July and August 1995, under the title, "Atomic Legacy."

Clearly, the best economic analysis of the military–industrial complex in the modern West comes from James L. Clayton, ed., *The Economic Impact of the Cold War: Sources and Readings* (New York: Harcourt, Brace and World, 1970). A good source for the consequences of the militarization of the American economy is Ann Markusen and Joel Yudkin, *Dismantling the Cold War Economy* (New York: Basic Books, 1993). Lamentations about the end of the atomic/military–industrial complex era include David Beers, *Blue Sky Dream: A Memoir of America's Fall from Grace* (New York: Doubleday, 1996); and Blaine Harden, "The Dark Side of Paradise: In Eastern Washington State, the Cold War Has Left Nature in Danger," *Washington Post Weekly Edition*, July 8–14, 1996.

An example of how scholars are trying to reassess earlier assumptions about the Cold War in the West can be found in Roger W. Lotchin, Guest Editor, "Special Issue: Fortress California at War: San Francisco, Los Angeles, Oakland, and San Diego, 1941–1945," *Pacific Historical Review* 63 (August 1994). Also of value in understanding the state of New Mexico during and after the Second World War are the essays in Richard W. Etulain, ed., *Contemporary New Mexico, 1940–1990* (Albuquerque: University of New Mexico Press, 1994), and Michael Welsh, *U.S. Army Corps of Engineers: Albuquerque District, 1935–1985* (Albuquerque: University of New Mexico Press, 1987). William Appleman Williams wrote a thought-provoking piece on the Cold War, the West, and U.S. diplomacy in "The Frontier Thesis and American Foreign Policy," *Pacific Historical Review* 24 (November 1955): 379–95.

CHAPTER SIX

PRO-DEFENSE, PRO-GROWTH, AND ANTI-COMMUNISM
Cold War Politics in the American West

TIMOTHY M. CHAMBLESS

During the decades of international conflict known as the Cold War between the United States and the Soviet Union and their respective allies, a "politics of patriotism" emerged in the American West. Politically, the Cold War was a "win-win situation" for western politicians who were pro-defense and pro-growth. These two positions, in time, became inseparable. In the political alchemy of the Cold War, anti-Communism was turned into defense dollars. And as it turned out, western politicians proved quite successful at gaining an extraordinary share of them. The reason for this success, which had enormous consequences for the economic development and growth of the region, is not hard to discover. Western politicians could make the strong case that undeveloped land, hundreds of square miles which only the American West possessed in abundance, was indispensable in waging the Cold War. Here, a combination of high technology and nuclear weapons could be easily and, if not always, safely tested; it was here that there was sufficient room to train and provide support for a military capable of mobilizing to fight a global war. This essay will examine the political dimension of this tremendous military presence in the region.

Evidence of the extent of the military buildup in the region during the Cold War era is available in the *Directory of Military Bases in the U.S.* (1991). Actually, this source provides three types of information. It identifies the number of military installations built before, during, and after World War II. But this data is almost certainly incomplete. The directory does not, for instance, include every military base that is known to exist. In certain instances, government officials at all levels have maintained a position of silence. In the name of

Table 6.1: Number of Military Bases in Western States for Three Time Periods

17 Western States	Pre-WWII Bases	WWII Bases	Cold War Bases	Total Bases
Arizona	4	5	2	11
California	16	41	31	88
Colorado	3	3	5	11
Idaho	0	2	2	4
Kansas	2	2	3	7
Montana	1	1	2	4
Nebraska	2	1	1	4
Nevada	1	2	2	5
New Mexico	3	2	1	6
North Dakota	0	0	7	7
Oklahoma	1	5	4	10
Oregon	0	2	7	9
South Dakota	2	1	1	4
Texas	9	15	11	35
Utah	2	4	3	9
Washington	6	7	8	21
Wyoming	2	0	1	3
TOTALs	54	93	91	238

Source: Directory of Military Bases in the U.S. (1991)

"national security," government officials who seek to be patriotic and protect their country from any disclosure that might render the country more vulnerable to foreign adversaries have chosen not to acknowledge the existence of selected military installations. The most prominent example of this official silence is a vast region in the Nevada desert, north of Las Vegas and near Nellis Air Force Base. This flight testing area cannot be found on any map, although its existence has been documented from various private sources. But elected officeholders and federal and state officials refuse to comment on the testing area, the so-called "Area 51," where secret spy planes were tested for years during the Cold War.

Still, these official omissions aside, the information from the directory is a powerful indicator of the Cold War's impact on the region when it is placed in a table that depicts the number of bases by state and at three different time periods. Table 6.1 reveals all of the West's Army, Navy, Air Force, and Marine bases as well as Coast Guard facilities. The number of existing military bases that had been created prior to World War II was fifty-four, a relatively small number that covered a time period of 150 years. In comparison, during the limited time period of only one-half decade (1940–45), in which the world was at war, almost twice as many military bases were created by the U.S. government—that is, created and funded by elected federal officials with taxpayers' money. From 1945 to 1991, between the end of World War II and the peaceful end of the Soviet Union, the Cold War emerged. During these years, there was unprecedented construction of military bases in the United States, which reflected the shift toward customized weaponry and preparation for the possible use of nuclear weapons in a future World War III. These Cold War expenditures were sought by post–World War II politicians who justified ongoing military spending on the basis of national security.

The table shows that certain western states received more military bases after World War II than during or prior to that conflict. For example, North Dakota was designated for seven bases during the Cold War, whereas it did not receive a single military installation during the Second World War. Oregon was the recipient of seven Cold War facilities in contrast to only two during World War II. Washington had seven military bases begun in the early 1940s, but then received eight more after the Second World War. Wyoming did not have a new base during World War II, but was designated for a large installation of ready-to-launch nuclear missiles during the Cold War. Utah received four large military facilities during the Second World War and three more during the Cold War years. These new facilities housed aspects of modern warfare: nuclear rocket motors, Strategic Air Command bombers, and nerve gas testing/storage facilities.

This large military infrastructure would not have been possible without local political support, which at no point was ever lacking. Indeed, throughout the Cold War western politicians consistently voted for huge military appropriations; they seized upon the threat of global Communism to expedite allocations for defense, which, in turn, they knew would help spur the region's rapid economic development. The nation's decision to wage an open-ended, expensive, and undeclared war on Communism had a profound effect on the western region's politics and economic development. The military's established presence and the growth of the defense industry in the region during the Cold War, both of which received wide political support, drew millions across the Mississippi River who were looking for job opportunities. Indeed, during this period America's demographic population center shifted westward across the Mississippi River.

The political advantages of supporting a strong defense, then, were clear, and prominent politicians became articulate defenders of appropriations for military spending during the Cold War—especially in their own states. Several, in fact, became candidates for the presidency during the Cold War era. California was the recipient of forty-one military installations during the Second World War, and added thirty-one more facilities during the Cold War. Not surprisingly, politicians such as Earl Warren, Richard Nixon, and Ronald Reagan were strong proponents of the nation's defense. Arizona received five military bases during World War II, and added two more during the Cold War. Arizona's Barry Goldwater supported the bases and believed that he was truly representing his constituents with a strong anti-Communist stance. Significantly, South Dakota received only one military installation during World War II and one during the Cold War; one may infer that George McGovern, the 1972 presidential candidate of the Democratic party, was not strongly influenced by a large military presence in his home state.

The Cold War involved forty-five years of heightened military preparedness, which was justified in the name of national security. Although few died as a direct result of the Cold War, this era had its frightening moments, the most famous of which was the Cuban Missile Crisis. Critics of the Cold War have pointed out, however, that more Americans were exposed to nuclear fallout than to Communist adversaries during nearly half a century of cold war (providing the losses that the country sustained during the Korean and Vietnam Wars are calculated on a separate ledger). Moreover, the greatest number of American casualties died in the western states from the effects of above-ground testing of nuclear weapons. Most of these "down-winders," as they were called, were unknowing or misinformed residents in the western states of Nevada and Utah. The costs of the Cold War, then, cannot be measured in just dollars and cents; real human and environmental factors must be taken into account as well.

From the perspective of many westerners, however, the Cold War years were not a period of sacrifice; on the contrary, they saw this time as one of unprecedented economic development and population growth. True, some westerners saw a challenge to their traditional grazing lands and agricultural way of life; but many others accepted these changes as part of the price of an economic expansion driven by military and strategic necessity. And politicians who saw the benefits of a strong defense recognized early that waging the Cold War was good politics.

Significantly, western politicians were able to base their appeal to constituents on more than just the prospect of high-paying jobs and a tremendous new infrastructure that would benefit the civilian sector as much as the military. They were also able to build on a regional heritage that celebrated the values of self-reliance, independence, and action. Westerners have traditionally seen themselves as different. The frontier hypothesis of Frederick Jackson Turner suggests several reasons for this difference in perspective. Although Turner's century-old thesis is controversial with such New Western History advocates as Patricia Limerick, Donald Worster, and Richard White, what can be said is that his description of frontier attitudes and values continued to resonate with westerners in the post–World War II era. Politicians were able to present the Cold War struggle against the spread of Communism in the same light as struggles of good versus evil in the Old West. Perhaps no one did this better than President and former California Governor Ronald Reagan. Indeed, these political figures tried to act like pioneers of old who faced the ordeals of an untamed land and hostile natives. Western lawmakers, in short, found it easy to portray the Cold War as another great challenge to America, just as winning the West had been to an earlier generation. And that great western industry, Hollywood, did its part by producing literally hundreds of westerns films and television shows depicting a world made up of white hats and black hats. The result of all this was a foreign policy that was as confident of its moral correctness as it was confrontational toward Communism.

If politicians could draw on the region's colorful heritage to link the ideology of nineteenth-century expansion with that of twentieth-century anti-Communism, the West's small population, public lands, and vast open spaces allowed these figures—along with military officials, scientists, federal officials, and others—to argue that the region was the ideal place to support, train, and test soldiers and weapons in the era of modern warfare. J. Robert Oppenheimer, a brilliant physicist of the first rank, was perhaps the first to make this case in arguing to locate the Manhattan Project on the Pajarito Plateau of New Mexico and to test the first atomic device near Alamagordo in the southern part of that state. Moreover, citizens in western states were aware of how the West was settled and defended—with superior weapons and a strong military presence. World War II only reinforced this sense of history. In 1945, voters and lawmakers in the western states continued to confront hostile conditions and external threats, as they believed they had always done.

Politicians who supported a strong role for the West in manning the Cold War's defenses found conditions in the western states highly suitable for other reasons as well. Not least of these was the region's relatively small population at the outset of the Cold War. Although the western states did have some cities of significant size, most land in the region was quite unpopulated in comparison to areas inhabited east of the Mississippi River. Low population meant several things: (1) relatively few people to govern; (2) few of the urban concerns of eastern states caused by high population density; (3) a people accustomed to difficult environmental hazards, such as extremes in weather and aridity; and (4) more opportunities for western lawmakers to have an impact on the debate over the nation's defense policy. To put all of this another way, elected officials who represented America's western states were in a position to take on a considerable number of international issues because they had relatively fewer constituents to represent than politicians from eastern states.

Indeed, at the outset of the post–World War II period, American senators and congressmen who represented western states faced relatively fewer domestic and/or statewide controversies than their colleagues from more populous states. (This apparent demographic disparity would move quickly toward a rough regional balance during the duration of the Cold War.) Frequently, western politicians emerged as committee chairmen who sought to represent their rural constituents' needs effectively, and at the same time these political figures could utilize their congressional authority to influence international issues. Members of Congress from western states had already grown accustomed to making governmental decisions about the region's vast open spaces; it did not require much to expand their horizons to include the entire world in their decision making. As the Cold War intensified, western lawmakers realized that the interests of their constituents and the interests of the nation were close if not identical; they could act "patriotically," in other words, while they were watching out for the economic interests of their state and region.

Politicians in eastern states certainly pursued their regional interests no less assiduously. A clear consequence of the Great Depression and the Second World War was a migration to cities in both the western and eastern states that promised jobs and greater opportunities. By 1945, most of America's cities faced urban problems directly linked to this substantial urban growth. Consequently, throughout the Cold War, urban politicians were more likely to confront domestic rather than international concerns. The eastern states, as well as certain populated areas in western states, tended to concentrate their energies on emerging domestic problems associated with postwar urban living. Rapid and concentrated population growth in cities and their suburbs, or "bedroom communities," was changing the priorities of urban policymakers. These new and growing population centers did not want the apparatus of the nation's defenses located near their neighborhoods—not as long as there were open spaces for military installations and test sites in the rural West available for such use. In this circumstance, at least, urban (mostly eastern) and rural (mostly western) interests coincided perfectly.

This was, of course, not always the case. For instance, a growing number of Americans wanted rural western lands protected from development of any kind. The wilderness movement that culminated in the Wilderness Act of 1964, which was enacted shortly after the Cuban Missile Crisis and just prior to the military buildup in Southeast Asia, was strongly supported by urban politicians; in more than three decades, many millions of acres of wilderness or road-less areas—the vast majority of which were situated in the public lands and wild country of the western states—were placed under federal protection. These actions stirred up much more controversy in the West than did the continued funding of the military–industrial complex, the presence of which was felt heavily in the region. Military reservations may have locked up the western region's lands every bit as much as designated wilderness areas, but the former, for the reasons discussed above, produced little of the controversy that was generated by wilderness protection.

Wilderness protection was a major source of political conflict between pol-iticians representing urban and rural constituencies, and to a related extent with eastern and western states. Preservation and development was an issue that would create a rivalry between eastern and western states. Residents of western states, in fact, often resented what was seen as manipulation and neglect by the congressional representatives from eastern states. Manipulation was strongly sensed when Congress acted to preserve western lands for recre-ation and tourism rather than allow western states and private sector interests to develop those lands. Neglect was perceived in the past when Congress limited congressional appropriations for the establishment of military forts and harbor facilities and the maintenance of Indian reservations and the public lands. Waging the Cold War, in contrast, was a point of regional agreement that seemed beneficial to everyone.

This regional win-win situation produced numerous politicians from west-ern states who emerged as "patriots" on the national scene. They articulated a vision for America as candidates for the presidency (successful and unsuccess-ful) in an electoral attempt to implement the pro-defense position of the western states. Among these were California's Earl Warren, Richard Nixon, Ronald Reagan and Jerry Brown; Arizona's Barry Goldwater; Idaho's Frank Church; Washington's Henry Jackson; Oregon's Wayne Morse; Colorado's Gary Hart; Texas's Lyndon Johnson and George Bush; South Dakota's George McGovern; and Kansas's Robert Dole. In addition, western states have sent articulate politicians to the U.S. Senate and highly visible figures to the U.S. House of Representatives.

One of the best known of these Cold War western politicians was Richard Nixon. Nixon was elected to California's Twelfth Congressional District in a bitter campaign over popular incumbent Jerry Voorhis, during which Nixon alleged that Voorhis was "soft on Communism." Nixon used this successful technique again in the 1949 Hiss–Chambers hearings, which helped catapult him into the U.S. Senate. That 1950 election was colored by campaign rhetoric in which Nixon characterized his opponent, popular Congresswoman Helen

Gahagan Douglas, as "the pink lady." Nixon continued to wave the anti-Communist banner, as he received his party's vice-presidential nomination two years later. He went on to serve two terms in that position, where he was a visible cold warrior, an advocate for a strong defense, and a supporter of the dangerous policy of "brinkmanship." Nixon used the fear of Communism in four more elections, during which time the state of California became the center of America's Cold War defense spending.

Ronald Reagan, in 1947, was president of Hollywood's Screen Actor's Guild when he testified in Washington before the House Un-American Activities Committee. His testimony helped to "blacklist" prominent authors and screenwriters whose works were alleged to be tolerant of Communism. Reagan appeared as a corporate spokesperson throughout the 1950s when California's defense industry was growing rapidly. In 1960, although he was a registered Democrat, he supported Richard Nixon for the presidency. In 1964 Reagan gave "the speech"—his impressive statewide television endorsement of Republican presidential candidate Arizonan Barry Goldwater—which helped him in his 1966 win over two-term California Governor Pat Brown. Reagan twice failed in short campaigns for the presidency, in 1968 and 1976, before winning that high office in 1980 and again in 1984. In the process, he brought to government a vision of greater defense spending and an aggressive anti-Communism that marked a return to the uncompromising rhetoric of the 1950s.

Lyndon Johnson had been a congressman who represented an economically depressed region of Texas during the late 1930s and 1940s, and had been primarily concerned with rebuilding a strong local and national economy. As a politician seeking election to the U.S. Senate, in 1948 he shifted his campaign strategy and called for a strong national defense. Robert Caro, one of his biographers, notes that LBJ was by this time already outspoken in his opposition to Communism. In 1955, as his party's new Senate Majority Leader, Johnson worked comfortably with President (and former General) Dwight Eisenhower. A shrewd politician, Johnson saw a clear relationship between a strong national defense and a strong Texas economy. Accordingly, Senator Johnson was a strong supporter of the Interstate Highway and Defense Act, which provided the nation with a network of divided superhighways, many miles of which would extend across the nation's largest state (prior to the admission of Alaska). As vice-president, LBJ would be a strong political force in the establishment of the NASA Manned Space Center in Houston, Texas. And finally, as president, he committed the nation to a (as it turned out) disastrous war in Southeast Asia in order to stop the spread of Communism in that part of the world. Throughout his three decades in elective office, Lyndon Johnson reflected the views of his constituents that anti-Communism and a strong national defense were good for the Lone Star state.

Barry Goldwater is a giant figure in the politics of the western states during the Cold War. Born in Arizona before it became a state, he inherited the pioneer spirit of his father, a Polish immigrant who had come to the American West to begin a new life. Barry Goldwater was a pilot in World War II, and maintained a membership in the Air Force Reserve following the war. He visualized the western states as a distinct region because of their arid mountainous terrain, which forced those who resided there to become hardened survivors. Quickly after the Second World War, Goldwater created a fortune as the owner of a chain of department stores; this business venture allowed him to seek elective office. In the late 1940s, as a local city councilman, he articulated the prevailing views of a fiercely independent politician. He is remembered by many Americans for an unsuccessful presidential candidacy in 1964, but for nearly a quarter of a century thereafter Barry Goldwater was a U.S. Senator with outspoken views on the need for a strong military to combat the spread of Communism. In commemoration of his strong pro-defense stance, his name appears on several military installations in western states, including the Barry M. Goldwater Air Force Range, which is the site of the world's largest gunnery range.

As early as 1946, which was the first federal election after the end of World War II, western states sent representatives and senators to Congress who would influence the course of the Cold War. The 1946 elections were momentous, in part, because Republicans regained control of Congress for the first time since 1930 and because foreign policy issues, despite the end of the war, continued to loom large. Not surprisingly, California, given its size, geography, and strategic location, produced the most candidates in response to growing Cold War tensions. The rest of the region's successful politicians would also emerge out of the pressures stemming from the Cold War, on the one hand, and from the economic development sparked by Cold War spending, on the other. Below are a few examples of this new breed of politician.

William F. Knowland, an enlisted man and officer during World War II, won a full term in the U.S. Senate (after having been appointed at the end of the war to finish the term of the old progressive leader Senator Hiram Johnson). This Republican anti-Communist from California soon emerged as the greatest recipient of federal funding for the Cold War; he was often characterized as the "Senator from Formosa" for his outspoken support of Taiwan and his unwavering criticism of mainland China's Communist government.

The state of Washington elected anti-Communist candidate Harry P. Cain, and through his efforts, the Puget Sound area became a naval center. Nevada benefited from George W. Malone's election to the Senate, where he joined ranks with cold warrior Pat McCarran; together, they helped Nevada become America's nuclear testing site. In Idaho, Henry Dworshak, a veteran of World War I and former state commander of the American Legion, was elected to the Senate. And in Utah, Arthur V. Watkins won election to the Senate as yet another outspoken anti-Communist.

In Montana, Zales N. Ecton was sent to Congress in reaction to the perception in his state of a Communist infiltration. Many Montana Democrats associated long-time Senator Burton K. Wheeler with isolationism before Pearl Harbor and with sensitivity toward the Soviet Union in the postwar period. Lief Erickson, a fellow Democrat, challenged Wheeler; he was perceived by many Montana Democrats to be more "patriotic" and more suspicious of the Soviet Union. In the primary election, the prominent incumbent was upset by Erickson, who was seen as more acceptable to Montana Democrats in the first U.S. Senate election following World War II. However, in the general election, Republican Ecton was narrowly elected by Montana voters in the new Cold War political climate.

But, on the whole, the election of 1948 went to anti-Communist Democrats, who regained control of Congress. These wins did not, however, settle the debate over how to meet the Communist challenge. In fact, the debate only intensified. Moreover, highly visible Republicans continued to exploit the growing fear of Communism as an issue and use it to win subsequent elections. In California, as we have already seen, Richard Nixon used tough anti-Communist rhetoric to be reelected to Congress, and then proceeded to make a national reputation by questioning Alger Hiss as a member of the House Un-American Activities Committee. (Until his death in November 1996, Alger Hiss proclaimed his innocence and identified himself as a victim of Cold War politicians. And Russian General Dimitri A. Volkogonov, a historian and chairman of a commission on the files of the KGB, announced that there was no evidence of Hiss involvement in Soviet intelligence.) In South Dakota, Karl Mundt used anti-Communist rhetoric as well as his affiliations with Christian organizations to win a seat in the Senate.

The Korean War erupted midway through the 1950 election campaign and reminded candidates and voters that the Cold War could become hot. Politicians in western states were quick to find political advantage in supporting this international "police action," which would nevertheless be handled and financed mainly by the United States. In Idaho, Republican Herman Welker, who had enlisted in the Army Air Corps in World War II, was elected to the Senate as a strong anti-Communist. In contrast, Wayne Morse, a fiery independent critic of repressive government, was reelected to the Senate in Oregon, and raised numerous questions about America's role in the world. In Utah, Elbert Thomas, an eighteen-year Senate veteran, was defeated by Wallace Bennett in a heated political campaign greatly influenced by Cold War issues. A brief examination of this Utah Senate campaign demonstrates how the fear of Communism had a major influence on the outcome of this western election.

Drew Pearson and Jack Anderson, the two most prominent investigative reporters in this period, wrote that "a prime target" of the National Republican Committee chairman was Elbert Thomas of Utah. And Thomas was, indeed, defeated by a previously unknown candidate. How did this Democratic incumbent, who had defeated strong opponents in three prior elections, somehow become vulnerable? Elbert Thomas, the incumbent Utah Democrat, was besieged by political allegations that he (1) leaned toward Communism; (2) was a "Communist sympathizer"; (3) had written a book which praised Communism and had been used by the American Communist Party as a recruitment tool; (4) sponsored rallies to honor the Communist party and the Soviet Union; (5) advocated socialism as a solution for America; and (6) contributed stories to the Communist press.

Given the premise that Communism was a terrible threat and Utah's incumbent Senator was somehow linked to this problem, Utah's voters reasoned that the clear solution was to replace Elbert Thomas with a Republican who would behave more patriotically. Critics contended that the breakout of war in Korea in 1950 was a result of the concessions made by Democratic President Franklin Roosevelt at the Yalta Conference (where Alger Hiss and other alleged Communist sympathizers had given away Eastern Europe and aided the spread of Communism throughout the world); also, only a year before, mainland China had been "lost" by another Democratic president, Harry Truman.

Thomas's opponents now declared that it was necessary to remove a Senator who had shown himself to be "soft" on Communism. Although there was never any evidence that Utah's senior U.S. Senator was a Socialist or Communist, the fact that Elbert Thomas had supported Franklin Roosevelt's New Deal programs and had expressed support for the Soviet Union as an American ally during the Second World War allowed his political critics to associate him with the emergence of the Cold War. In 1950, Utah's voters agreed.

In 1952 Texan Martin Dies rode the political wave of anti-Communism and was reelected to Congress in an at-large election. Dies, a former fourteen-year congressman who had retired in 1945, had sponsored the 1938 House resolution that created the Special Committee to Investigate Un-American Activities. In Wyoming, Republican Governor Frank Barrett, a veteran of World War I, won a seat in the U.S. Senate—defeating the prominent Democratic incumbent Joseph C. O'Mahoney. Henry "Scoop" Jackson was elected in the state of

Washington, where he became quickly known as the "Senator from Boeing." In Utah, Republican conservative and anti-Communist Arthur V. Watkins was reelected.

The election of 1954 saw Republicans lose control of the Congress. Still, Cold War politics were evident in Colorado, where Republican candidate, Gordon Allott, a veteran of World War II and a state commander of both the American Legion and Veterans of Foreign Wars, won election to the U.S. Senate. But in December of 1954, the Senate vote to censure Joseph McCarthy and strip him of his committee assignments marked a turning point in the behavior of politicians, whether they were from the north, south, east, or west. As the domestic "nightmare in Red" came to a slow end after 1954, politicians from western states found themselves less vulnerable to McCarthyite tactics and excesses.

Running straight through the peaks and valleys of the anti-Communistic rhetoric of the Cold War was a keen appreciation for the regional benefits of a strong defense. Perhaps nowhere was this more evident than in the support western lawmakers gave to the Interstate Highway and Defense Act of 1956. Authorized by the Eisenhower administration, this action was intended to strengthen the nation's security. The vast majority of road miles, however, were located in the western states, where local politicians greeted this latest federal expenditure as an act of patriotism. Western politicians who had repeatedly called for a balanced federal budget could justify the unprecedented billions to be spent for transportation in their states in the name of defense preparedness and mobility during a nuclear attack. It took four decades to complete the Interstate highway system of safe and efficient divided roadways throughout America. Its completion roughly coincided with the end of the Cold War and provided an incalculable boon to the American West's economic development.

But if there were benefits to waging the Cold War, such as a modern, safe, and efficient highway system, what were the costs? In mid–July 1995 the United States Nuclear Weapons Cost Study Project produced a study on the costs of the Cold War. This project, commissioned by the government, drew upon the expertise of researchers from several private-sector organizations, including the Brookings Institution, the National Security Archive, the Natural Resources Defense Council, and the Defense Budget Project. The study concluded—using a U.S. Department of Defense formula—that $3.9 trillion had been spent on nuclear weapons between 1945 and 1995. This figure represented from one-fourth to one-third of the entire military budget in that fifty-year period, and exceeded the cost for either the army or the navy since 1945. In 1995 dollars, the $3.9 trillion spent represents roughly the equivalent of America's entire goods and services for seven months. This cost far exceeds all previous estimates of the cost of nuclear weapons to the American taxpayer and calls into serious question the 1950s slogan "more bang for the buck," which was used to justify nuclear weapons programs over conventional ones. And a large portion of that funding was spent in the American West, given that it was the site of much of the nation's military research and development, testing, weapons delivery systems, security, communications and control systems, dismantlement, and environmental cleanup.

The environmental costs associated with nuclear weapons, from their manufacture to their deployment, are particularly noteworthy. The Cold War may be over, but the contamination and waste of nuclear sites will require billions of dollars and many years, if not decades, to render safe again. A dramatic example of this problem is illustrated by the fact that between 1945 and 1992, approximately nine hundred nuclear blasts—above ground and in the atmosphere—were authorized and conducted by the U.S. government in the western state of Nevada. More than any other factor, the detonation of nuclear bombs reminded American citizens living in western states that the Cold War was very real and that its legacy, measured in atomic half-lives, would endure virtually forever. There is also the problem of what to do with the leftover military hardware of the Cold War, which is currently being stockpiled in the western states. There are navy ships moored in the Columbia River west of Portland, Oregon, and fighter planes parked on the southern Arizona desert.

Another enduring cost of the Cold War, which has emerged as one the most important and divisive political issues of the 1990s, is the ballooning national debt. In the mid–1990s, the national debt exceeded $4.1 trillion. Throughout U.S. history, America had accumulated a $1 trillion debt, from the administration of George Washington up to that of Jimmy Carter. However, during the twelve years of the Ronald Reagan and George Bush presidencies, the U.S. debt grew to nearly $4 trillion. This astronomical increase was due in no small part to the Reagan' administration's military buildup, which was part of a calculated strategy to force the Soviet Union to capitulate and bring an end to the Cold War. Although the growth of the federal deficit has slowed significantly under President Bill Clinton, it nevertheless continues to increase. Today, each party tries to blame the other for the huge size of the national debt, but certainly Cold War spending since 1945, which had wide bipartisan support, especially for nuclear weapons, was a major contributing factor to the problem. Ironically, western conservatives are often the loudest in their calls for a balanced budget, even though their region has perhaps benefited more from defense spending since 1945 than any other region.

With the fall of the Berlin Wall on November 9, 1989, the politics of patriotism had largely run its course. Other issues, including battling over the budget, have since taken their place. This political change occurred quickly. In 1990 Congress enacted the Base Closure and Realignment Act. Its purpose was to save the United States billions of dollars by the year 2000 in an attempt to move toward a balanced federal budget. The act was supported by the West's representatives in Washington, who had decried the succession of budget deficits even as they benefited from them. These same members of Congress, who identified themselves as "fiscal conservatives," were also aware that reductions in Pentagon expenditures would impact the western states to a far greater extent than the eastern states. They and their constituents reluctantly accepted that the elimination and merging of large military bases would almost certainly have a negative impact upon the region, where many of them were located.

It should be noted that the western political establishment was not entirely uncritical of the benefits of military spending in the region, as the debate over the MX antiballistic missile system revealed. During the Carter Administration, the Pentagon and powerful executive branch officials proposed the construction of an unprecedented network of military bases and missile sites. In the late 1970s Air Force planners and the Carter administration proposed the construction of an anti-missile defense system, which, if built, would have covered a substantial portion of western Utah and eastern Nevada. This MX anti-missile system proposal was unprecedented in its magnitude, and involved incalculable damage to the environment. The resulting controversy was just as unprecedented.

At first, western politicians echoed the arguments of Pentagon planners that the MX system would provide the entire nation with comprehensive protection against Soviet aggression, and that the peoples of the arid and rural mountain desert states of Utah and Nevada would experience stronger economies while performing a patriotic service. However, as the full extent of the proposal became known during a series of public hearings in the region, western politicians and other traditional friends of the military began to have misgivings about the project. Specifically, the congressional delegations, governors, and state politicians of Utah and Nevada communicated their concerns about the wisdom of removing thousands of acres of land from potential development. Also, there was considerable debate about whether the proposed defense system would actually work, and whether, if proven reliable, it would upset the "balance of terror" that assured neither the U.S. nor the Soviet Union would launch a nuclear first strike. Moreover, the idea of making the western states of Utah and Nevada the potential primary targets for Russian missiles caused such diverse groups as the Mormon Church (headquartered in Salt Lake City) and numerous environmental organizations to oppose loudly the federal government's defense proposal. Ultimately, in 1981, President Reagan, himself a former governor of a western state who had close political ties to politicians in Nevada and Utah, formally withdrew the MX proposal. Ronald Reagan, as president, was able to maintain his tough anti-Communist stance by authorizing the upgrade of existing missile silos and related military installations.

The controversy over the MX, however, was an exception to the rule. In the years following the Second World War, politicians from the western states came forward to support the nation's defenses. These politicians reflected their region's traditional political values and outlook. A significant number of them even rose to national prominence because of their words and deeds. Indeed, no less than seven received the presidential nominations of their respective parties; four went on to win the White House. And just as visible as these political figures was the large defense apparatus built and maintained in the region. Western politicians' repeated efforts to strengthen America's role as defender of the free world was a complete success. They would have no doubt been greatly angered to have their patriotism questioned, for they saw dollars targeted for defense spending as essential to the nation's security. But perhaps the real point here is that the anti-Communism and pro-defense positions of the Cold War significantly influenced the political debate in the region for over four decades and gave the American West a regional outlook that it would not otherwise have possessed.

BIBLIOGRAPHIC ESSAY

There are relatively few works in the field of Cold War history and scholarship that focus entirely on the Cold War in the American West, and none at all that examine the impact of the Cold War on the politics of the region as a whole. Still, I have found the following works helpful in writing this essay. Especially useful is the data compiled by William R. Evinger, which is available in his edited work, *Directory of Military Bases in the U.S.* (Phoenix: Oryz Press, 1991). I have also consulted closely the work of Frank Jonas, who edited *Political Dynamiting* (Salt Lake City: University of Utah Press, 1970). Jonas provides valuable insights into the post–World War II politics of Utah and Montana. Also very helpful is Michele Stenehjem Gerber's discussion of Cold War politics in the American West in *On The Home Front: The Cold War Legacy of the Hanford Nuclear Site* (Lincoln: University of Nebraska Press, 1992).

There are also several valuable firsthand accounts available. Arizona Senator and presidential candidate Barry Goldwater, an outspoken anti-Communist lawmaker, reveals the thinking of western politicians with his two books, *Goldwater* (New York: Doubleday, 1988), and *Why Not Victory?* (New York: McGraw-Hill, 1962). I have been very impressed with Robert Alan Goldberg's recent book entitled *Barry Goldwater*, (New Haven: Yale University Press, 1995) which has unique insights into Goldwater's thinking. In contrast, Stewart L. Udall, a former Arizona congressman and Secretary of the Interior, has written a book critical of nuclear defense in the region entitled *The Myths of August: A Personal Exploration of Our Tragic Cold War Affair with the Atom* (New York: Pantheon Books, 1994). Udall later represented citizens of Nevada and Utah who were seeking financial compensation through the courts for their exposure to aboveground testing of atomic bombs and nuclear fallout.

Perhaps the best source on politics in America's western states is Paul Kleppner's essay, "Politics without Parties: The Western States, 1900–1984," in *The Twentieth-Century West: Historical Interpretations*, ed. Gerald D. Nash and Richard W. Etulain (Albuquerque: University of New Mexico Press, 1989). Kleppner's study, *The Evolution of American Electoral Systems* (Westport, CT: Greenwood Press, 1981), provides additional insight into the political environment of the post–World War II period in the country as a whole. Still valuable is Gerald D. Nash's text, *The American West in the Twentieth Century: A Short History of an Urban Oasis* (Englewood Cliffs, NJ: Prentice-Hall, 1973).

I found Richard W. Etulain's bibliographies, edited works, and texts to be indispensable to this study. See *The American West in the Twentieth Century: A Bibliography* (Norman: University of Oklahoma Press, 1994*); The Twentieth Century West: Historical Interpretations* (Albuquerque: University of New Mexico Press, 1989), which he co-edited with Gerald D. Nash; *Western American Literature: A Bibliography of Interpretative Books and Articles* (Vermillion, SD: Dakota Press, 1972); and *The American West: A Twentieth-Century History* (Lincoln: University of Nebraska Press, 1989), which he co-authored with Michael P. Malone. Also useful is Michael P. Malone's *The American West, as Seen by Europeans and Americans* (Amsterdam: Free University Press, 1989).

For insights into the politics of the environment, see Roderick Nash's *Wilderness and the American Mind*, 3rd. ed. (New Haven: Yale University Press, 1982); *The American Environment: Readings in the History of Conservation*, 2nd ed. (Reading, MA: Addison-Wesley, 1976); and *A River Too Far: The Past and Future of the Arid West* (Reno: University of Nevada Press, 1991). For more recent interpretations, see Richard White's *Land Use, Environment, and Social Change: The Shaping of Island County, Washington* (Seattle: University of Washington Press, 1992), and especially his *"It's Your Misfortune and None of My Own": A History of the American West* (Norman: University of Oklahoma Press, 1991).

As for insights into the thinking of ordinary Americans during the latter half of the twentieth century, I found the following works particularly useful: H. W. Brands *The Devil We Knew: Americans and the Cold War* (New York: Oxford University Press, 1993); Guy Oakes *The Imaginary War: Civil Defense and American Cold War Culture* (New York: Oxford University Press, 1994). For analysis of the language of politicians, consult Martin J. Medhurst, Robert L. Ivie, Philip Wander, and Robert L. Scott, *Cold War Rhetoric: Strategy, Metaphor, and Ideology* (New York: Greenwood Press, 1990). Lynn Boyd Hinds highlights the early years of the Cold War debate in *The Cold War as Rhetoric: The Beginnings, 1945–1950* (New York: Praeger, 1991). See also Tobin Siebers' *Cold War Criticism and the Politics of Skepticism* (New York: Oxford University Press, 1993).

Of the works on the economic dimension of the Cold War, James L. Clayton's *The Economic Impact of the Cold War: Sources and Readings* (New York: Harcourt, Brace & World, 1970) is important. For a more recent analysis, see "Four Trillion Dollars and Counting," by the Nuclear Weapons Cost Study Project Committee, Stephen I. Schwartz, ed., in the *Bulletin of the Atomic Scientists* (November/December 1995). See also the work of Mark J. Madrian and Douglas A. MacDonald, who treat Utah's economy as a case study in *The Outlook for Utah's Defense Industry in the Post–Cold War Era* (Salt Lake City: Economic and Statistical Unit, Utah Tax Commission, 1990).

Finally, there is a growing literature of a general nature on politics and the Cold War. Key works here include William Dudley, *The Cold War: Opposing Viewpoints* (San Diego: Greenhaven Press, 1992); Melvin P. Leffler, *A Preponderance of Power: National Security, the Truman Administration, and the Cold War* (Palo Alto: Stanford University Press, 1992). Mary McAuliff's *Crisis on the Left: Cold War Politics and American Liberals, 1947–1954* (Amherst: University of Massachusetts, 1978) studies the dilemma faced by many Americans who were "liberal" on social policy but "conservative" on foreign policy. Moti Nissani's *Lives in the Balance: The Cold War and American Politics, 1945–1991* (Wakefield, NH: Dowser Publican Group, 1992), also focuses attention on how lives were changed during an undeclared war of nearly fifty years. And Lary May has edited a useful work, *Recasting America: Culture and Politics in the Age of Cold War* (Chicago: University of Chicago Press, 1989), which depicts the impact of the Cold War on America's changing culture. See also Michael Beschloss's *The Crisis Years: Kennedy and Khrushchev, 1960–1963* (New York: Edward Burlingame Books, 1991) and *At The Highest Levels: The Inside Story of the End of the Cold War* (Boston: Little, Brown, 1993), which he co-authored with Strobe Talbott. And, finally, Anthony Dolan highlights Ronald Reagan's role in fighting the Cold War in *Undoing the Evil Empire: How Reagan Won the Cold War* (Lanham, MD: University Press of America, 1990).

CHAPTER SEVEN

CRUSADERS AGAINST COMMUNISM, WITNESSES FOR PEACE

Religion in the American West and the Cold War

MARK STOLL

In 1952 the Korean War still raged. The United States and the Soviet Union were testing and expanding their nuclear arsenals. The specter of Communist spies and infiltrators haunted the nation. That year Hollywood released a movie of H. G. Wells's *War of the Worlds*. Set in California among a painfully wholesome group of Americans, the film captured in a science-fiction story popular fears about invasion, the terrors of modern war, and annihilation of civilians and civilization. Invincible invading Martians with their heat rays destroyed everything in their path. But whereas the only religious figure in Wells's novel had been a curate gone mad, Hollywood made religion the film's central theme. In one scene, for example, a venerable clergyman from the "Community Church" walks toward the menacing Martians, reciting the Twenty-third Psalm and holding aloft a Bible with a gleaming silver cross on its cover, only to be incinerated by their heat ray. Later, when the Martians attack Los Angeles, its streets are empty—the population is in the city's houses of worship praying for a miracle. At the exact moment when the Martians aim their weapons at the churches, they die—struck down by bacteria, against which they have no immunity. The narrator concludes that mankind had been saved by the littlest things that God had put on this earth, and the film ends with a hymn. The moral of this Cold War morality play was that God, and only God, could save the United States against an enemy who was not only godless but rejected the offer of redemption—an enemy such as the Communist Soviet Union.

The Cold War signified many things: a political rivalry between two great powers; an economic competition; an arms race; a struggle for global influence. But Americans did not generally think about the Cold War in terms of naked struggle for world dominance between to self-interested nations. The Cold War for most Americans was a moral confrontation with the earthly embodiment of evil, a struggle for the world's hearts and minds—and souls. With World War II, a "good war" against manifest evil, fresh in memory, inevitably Americans imagined the Cold War as a contest between Christian (and Jewish) democratic liberty and atheist totalitarian slavery.

Westerners had a distinctive impact on American religion during the Cold War, even though the West does not, like the South, have a distinctive regional denominational character. The geographical denominational distribution across the West corresponds to historical migration patterns. Some northern churches spread in a band from the Midwest to the Northwest, while conservative denominations associated with the "Okies" are strongly represented in the Southwest and Southern California. Strong in much of the West (70 percent of American Catholics live west of Denver), the Roman Catholic Church benefits from the region's proximity to Latin America and predominates along a broad swath that stretches across the Southwest from San Francisco to Brownsville, Texas. Mainly migrants from New York, western Jews are primarily urban, with a particularly large presence in Los Angeles. Unique among western denominations, the Church of Jesus Christ of Latter-Day Saints, or Mormon church, dominates only one region, in and around Utah, in the heart of the West.

That no one church characterizes the West does not mean, however, that the West has no real religious identity. Strong individualists, western Protestant believers tend less to be churchgoers and have weaker denominational identification, while western Jews have more of a cultural than a religious identity. Due in part to their individualism, westerners have a greater tendency to take up more extreme positions on the religious right or left. Isolation of West Coast denominations from the rest of the nation has also tended to make sectarianism more exaggerated. Consequently, western religious responses to the Cold War have been particularly extreme, prominent, and vocal.

The issues of the Cold War, of course, had no sectional boundaries. All major American denominations are national, and no significant religious group exists solely in the West. On the institutional level, the religious response to the Cold War is a national one. Nevertheless, many western individuals, churches, movements, and actions made their distinctive marks on the religious history of the Cold War in America.

One thing to note about the religious response to the Cold War is that a brief history such as this one can be misleading, particularly about gender issues. Probably due to the weight of religious history, practically no women appear in the leadership of major religious organizations. But on both the religious right and left, women usually make up the majority of members, and sometimes the great majority. Women also often operate as lieutenants and organizers in groups and movements ranging from Robert Thieme's ministry to Sanctuary.

Religious response to the Cold War breaks into three general periods. In its earliest phase, from World War II to the early 1960s, religious bodies united nearly unanimously behind the effort to contain "godless Communism." A second period followed Vatican II's condemnation of nuclear weapons and modern war, which inspired other denominations to rethink their support of American Cold War policy. Religious opposition to American Cold War policies increased throughout the Vietnam War era. Deep polarization of the religious community on foreign policy issues characterized the third period, from the late 1970s to 1989, when President Ronald Reagan revitalized Cold War rhetoric and policy with the enthusiastic backing of the religious right, but without the religious unanimity of the 1950s.

CRUSADING AGAINST COMMUNISTS, 1949–1963

For most religious leaders in the 1940s, there was no hesitation about linking arms in a common front against the Communists. Not only did Communist totalitarianism threaten virtually every traditional American value, it was officially atheist and materialist. Prewar radicals and participants in the peace movement fell silent or climbed aboard the anti-Communist bandwagon. Mormons and Catholics, two groups who had traditionally distanced themselves from the American government and its foreign policies, adopted "hyper-American" conservative foreign policy views. Protestants held greater diversity of opinion than other religious groups. They disagreed whether the Communist challenge called for a worldwide revival of religion as a potent means to combat it, or whether Communism was a moral challenge to the United States that it should meet by helping other nations with their social and economic problems. A very small number, mostly liberal Protestants like the liberal Quakers, objected to containment and American militarism as unchristian, and saw no ideological or political threat in Communism. Black Protestants tended to be far more liberal on foreign policy issues than White Protestants of the same education and income, if about on par with White Protestants as a whole, yet their primary interest in social issues directed their activity away from foreign policy concerns.

Beginning after World War II and culminating with the election of the nation's first Catholic president, John F. Kennedy in 1961, Catholics felt themselves fully accepted as Americans for the first time in American history. Will

Herberg's *Protestant, Catholic, Jew* expressed the widely held view that in prosperous 1950s America, these historically antagonistic religions all were paths to "American" values. A long tradition of hyper-Americanism rooted in a desire to be accepted as Americans combined with an absence of a Catholic dissenting tradition to make Catholics enthusiastic Cold Warriors. The vigorous prewar Catholic peace movement, led by Catholic-convert Dorothy Day's Catholic Worker movement, practically disappeared. Catholics avidly supported fellow-Catholic Senator Joseph McCarthy's ceaseless pursuit of Communists in government. Church hierarchy quickly applied to the Cold War the traditional "just-war" theory that it had used to justify World War II. Communist action against the Church in heavily Catholic Eastern Europe hardened attitudes further. A strong foe of Communism, Pope Pius XII in 1949 excommunicated all Catholics who supported Communism and later linked pacifism with Communism. Catholic conservatism was so strong that well into the Vietnam War, Catholics took conscientious objector status in disproportionately low numbers.

Fundamentalist Protestants were especially disposed to see the Cold War in terms of good and evil and in terms of Armageddon, the final battle between good and evil before the Second Coming of Christ. After the Bolshevik Revolution of 1917, fundamentalists had not immediately attached great significance to the Soviet Union. As Communism's appeal grew during the crisis of the Depression, Russia loomed as a greater menace and assumed the form of the embodiment of evil that it retained for fundamentalists throughout the Cold War. As early as 1931, leading Texas fundamentalist J. Frank Norris preached a sermon entitled, "The World-Wide Sweep of Russian Bolshevism and its Relation To The Second Coming of Christ." The atomic bomb whipped conservative Protestants into an apocalyptic fervor and greatly increased Protestant interest in the prophetic portions of the Bible. A number of verses seemed to foretell nuclear warfare, the most widely quoted being II Peter 3:10: "The heavens shall pass away with a great noise, and the elements shall melt with fervent heat, the earth also and the works that are therein shall be burned up." Other passages appeared to refer to Russia and other contemporary nations. The end-time theory which fundamentalists favored, premillennial dispensationalism, was easily adaptable to Cold War events. In this theory the gathering to heaven of the saved ("rapture") preceded punishment of the wicked in a violent apocalypse ("tribulation"), which ended in the thousand-year reign of Jesus Christ on earth. This theory gave Israel and the Soviet Union, with other nations mentioned in the Bible, prominent roles in the violent destruction of the tribulation. The best-known early interpreter of prophecy for the atomic era was the prolific Wilbur M. Smith of the Fuller Theological Seminary in

Pasadena, California, whose "The Atomic Age and the Word of God" appeared in the January 1946 *Reader's Digest*. Smith's interpretation influenced many fundamentalists, including evangelist Billy Graham.

All fundamentalists were anti-Communists, but the leading crusaders against godless Communism operated in the West, close to a Tulsa–Dallas–Los Angeles axis. The senior crusader, J. Frank Norris, was pastor of Fort Worth's largest Baptist church from 1909 to 1952; founded Fort Worth's Baptist Bible Seminary; founded and edited *The Fundamentalist* periodical; and owned a powerful radio station. An outspoken anti-Communist since 1930, Norris and like-minded fundamentalists linked Communism with modernism (including evolution and integration), social programs, and the ecumenical Federal Council of Churches (FCC, later the National Council of Churches, or NCC), which conservatives frequently labeled "soft on Communism." Norris and other fundamentalists took it very hard when China "fell" to the Communists in 1949, since many Americans had long supported missionaries there and believed Nationalist ruler Chiang Kai-Shek and his wife to be devoted Christians. Norris defended nuclear weapons and an American first-strike policy; he felt that although nuclear war might destroy the world, it would be part of God's plan to bring "a new earth and a new heaven" as predicted in Scripture. When Southern Baptist Convention president Louis Newton made some favorable comments about the Soviet Union after a 1946 visit, Norris played on fundamentalist fears of Communist infiltration by accusing him of Communist sympathies and began an extended, unsuccessful campaign to oust him. Norris actively worked to form a united anti-Communist front with the Catholic Church, for which many of his religious allies roundly criticized him. Much to their dismay, Norris had an audience with Pope Pius XII in Rome and supported the Truman administration's controversial plan to send an ambassador to the Vatican.

The most prominent among Norris's anti-Communist fundamentalist allies were Carl McIntire and Gerald L. K. Smith. A close associate of McCarthy, Calvinist McIntire was founder of the Bible Presbyterian Church, a religious publication and radio empire, and Highland College in Pasadena, California, as well as a seminary and another college in the East.

Norris broke bitterly and publicly with Smith in 1947 when Norris, a supporter of a new state of Israel because of its putative eschatological role, denounced Smith's outspoken anti-Semitism. Smith saw Communism as a Jewish conspiracy. Headquartered in Los Angeles, Smith was one of the main sources of the White-supremacist "Christian Identity" movement. Christian Identity combined anti-Semitism, racism, survivalism, and millennialism into a violent "church" that has since been preparing for an Armageddon of Whites against browns, Blacks, and Jews. The Christian Identity movement claims that the Whites of Western Europe are the true descendants of the Biblical patriarchs, while Jews are demonic impostors. Christian Identity gradually became the theological center for a number of Ku Klux Klan members, neo-Nazis, skinhead racists, and "Aryan" groups.

An ordained Disciples of Christ minister, Smith had been an assistant in the 1930s to the anti-Semitic "radio priest" Father Coughlin, an associate of Henry Ford and Huey Long, and a member of the American Nazi group, the Silver Shirts. Following World War II, Smith founded the Christian Defense League, a survivalist group, and spread Christian Identity theology in his periodical, *The Cross and the Flag.* One of the newspaper's editors, Dr. Wesley Swift, a Methodist minister from Alabama and former KKK Kleagle, founded the Church of Jesus Christ-Christian, which operates today from Hayden Lake, Idaho. Since Swift's death in 1970, the "Reverend" Richard G. Butler (a mail-order minister) has led the church. Swift was also associated with such racist paramilitary groups as the California Rangers and the Minutemen. Groups associated with the Christian Identity movement have perpetrated numerous violent and deadly "hate-crimes" across the West from North Dakota to California, with the avowed purpose of stopping a Zionist-Communist conspiracy from subverting the United States.

As Norris's health declined after 1950, his star was eclipsed by Billy James Hargis, the most vocal fundamentalist Cold Warrior during the next two decades. Hargis was the anti-Communist protégé of A. B. McReynolds. Influential in the Independent Christian Churches, McReynolds ran an operation throughout the Cold War from his Kiamichi Mountain Mission in Talihina, Oklahoma. He conducted an annual men's clinic in the 1960s which trained thousands of church leaders. During the 1960s and early 1970s, he appeared with Dr. Gerald F. Winrod, who mixed anti-Communism with anti-Semitism, on Dallas oilman H. L. Hunt's "Defender Hour" on border radio.

Rising on the strength of his anti-Communist "crusade" to join the leadership of evangelical fundamentalists, Hargis operated the Christian Crusade from Tulsa, Oklahoma. In the 1950s and 1960s, his organization's literature reached millions of readers. Hundreds of radio stations carried his broadcasts. In the early 1960s, Hargis established the Anti-Communist Youth University in Manitou Springs, Colorado, at the foot of Pike's Peak, which offered two-week classes with a curriculum consisting, in Hargis's words, of "the Bible, the free enterprise system, Constitutional government, how to fight communism, and how to organize anti-Communist youth chapters." Hargis identified the United States (along with Jesus Christ and the Bible) as God's gift to humanity, and the Soviet Union as the Antichrist and the Devil. His most famous anti-Communist stunt was the 1953 Bible Balloon project, in which he and Carl

McIntire launched tens of thousands of balloons from Germany, laden with Bibles and religious tracts, to float across the Iron Curtain. Semi-retired since 1974, Hargis moved his Christian Crusade to Neosho, Missouri, in 1976, where it has fallen into increasing obscurity.

At McIntire's invitation, Frederick Schwarz, another Western anti-Communist crusader, immigrated from Australia in 1953 and established the Christian Anti-Communist Crusade in Waterloo, Iowa. He eventually downplayed association with McIntire and moved his headquarters to Long Beach, California. While neither a true fundamentalist nor a millennialist, Schwarz regarded conservative Christianity as Communism's only alternative. He spread his message through radio programs and presentations given throughout the nation. An appearance before the House Committee on Un-American Activities (HUAC) in 1957 increased his prominence. Schwarz took his anti-Communist message abroad in the 1970s to countries like El Salvador and the Philippines. He and his Christian Anti-Communism Crusade are still active.

A more secular ally of the fundamentalists, the John Birch Society, founded by North Carolinian Robert Welch in Indianapolis in 1958, found fertile soil in the West. Welch named the society after John Birch, a young Baptist missionary and graduate of Norris's Baptist Bible Seminary whom Chinese Communists allegedly killed during World War II ("the first casualty of World War III"). The society's strongholds were Texas and southern California, particularly in Los Angeles and Houston. In the early 1960s, the mayor of Amarillo, Texas, the school board of Midlothian, Texas, and several congressmen from Southern California were "Birchers." Convinced that Communists were already well on the road to controlling the nation—Welch at times called Eisenhower a "dedicated, conscious agent of the Communist conspiracy" and Reagan its "lackey"—Welch also accused the majority of the nation's clergy of Communist sympathies. Although raised a fundamentalist Baptist, Welch was theologically liberal. His closest clerical friend and supporter was James W. Fifield, Jr., minister of the First Congregational Church of Los Angeles, a theological liberal who always welcomed Welch to his church. Fundamentalists attracted to Welch's politics overlooked his theological peccadilloes. Mormon Apostle and former U.S. Secretary of Agriculture Ezra Taft Benson and his son Reed aided Birch recruitment efforts among Mormons. McIntire and Hargis had close ties to the "Birchers." Welch's influence declined after the 1960s, and he stepped down as John Birch Society president in 1983.

Gerald L. K. Smith's activity in the Los Angeles area, home of one of the nation's largest Jewish communities, worried Jews, who feared a popular association of Judaism with Communism. Their fears grew with the rise of McCarthyism. A high proportion of West Coast Jews had been convinced radicals in the

1930s, and had had influence in a number of mainstream Jewish organizations. At the same time, many of the Communist spy trials in the early 1950s involved Jews, such as Julius and Ethel Rosenberg, Judith Coplon, Robert Soblen, Jack Soble, Morton Sobell, and even Klaus Fuchs, who many falsely assumed was Jewish.

In such an atmosphere, and with the Nazi Holocaust a fresh memory, HUAC's investigations of the Jewish-dominated Hollywood film industry especially alarmed Los Angeles Jews—more especially since John Rankin, who publicly linked Jews and Communism, was a committee member. Six of the Hollywood Ten were Jewish. Fearful that anti-Communism could easily transform into anti-Semitism, Los Angeles Jewish organizations like the Western Division of the American Jewish Committee conducted purges of leftists and affiliated leftist Jewish organizations such as the Jewish People's Fraternal Order, and waved the flag as prominently as they could.

The first major challenge to the relatively unanimous anti-Communism of American churches was the Korean War. The churches did not waver in their opposition to Communism, but they did disagree whether Truman's policy of containment was the best policy. However, most religious groups patriotically closed ranks in support of American troops at war overseas. In 1950 liberal Protestant clergy called for condemnation of the hydrogen bomb, but the NCC was so divided on the issue that it could resolve on no action but prayer. Significant religious divisions over the Cold War would await the Vietnam War.

MORAL CHALLENGE TO THE COLD WAR, 1963–1975

The first large challenge to American Cold War policy was to its most terrifying aspect: nuclear war. The challenge came from an unexpected source, the Catholic Church. The election of John XXIII marked a dramatic change in the Catholic position in international affairs. John's first encyclical, the 1961 *Mater et Magistra*, emphasized social justice rather than international order as the key to peace. In his 1963 *Pacem in Terris* (*Peace on Earth*), John condemned nuclear war, called for international disarmament, and appealed for the development of international bodies to protect the common good. In 1962 the pope convened Vatican II, which in its 1965 *Gaudium et Spes* reaffirmed John's encyclicals and condemned the policy of nuclear deterrence. Continuing John's work for peace, his successor Paul VI expanded on Vatican II and approved conscientious objection in his *Populorum Progressio* of 1967.

During much of the first decade of the Cold War, religious leaders had nearly unanimously supported anti-Communism and discouraged criticism of the United States as actually or effectively subversive. Dr. Martin Luther King, Jr., and the Southern Christian Leadership Conference showed that the church could mount an effective moral criticism of domestic policy. Now the Catholic Church had begun the erosion of moral support for American foreign policy. The Vietnam War dramatically accelerated that erosion.

Disillusionment with U.S. foreign policy in Vietnam grew slowly. The religious and political right wing, of course, never wavered in its anti-Communism and support for nuclear weapons and the Vietnam War. Even Catholics only slowly came to oppose the war, in part because many Vietnamese were Catholic. The Catholic hierarchy (and most of the Catholic laity) supported the war as a "just war" until the end of the decade. (A Catholic pacifist movement, inspired by Dorothy Day and Catholic-convert Thomas Merton, and the "Catholic Left," led by the priests Daniel and Philip Berrigan, opposed the war from nearly the beginning, but were active mainly in the East.) In the 1971 Resolution on Southeast Asia the bishops finally condemned the war as unjust, the first time the Catholic church opposed the government on a major foreign policy issue. Yet mainline Protestant churches had already been condemning the war for two or three years.

Religious opposition to Cold War policy does not lend itself to easy summary. It lacked the visible charismatic figures, funding, organization, publication and broadcasting empires, and educational institutions that fundamentalism had. Religious liberals tended to act locally and independently in small organizations or loose regional or national affiliations. Their story is much more diverse and diffuse. The largest, most respected, and most moderate religious anti-war group was the nondenominational Clergy and Laymen Concerned About Vietnam (CALCAV), organized in 1965 and 1966. Like the other religious anti-war groups—Fellowship of Reconciliation, Interreligious Committee on Vietnam, American Friends Service Committee, Catholic Peace Fellowship, Pax Christi (Catholic), and Catholic Worker Movement—most of CALCAV's leadership and activity lay in the East. Its only major western leader was Stanford theologian Robert McAfee Brown. Nevertheless, chapters were organized in Seattle, Portland, San Francisco, Palo Alto, San Jose, Los Angeles, Denver, Minneapolis, and even Dallas. Local activity ranged from organizing discussions in churches on the war to civil disobedience. For example, in 1967 Denver CALCAV established a military counseling center; in 1968 clerics from San Francisco CALCAV chained themselves for a two-day service to nine soldiers who went AWOL to protest the war; and in 1971 Minnesota CALCAV organized a 440-mile Peace Walk across the state. In the 1970s, CALCAV changed it name to the gender-neutral Clergy and Laity Concerned (CALC) and shifted its focus to social concerns.

The San Francisco area became the religious countercultural counterpart to Los Angeles fundamentalism. Yet, although many new and Asian-influenced religious groups emerged in the Bay Area, few had strong political interests. Exceptions were those groups closely associated with campuses, especially at the University of California at Berkeley and Stanford University. In Berkeley, the campus Unitas involved Protestants against the war, and the University Lutheran Chapel (Missouri Synod) under Gus Schultz provided sanctuary for Vietnam draft resisters. The Catholic Newman Center at Stanford, defying the hierarchy's hostility to anti-war protest, actively participated in anti-war activity. A Catholic Stanford professor, Michael Novak, joined Robert McAfee Brown in radical opposition to the war. (In the 1970s, Novak became a prominent neoconservative; in the 1980s, he voted for Reagan, wrote a religious defense of capitalism, and was appointed to a position in the Reagan Administration.) *Ramparts*, a liberal lay Catholic magazine founded in Menlo Park, California, in 1962, moved to San Francisco to become a leading journal of the New Left.

THE LAST BATTLES: 1975–1989

In the 1970s, as the Vietnam War ground to a dispiriting halt and as the United States opened up relations with Communist China and negotiated arms limitations with the Soviet Union, the religious left abandoned foreign policy concerns for social and environmental issues. By the end of the decade, the religious right was making a comeback from a decade of defensiveness and retreat. In the election of 1980, its forces swept the political field. In doing so, and in reviving the Cold War rhetoric of the 1950s, they also revived the flagging spirit of the religious left.

Ronald Reagan was a typical westerner in that his conservative religious beliefs did not accompany involvement in a particular church, or even regular church attendance. He associated closely with conservative Christian figures and organizations, especially Billy Graham, Hollywood minister Donn Moomaw, and born-again singer Pat Boone. He was the only Republican candidate to attend the National Affairs Briefing in Dallas in August 1980, organized by Southern Baptist layman Edward A. McAteer's fundamentalist Religious Roundtable. As president, Reagan had close ties to such California fundamentalists as Robert Grant of Christian Voice, founded in 1979 in Pasadena, California. An effective lobbying organization throughout Reagan's first term, Christian Voice won notoriety for issuing "report cards" rating congressional and presidential candidates on domestic and foreign issues (for instance, labeling the Strategic Defense Initiative, or "Star Wars," pro-biblical).

Reagan's hard-line anti-Communism and belief that the Soviet Union was an "evil empire" (in an oft-quoted phrase) endeared him to the religious right. His ascent to power also exposed to media light the culture of the premillennialist apocalypse that the Cold War had nursed mainly along the fringes of the religious world since World War II. For the alert fundamentalist, the Cold War afforded signs aplenty of the impending apocalypse. An atheistic, apparently expansionist enemy in military and cultural competition with a (or even "the") "Christian" nation (the United States) for domination of the world fit into visions of a final battle (World War III) between the forces of good and evil at Armageddon. The atomic bomb offered the postwar world a vivid realization of fiery Biblical scenes of end-time destruction. The establishment of Israel in 1948 and the reunion of Jerusalem in 1967, allowing the regathering of the Jews and the rebuilding of the Temple, were also predicted events signaling the completion of history. The "signs" of the 1980s created renewed excitement: Reagan labeled the Soviet Union an "evil empire"; Gorbachev carried "the mark of the Beast" on his forehead; "Chernobyl" was Russian for "wormwood"; and many other more-or-less "predicted" events abounded. Reagan's top appointees who took Biblical prophecy seriously included Secretary of Defense Caspar Weinberger, Secretary of the Interior James Watt, and Surgeon General C. Everett Koop.

In the 1970s and 1980s the greatest popularizer of apocalyptic scenarios was Hal Lindsey. A native of Houston, Lindsey graduated from the Dallas Theological Seminary in 1962 and became a speaker in the Campus Crusade for Christ. The Dallas Theological Seminary has long been the leading American institution of apocalyptic studies. In 1970 Lindsey published a phenomenal best-seller, *The Late Great Planet Earth*, which sold twenty million copies in fifty-two languages and in 1978 was made into a movie. In this and his many other "apocalyptic thrillers," Lindsey combined biblical prophecy with up-to-date knowledge of weapons systems and world politics. He influenced most prophecy writers who followed him in that he believed that the prophets' archaic imagery simply meant they had no words or concepts to describe modern weapons and their effects. For instance, the image in Revelations of horses with lion-like heads and fire, smoke, and brimstone issuing from their mouths represented "some kind of mobilized ballistic missile launcher."

A flurry of millennial excitement came at the end of Reagan's presidency. Former space engineer Edgar Whisenant of Arkansas predicted an exact moment when the rapture would come in *88 Reasons Why the Rapture Will Be in*

1988 (Nashville, 1988). The book sold two million copies (or more—figures vary).

George Bush's vice-president, Dan Quayle, and his wife, Marilyn, had a close connection with the apocalyptic wing of conservative Protestantism. The Quayles and their parents were followers of Robert Thieme, pastor of the Berachah church in Houston. Thieme attended the Dallas Theological Seminary before taking the ministry of his Houston church. Thieme's church services resembled lectures. His "tape ministry" sent out 30,000 cassettes of his lectures each month and spread his fundamentalist, anti-Communist, and procapitalist millennialist message. Contemptuous of most other fundamentalists, Thieme was isolated from the fundamentalist world and strictly apolitical. Nevertheless, his influence extended far; Hal Lindsey dedicated his 1989 book, *The Road to Holocaust*, to his "spiritual father, Col. Robert B. Thieme, Jr." Another apocalypticist with a huge following, Charles Swindoll of the First Evangelical Free Church in Fullerton, California, was converted in Thieme's church and went on to the Dallas Theological Seminary (of which he subsequently became president).

Although the early 1980s were the heyday of fundamentalist Protestantism, developments since the 1960s ensured significant division among the churches on international issues. The experience of civil rights and Vietnam accustomed the churches and their leaders to letting their voices be heard. Two major issues prompted religious dissent: nuclear weapons and Central America. Moreover, unlike the Vietnam era when most of the liberal leadership had come from the East, during the 1980s westerners frequently led the way.

Vatican II had gradually grown in importance among Catholic bishops, particularly as the older, conservative bishops died or retired and younger, more radical bishops took their place. Archbishop John R. Quinn of San Francisco supported homosexuals, and Archbishop Roger Mahony of Los Angeles had worked closely with César Chavez, but it was Archbishop Raymond Hunthausen of Seattle who led the bishops on foreign policy issues. A native Montanan, Hunthausen was made bishop of Helena in 1962 and archbishop of Seattle in 1975. He had signed a protest against deployment of nuclear missiles in Montana, but in Seattle Hunthausen began to make himself known as a peace activist. Inspired by Jim Douglass, Seattle author of *The Nonviolent Cross* and Catholic activist and pacifist, Hunthausen took part in civil disobedience against deployment of the Trident nuclear submarine at the Bangor, Washington, naval base across the Puget Sound from Seattle, which he called "an American Auschwitz." He appealed for unilateral nuclear disarmament and urged people to withhold taxes from the "nuclear-armed Caesar." Beginning in 1982 Hunthausen withheld half his federal income tax, the portion that would go to the military, and donated it to charity. He also supported the Central American Sanctuary movement. In the meantime, the new pope, John Paul II, was moving the church in a more conservative direction. John Paul's experience as a bishop in Communist Poland led him to take a dim view with tampering with tradition, dogma, and ecclesiology. In 1983 the Vatican began an "apostolic investigation" of Hunthausen, and in 1986 stripped him of some of his powers. Suspicions emerged that Hunthausen was being made an example, since no other bishop underwent this extraordinary process. Widespread protest from his diocese and across the country forced the Vatican to restore his powers in 1987. Hunthausen retired five years early in 1991, leading to further suspicion of coercion.

The Reagan Administration had increasing difficulties with the Catholic Church. The government was rebuked in 1981 when it christened a nuclear submarine the USS Corpus Christi (named for the Texas city, but Latin for "the body of Christ"). The National Conference of Catholic Bishops, along with the NCC and many other religious bodies, requested a name change, and the navy ended the controversy by changing the submarine's name to USS City of Corpus Christi. Also in 1981, Bishop Leroy Matthiesen of Amarillo, Texas, made headlines when he urged workers to resign from jobs at the local Pantex plant, which assembled nuclear weapons. Scandalized Amarillans regarded the Pantex plant as the mainstay of both the local economy and the Free World. The local United Way evicted Catholic charities in response, but twelve Texas Catholic bishops issued a statement supporting Matthiesen.

By far the most visible of Catholic dissent from Republican foreign policy was the bishops' 1983 pastoral letter, *The Challenge of Peace: God's Promise and Our Response.* Prompted by Reagan's 1980 election rhetoric on defense, the letter condemned first use of nuclear weapons and all use of nuclear weapons against unarmed populations, expressed extreme skepticism about "limited" nuclear war, and criticized the policy of deterrence. It also urged immediate negotiations aimed at freezing and reducing production, implementing a test ban, and enforcing nonproliferation of nuclear weapons. By this time, Archbishops Quinn and Mahony had condemned administration nuclear policies. Half of all active bishops were involved in the growing nuclear freeze movement, and about a third joined Pax Christi. Within two years, the Episcopal and Methodist churches had followed up with strongly worded anti-nuclear weapons statements of their own.

Religion played a major role in defeating the MX missile mobile basing plan, which the governments and people of Nevada and Utah originally supported. As soon as the Carter administration proposed it, CALC, the American Friends Service Committee, and the secular National Committee for a Sane

Nuclear Policy (SANE) began attempts to organize local resistance. Incensed over plans to place the MX on tribal lands, Nevada Indians organized the Western Shoshone Sacred Lands Association and sued the government, saying the MX was a threat to their land, religion, and way of life. In 1980 MX opponents began recruiting area religious leaders, and won active support of Salt Lake City's Unitarian, Methodist, Episcopalian, and Catholic clergy and bishops, Reno's Episcopalian bishop, and the Catholic priests and Franciscan community of Las Vegas. SANE received donations or support from most mainline Protestant denominations, nationally based religious peace groups, the NCC, and the Catholic Maryknoll Order. CALC financed a national speaking tour of MX opponents, who spoke primarily in churches and synagogues and were fed and housed by local CALC groups. University of Utah law professor Ed Firmage, an active CALC member, knew the importance of the Mormon church, whose adherents made up the vast majority of area residents. A liberal Democrat as well as a descendant of Brigham Young, Firmage began extended talks with the Mormon leadership, in which he drew heavily on traditional Mormon beliefs and texts. As a result of his efforts, the Mormon church stunned the country when in May 1981 it announced its opposition to the MX missile, based on Mormon tradition and the Saints' vision of Zion in Utah. Cynics noted that Mormons first spoke out against nuclear weapons when the issue affected their home territory, but nevertheless momentum for the MX was lost and in October Reagan announced his rejection of the mobile basing plan.

Shock over the Mormon rejection of the MX missile was all the greater because the church had unofficially long been solidly in the Republican camp. Utah right-wing groups were very influential in state Republican politics. The most successful of those groups was the Freemen Institute, founded by Mormon and former FBI agent W. Cleon Skousen. Skousen feared a conspiracy of the super-rich to take over the world using socialism and Communist revolution and saw American history as fulfillment of Mormon millennial prophecy. The Freemen Institute used Mormon religious terms and ideas and had close interconnections with the church. Nevertheless, as the MX statement shows, there have been various currents at work within the church for some time. Mormon anti-Communist rhetoric first eased during the 1970s as the church—more successfully than any other denomination—began to create and exploit openings to proselytize in Eastern Europe and China.

Opposition to Reagan's nuclear buildup continued throughout his presidency. Most NCC churches opposed the Trident submarine, the MX missile, the cruise missile, the Strategic Defense Initiative (or "Star Wars"), and endorsed nuclear freeze. Naturally, western religious groups actively opposed government policy since so many nuclear weapons-related sites were located in the West. Catholic Workers began protests at the Nevada Test Site as early as the 1950s. The Lutheran Peace Fellowship worked for peace and against nuclear weapons throughout the 1980s in such actions as protests against the "White trains" bringing nuclear materials to the Bangor Trident submarine base. The ecumenical Church Council of Greater Seattle, under the direction of William B. Cate, organized peace initiatives and the anti-nuclear protests in which Archbishop Hunthausen participated. The Nevada Desert Experience, founded by Franciscan communities in Las Vegas and San Francisco in 1981, led faith-based nonviolent opposition to nuclear testing at the Nevada Test Site, and has coordinated action with Pax Christi, Sojourners, Catholic Worker, Fellowship of Reconciliation, Jewish Peace Fellowship, Buddhist Peace Fellowship, and the Catholic Peace Coalition. Members of the Buddhist Nipponzan Myohoji sect of Los Angeles beat drums at hundreds of demonstrations. The Ecumenical Peace Institute of the San Francisco Bay Area protested at Lawrence Livermore Laboratory. As in the Vietnam era, many protests involved campus ministries from universities across the West. Other protests took place at Rocky Flats Nuclear Weapons Plant near Denver; Amarillo's Pantex plant; Hanford Nuclear Reservation in Washington; the ICBM missile silos in Montana, Wyoming, Missouri, and the Dakotas; and Davis-Monthan Air Force Base in Tucson.

Perhaps no single issue of the 1980s split the churches like Reagan's Central American policy. In addition to their support of administration policy, fundamentalists actively proselytized in Central America. Pentacostals, in particular, were remarkably successful. Their message emphasized personal salvation and was apocalyptic, non-political, anti-activist, anti-Catholic, and pro-American. Religious people and organizations from across the West were at the forefront in saving Central Americans from Satan, Communism, and Catholicism. Bankrolled by right-wing Dallas oilman Nelson Bunker Hunt, Campus Crusade for Christ under Bill Bright operated in Latin America while supporting U.S. foreign policy. Louisiana Pentecostal evangelist Jimmy Swaggart's organization was very active in Central America and served as a covert conduit for aid to the Contras in Nicaragua. Newman Peyton, Jr., and Glen Norwood, Texas businessmen and leaders of the Full Gospel Fellowship, personally evangelized leaders across Latin America, from Paraguay's Alfredo Stroessner to Nicaragua's Daniel Ortega. California was the American capital of missions to Latin America. Los Angeles was the home of the Fuller School of World Mission, the Missions Advanced Research Center at World Vision, and the U.S. Center for World Mission, and headquarters for Wycliffe Bible Translators, World Vision, and Campus Crusade for Christ. Guatemala General Efraín Ríos Montt, whose bloody regime ruled during much of 1982 and 1983, belonged to the Church of the Word, a branch of Eureka, California–based Gospel Outreach. Ríos Montt preached on TV every Sunday and used his power to spread fundamentalist evangelical Protestantism in Guatemala.

Among liberal, pacifist, and mainline Protestant churches and within the Catholic Church, there was considerable interest in and support for liberation theology and resistance to Reagan's Central American policies, resistance which for the first time in the Cold War was led and dominated by religious groups and individuals. These groups came together in the Sanctuary movement. In the early 1980s, immigration officials usually awarded political asylum to refugees from governments the administration opposed, like Nicaragua, and deported refugees from those it supported, like El Salvador and Guatemala. Sanctuary started in Tucson, Arizona, where many Salvadorean and Guatemalan refugees were caught trying to cross the border. Catholic Father Ricardo Elford and Presbyterian minister John Fife were key early figures in a movement that began as a refugee advocacy network and spread across the Southwest and then north to Chicago, Seattle, New York, and Boston. Faced with hostile government policy, in 1981 Quaker Jim Corbett proposed creating religious refugee sanctuaries on the model of the antebellum underground railroad for escaped slaves. California groups from Los Angeles to San Francisco soon joined, including Gus Schultz's University Lutheran Chapel in Berkeley, which had pioneered sanctuary for draft resisters in the 1960s. At its height, six hundred congregations and religious organizations nationwide were Sanctuary cosponsors, although the movement developed tension between the Tucson-based group, which was Protestant-led, decentralized, and inspired by civil disobedience, and the Chicago-based group, which was Catholic, centralized, and inspired by liberation theology. At first wary and ambivalent about Sanctuary, the government finally moved to prosecute in 1984. Of several scattered trials, the most publicized was a trial of sixteen Tucson Sanctuary leaders in 1985. Most were convicted, but the judge suspended the sentences. Publicity from the trial led hundreds of churches, along with a few synagogues and city councils, to declare themselves sanctuaries, and three somewhat separate sanctuary movements emerged by 1987–88 in Southern California, southern Arizona, and South Texas. Other national resistance movements included Witness for Peace and Pledge of Resistance, whose most prominent organizer was Ken Butigan, a student at Berkeley Graduate Theological Union.

The "War of the Worlds"—the Communist and capitalist worlds—ended in 1989. The 1952 science fiction movie had been prescient in one sense: the Communist threat collapsed due to its own internal weakness and not to military attack. Otherwise, the film was wide of the mark. Long before 1989, the religious consensus that had given the Cold War its moral backbone had collapsed. It is true that a growing string of fundamentalist seminaries, institutions, communications empires, sects, and churches from Texas to California and Idaho drew nourishment from the tensions and moral issues of the Cold War. Yet by the 1980s, even old stalwart supporters of American policy like the Catholic and Mormon churches deserted the administration on crucial issues. No amount of 1950s-style apocalyptic rhetoric about the "evil empire" could convince most Americans that the Soviet Union was the source of the world's evil. Indeed, one important religious legacy of the Cold War in the West is the network of peace organizations now engaged in social, environmental, and political activism. The faith-based activism that the Cold War inspired lives on in the recent battles across the West on domestic issues.

BIBLIOGRAPHIC ESSAY

There are no general historical works on American religion and the Cold War, or on religion in the West. (Researchers and dissertation advisors take note!) The best starting point for research is Richard W. Etulain, *Religion in the Twentieth-Century American West: A Bibliography* (Albuquerque: Center for the American West, Department of History, University of New Mexico, 1991). A general overview can be found in Melvin B. Endy, Jr., "War and Peace," in *Encyclopedia of the American Religious Experience: Studies of Traditions and Movements*, ed. Charles H. Lippy and Peter W. Williams (New York: Scribners, 1988). A good general introduction to West Coast religious history can be found in Eldon G. Ernst, "American Religious History From a Pacific Coast Perspective," in *Religion and Society in the American West*, ed. Carl Guarneri and David J. Alvarez (Lanham, MD: University Press of America, 1987); see also Ferenc M. Szasz and Margaret Connell Szasz, "Religion and Spirituality," in *The Oxford History of the American West*, ed. Clyde A. Milner II et al. (New York: Oxford University Press, 1994). For religion during the early Cold War, see Stephen J. Whitfield, *The Culture of the Cold War*, 2nd ed. (Baltimore: Johns Hopkins University Press, 1996), chapter 4.

An excellent starting point for investigating fundamentalism is Glenn H. Utter and John W. Storey, *The Religious Right: A Reference Handbook* (Santa Barbara, CA: ABC-CLIO, 1995). See also Garry Wills, *Under God: Religion and American Politics* (New York: Simon and Schuster, 1990); Arnold Forster and Benjamin R. Epstein, *Danger on the Right* (New York: Random House, 1964); Seymour Martin Lipset and Earl Raab, *The Politics of Unreason: Right-Wing Extremism in America, 1790–1970* (New York: Harper & Row, 1970); Erling Jorstad, *The Politics of Doomsday: Fundamentalists of the Far Right* (Nashville: Abingdon Press, 1970); and Alfred O. Hero, Jr., *American Religious Groups View Foreign Policy: Trends in Rank-and-File Opinion, 1937–1969* (Durham, NC: Duke University Press, 1973). On apocalypticism, see Paul Boyer, *When Time Shall Be No More: Prophecy Belief in Modern American Culture* (Cambridge: Belknap Press of Harvard University Press, 1992). For J. Frank Norris and Billy James Hargis, see Barry Gene Hankins, *God's Rascal: J. Frank Norris and the Beginnings of Southern Fundamentalism* (Lexington, KY: University Press of Kentucky, 1996); John Harold Redekop, *The American Far Right: A Case Study of Billy James Hargis and Christian Crusade* (Grand Rapids, MI: W. B. Eerdmans, 1968). For the controversy between J. Frank Norris and Louie D. Newton, contact William R. Glass of Mississippi University for Women; and for A. B. McReynolds, contact Kevin Kragenbrink of Auburn University. Information on Gerald L. K. Smith and the racist, anti-Semitic Christian right can be found in Glen Jeansonne, *Gerald L. K. Smith: Minister of Hate* (New Haven: Yale University Press, 1988); *Extremism on the Right: A Handbook*, rev. ed. (New York: Anti-Defamation League of B'nai B'rith, 1988); and Michael Barkun, *Religion and the Racist Right: The Origins of the Christian Identity Movement* (Chapel Hill: University of North Carolina Press, 1994). Jewish fear of Cold War anti-Semitism is discussed in Max Vorspan and Lloyd P. Gartner, *History of the Jews of Los Angeles* (San Marino, CA: Huntington Library, 1970); and Victor S. Navasky, *Naming Names* (New York: Viking Press, 1980).

The religious response to the Korean War is the subject of Harold H. Osmer, *U.S. Religious Journalism and the Korean War* (Lanham, MD: University Press of America, 1980).

For the Catholic Church's changing role, see Patrick Allitt, *Catholic Intellectuals and Conservative Politics in America, 1950–1985* (Ithaca, NY: Cornell University Press, 1993); Ronald G. Musto, *The Catholic Peace Tradition* (Maryknoll, NY: Orbis Books, 1986); Timothy A. Byrnes, *Catholic Bishops in American Politics* (Princeton: Princeton University Press, 1991); William A. Au, *The Cross, the Flag, and the Bomb: American Catholics Debate War and Peace, 1960–1983* (Westport, CT: Greenwood Press, 1985); and James Terence Fisher, *The Catholic Counterculture in America, 1933–1962* (Chapel Hill: University of North Carolina Press, 1989). On CALCAV, see Mitchell K. Hall, *Because of Their Faith: CALCAV and Religious Opposition to the Vietnam War* (New York: Columbia University Press, 1990).

A number of books deal with the Christian Right in the 1980s. See Garry Wills, *Under God*; Matthew C. Moen, *The Christian Right and Congress* (Tuscaloosa, AL: University of Alabama Press, 1989); Richard V. Pierard and Robert D. Linder, *Civil Religion and the Presidency* (Grand Rapids, MI: Academie Books, 1988).

Archbishop Hunthausen has generated volumes of press comment, but the best summary of his career is his entry in the *Current Biography Yearbook* for 1987. A. G. Mojtabai, *Blessèd Assurance: At Home with the Bomb in Amarillo, Texas* (Boston: Houghton Mifflin, 1986), describes the Pantex controversy. On the bishops' 1983 pastoral letter, see Jim Castelli, *The Bishops and the Bomb: Waging Peace in a Nuclear Age* (Garden City, NY: Image Books, 1983).

On the MX controversy, see Matthew Glass, *Citizens against the MX: Public Languages in the Nuclear Age* (Urbana, IL: University of Illinois Press, 1993); and Steven A. Hildreth, "Mormon Concern Over MX: Parochialism or Enduring Moral Theology?," *Journal of Church and State* 26 (spring 1984): 227–54. On Mormons at home and abroad, see Anson Shupe, *Wealth and Power in American Zion* (Lewiston, NY: E. Mellen Press, 1992); and Robert Gottlieb and Peter Wiley, *America's Saints: The Rise of Mormon Power* (New York: Putnam's, 1984). A detailed discussion of the position of various denominations on nuclear weapons in the early 1980s is the subject of Donald L. Davidson, *Nuclear Weapons and the American Churches: Ethical Positions on Modern Warfare* (Boulder, CO: Westview Press, 1983).

For Central America, see David Stoll, *Is Latin America Turning Protestant? The Politics of Evangelical Growth* (Berkeley: University of California Press, 1990). The book to start with on the Sanctuary movement is Hilary Cunningham's *God and Caesar at the Rio Grande: Sanctuary and the Politics of Religion* (Minneapolis: University of Minnesota Press, 1995); see also Christian Smith, *Resisting Reagan: The U.S. Central America Peace Movement* (Chicago: University of Chicago Press, 1996); Robert Tomsho, *The American Sanctuary Movement* (Austin: Texas Monthly Press, 1987); and Ann Crittenden, *Sanctuary: A Story of American Conscience and the Law in Collision* (New York: Weidenfeld & Nicolson, 1988).

The history of faith-based peace movements is yet to be written. I wish to thank the following people for providing me with names and information: Gary Cavalier, Nevada Desert Experience; Felice and Jack Cohen-Joppa, eds., *Nuclear Resister,* Tucson, Arizona; Patricia McIntyre, Texas Christian University; and Mr. Phillip Runkel, Assistant Archivist, Marquette University Libraries, which has the Dorothy Day–Catholic Worker Archives.

CHAPTER EIGHT

FROM THE BEAT GENERATION TO THE SANCTUARY MOVEMENT

Cold War Resistance Cultures in the American West

℞

STEVE FOX

In October 1964 University of California–Berkeley officials tried to arrest student Jack Weinberg for distributing civil rights leaflets at the edge of campus. Six thousand students of all political persuasions jammed the campus plaza preventing the police from taking Weinberg away. This sudden showdown created the Berkeley Free Speech Movement (FSM). The first White student movement in the United States since the 1930s, the FSM's mass clash with Chancellor, Regents, and police revealed a faultline dividing California's affluent Cold War cultures. In demanding that their educators pay attention to social injustice, the Berkeley students were also demonstrating that open protest of Cold War social policies had spread from African Americans in the South to the White student population of the West, and thus from the working classes to the middle and upper-middle classes of the nation's most powerful state.

One generation later, in October 1990, teacher Carrie Gassman walked to the blackboard in her fourth-grade class in Albuquerque, wrote the word *War*, and asked the class what they might do about it. Her students began organizing that day and, four years later, after attracting the help of 64,000 other children in one hundred countries, they had designed a Peace Statue cast in bronze that today, rejected by Los Alamos, sits at the entrance to the Albuquerque Museum. The stubborn Albuquerque "peace kids" demonstrated that anti-war activism had been transferred from adults to children in a western metropolis that owed its modern growth to nuclear age military spending.

Historian George Lipsitz has characterized the Cold War social landscape as "the mysterious nightmare of life in postwar America." Across this social landscape, between the years 1949 and 1989, social movements arose among racial and ethnic minorities, students, women, and churchgoers. Recoiling from the horrors of wartime genocide and from the United States's continuing racial and economic inequalities, these movements protested that they could not return to business as usual. They could not resume pursuit of a consumer's American Dream in a militarized and divided society.

The experience of the Cold War years was different in the western states from experiences in other regions of the country because the vast landscapes of the West were home to competing factions: Native American and Mexican American cultures with many generations of resistance to mainstream forces; military installations—nuclear and aerospace—that had mushroomed during and after World War II; and an ethos of the new, of the ability to start life over. Many of the significant events and personalities of Cold War resistance cultures appeared on the national stage first in the West, particularly in California. To understand how this happened, we must entertain a brief prologue linking the tectonic realignments of World War II with those of the Cold War. In short, World War II's mobilization, social mixing, and inclusion was followed by the Cold War's return to exclusion and the politics of status quo dominance. This essay is not an index to all notable movements; it is a survey of representative figures and movements that illustrate the thesis that people experienced the Cold War in the western states differently from those living in other regions.

PROLOGUE TO REBELS WITH CAUSES

The war effort required unprecedented inclusion of women and once-excluded ethnic groups. Round-the-clock production at ship, plane, arms, electronics, and clothing factories demanded full employment, giving workers pride and power they had never before enjoyed. Women, personified by Rosie the Riveter, welded the steel plates of ships and planes and revolutionized their roles forever. Six million African Americans increased their great migration out of the South just as the war broke out. Perfection of a cotton-picking machine in the late-1930s had ended sharecropping and forced southern Blacks off the land and into cities.

In 1941 A. Philip Randolph of the Brotherhood of Sleeping Car Porters threatened a march on Washington if President Franklin Roosevelt did not open defense plants to Black workers. The president complied. Again, in 1948 Randolph threatened a march on Washington if President Truman did not integrate the armed forces. Again, the President complied. When the war ended, workers of all colors assailed the sudden cuts in jobs and workweek pay:

1946 was the biggest year of strikes in U.S. history, with wildcat walkouts leading to general strikes that shut down whole cities.

African Americans who had migrated thousands of miles to work alongside Whites or had traveled around the globe to fight fascism had new knowledge, new skills, and new motivation for fighting racism. But social gains made in wartime were being reversed, and returning home, Blacks faced double and triple the rates of unemployment Whites faced. This encouraged many of them to re-enlist. When the first shots of Cold War combat were fired in Korea in the summer of 1950, African Americans made up 28 percent of the front-line soldiers. And even though Black soldiers shared an ethic of trying to exceed all common standards of deportment to avoid trouble, almost 90 percent of troops charged with cowardice were Black. As George Lipsitz notes,

> The Black community at all levels responded . . . vehemently to the racism in the military . . . from Thurgood Marshall to Ivory Perry, Blacks drew upon a common political stance to oppose a trend that threatened to turn back the clock on justice. . . . Military officers and mass media figures might insist that Black troops in Korea caused their own problems, but an independent network of communication and organization challenged those views on a wide variety of fronts. The very same network would be in the vanguard of the civil rights movement in the decades that followed.

Ironically, the military that White students would fight so bitterly during the Vietnam era had been, and would continue to be, an important incubator of the Black equality movement which first inspired them to protest.

The African American freedom struggle based in the South is the prototypical twentieth-century U.S. resistance movement. Its roots were five generations old by World War II, and the substance and style of the Civil Rights Movement that burgeoned after World War II influenced all dissenting movements that arose after the war. Direct action, student demonstrations, nonviolent civil disobedience—all came from Black civil rights organizers. Civil rights training became the wellspring of White student activism. However, the civil rights struggle was not only waged in the South. New Mexico and Arizona activists won victories at local and state levels before the 1954 *Brown v. Board of Education* landmark case—which was, after all, from the western state of Kansas.

In Phoenix, African American plaintiffs and White allies, including Barry Goldwater, got Arizona's segregation laws ruled invalid in 1953. Said White activist William Mahoney: "The die is cast in the South or in an old city like

New York , but we here [in Phoenix] are present for creation. We're making a society where the die isn't cast." Similarly, in Albuquerque, two Black students, including the first president of the main dormitory, were repeatedly denied service at local restaurants in 1948–49. Students led successful boycotts of Oklahoma Joe's and Walgreen's and threatened any others who barred Blacks. A main argument presented to the City Commission in 1950 was that Albuquerque, a center of defense spending, must be a model of democracy. On Lincoln's birthday in 1952, Albuquerque joined a town in Oregon as the first U.S. cities since Reconstruction to pass antidiscrimination ordinances. Recognizing the city's success, the state passed the New Mexico Civil Rights Act of 1955 outlawing discrimination in public places. A mixture of ex-soldiers, Old Western egalitarian thinking, and well-educated defense workers took a stand against White southern immigrants who wanted the West to be like the Old South.

By the 1950s, many conservative military values had been transferred to civilian life. Dwight Eisenhower, Supreme Allied Commander in the war, was president of Columbia University. His brother, Milton, was president of The Pennsylvania State University and, later, Johns Hopkins University. A retired Women's Navy Commander was president of Barnard. Overall, 40 percent of college presidents in the 1950s had served in the Defense or State departments during the war. But the conformity, obedience, and mechanization required to win the global war were at odds with other American values—individual creativity, dissent, and freedom. The wartime social contract that had offered good pay for teamwork now was open only to White men. The Federal Bureau of Investigation (FBI) expanded its files on people who voiced criticism. Willa Cather, James Agee, James Baldwin, F. Scott Fitzgerald, William Faulkner, Ernest Hemingway, Jack London, Robinson Jeffers, Joseph Wood Krutch, Tennessee Williams, Allen Ginsberg, and 136 other major authors were all investigated by the FBI. The House Un-American Activities Committee (HUAC) and the McCarthy hearings raised the terms "blacklist" and "un-American" to chilling prominence. Inevitably, people began to resist this intolerance. Many opening shots in what were to become cultural wars were fired in the West, the landscape of the new, the cradle of the atomic and microelectronics ages, and home to their opposition.

In studying the Cold War West, we must acknowledge the prominent role California played as a laboratory of social change. Gerald Nash and Richard White have noted the shift of power to California after the war. Over the Cold War period, the state's economy surpassed all but four *nations* in the world. In the state's fluid cultural climate, high technology districts, nuclear laboratories, and youthful rebellion developed side by side. California was home to the first urban race riot of the 1960s (the Watts riot of 1965); the first White student movement since the 1930s; the first mass demonstration against the Vietnam War; the first public performances of the Beat Generation and Hippie counter-cultures; and the ethnic political awakenings of myriad groups. These included Mexican Americans; the Black Panthers of Oakland, who evolved from a ragtag group who could not pay the rent to stars of magazine covers around the world; and the Red Power movement of Native American activism. Bay Area and Los Angeles Native American students and activists seized the abandoned federal prison on Alcatraz Island. The American Indian Movement (AIM), founded in Minneapolis in 1968, was modeled on the Black Panthers and inspired to direct action by Alcatraz. The Chicano Movement flowered in New Mexico, Colorado, Texas, and California after symbolic events in Rio Arriba County, New Mexico, and in Denver.

The radical environmental movement Greenpeace appeared in Vancouver, British Columbia, in 1971 and Earth First! was born in New Mexico in 1980. In the 1980s and 1990s an ecumenical coalition of church members organized against the nuclear industry, which was concentrated in Washington state, along Interstate 25 from Wyoming to El Paso, and between Albuquerque, New Mexico, and Amarillo, Texas (nuclear centers linked by Interstate 40). The Sanctuary Movement, another ecumenical, multicultural movement born in Arizona and Texas in 1981, defied official federal policy and smuggled Central American political refugees into the United States. The Peace and Sanctuary movements had prominent women strategists, and the most recent demonstration of resistance to the Cold War, the Children's Peace Statue project of 1990–95, was conceived, organized, and carried out by Albuquerque fourth-graders. Indian and Hispanic pilgrimage traditions that criss-cross the Southwest and Mexico gave these movements grassroots authenticity, as peace pilgrims walked in symbolic resistance on the highways and nuclear test ranges.

And so by the Cold War's end in 1989, life in America showed many layers of resistance to mainstream consumer and arms-race culture. Let us now trace the development of several key movements strongly associated with the Cold War West.

THE "BEAT GENERATION"

Who were the Beats? Jack Kerouac, a handsome French Canadian from the decaying mill town of Lowell, Massachusetts; Allen Ginsberg, son of a Jewish lyric poet and schizophrenic mother from Newark, New Jersey; Gary Snyder, a student of Oriental thought from a Washington State Socialist family; Neil Cassady, a delinquent rogue and performance talker from Denver; and a handful of others. They were a circle of writers who formed a literary movement, the first to seize the imagination of the young since F. Scott Fitzgerald's Lost Generation of the 1920s.

Together, the Beats rocked a staid literary landscape with one innovation after another: personal reportage, confessional fiction, and poetry modeled on vernacular speech and jazz music. Their subject was postwar America's paradoxes and fading promise. Their sources flowed from a quest for spiritual and physical ecstasy and a generous democracy. Their techniques were improvisational. There was an audience for their flouting of postwar conventions and ridiculing of conformity because the tradition of protest and dissent is the American tradition—individual against community, spirited minority against sullen majority.

The Beat writers developed many of the themes that formed the foundations of later and larger social movements. They wrote of industrial abuses of nature and the need for reconciliation with the nonhuman. They wrote of White hunger for more contact with nonWhite races. They wrote of the mysteries of sex and spiritual disciplines; they wrote of dancing, drugs, and bold, mystical talk. They said their name reflected both the damage done to their generation by the war and the antidote to it: beat and beatitude. During and just after World War II, Black jazz musicians and Times Square drug users had a phrase for psychic exhaustion: "Man, I'm beat." Allen Ginsberg and Jack Kerouac passed the term into their circle, and by 1947 Kerouac defined the era: "It's a sort of furtiveness . . . a weariness with all the forms of the world. . . . I guess you could say we're a beat generation."

The war and its industrial aftermath may have beaten them down, but in compensation military work paid good wages: Kerouac and Ginsberg survived by joining the Merchant Marine. As late as 1956, Ginsberg supported his poetry by shipping out on a California freighter delivering parts to Arctic radar installations. As a Yeoman Storekeeper, he made $5,040 a year, excellent wages that fueled months of writing. Gary Snyder recently pointed out that the good jobs and affordable rents of the expanding postwar economy gave the bohemian underground a freedom of movement unimaginable by the later 1970s.

The Beats exploded onto the literary landscape and into the popular imagination through the San Francisco poetry renaissance. In 1955 Ginsberg organized a reading at Six Gallery on Fillmore Street to showcase his friends' work and introduce his idol Kerouac to the city. Ginsberg's own poem *Howl*, written for the occasion with the assistance of peyote and Benzedrine inhalers, seized the imagination of those present and of the literary community nationwide. With his opening line and the long choruses following, Ginsberg placed his

personal anguish in the context of a generation longing for spiritual catharsis.
He began:

> I saw the best minds of my generation destroyed by madness, starving
> hysterical naked,
> dragging themselves through the negro streets at dawn looking for an
> angry fix,
> angelheaded hipsters burning for the ancient heavenly connection to the
> starry dynamo in the machinery of night . . .

Moloch! shouted Ginsberg at the militarized world, as he pleaded for social
renewal. Federal authorities publicized the poem and the Beats by indicting
writer and publisher for obscenity. *Howl* was soon translated into thirty languages.

Many of the tortured minds Ginsberg had seen destroyed by madness were
women—his friend Natalie Jackson, whose suicide came as he was finishing *Howl*; William Burroughs's wife Joan Vollmer, whose proto-pad was the
household where many of the writers developed their early connections; and
Ginsberg's mother Naomi, lobotomized and institutionalized when he was
thirteen. Kerouac met Ginsberg and William Burroughs through connections
set up by his girlfriend, Edie Parker, who is never mentioned by the literary
biographers. These women's experiences and influence were uncelebrated in
the male-oriented Beat scene.

Allen Ginsberg exploited the press's role in packaging the deviant and the
sensational for a quiescent public. Ginsberg became not only the Whitman of
his age, but also a tireless promoter who kept his address book current with
telephone numbers that helped mainstream writers, the underground, gallery
owners, and academic powers keep in contact with each other. In contrast to
the McCarthyist boundaries drawn by most mainstream cultural leaders, the
Beats were paragons of democratic discourse and civic concern. Memoirist
Joyce Johnson described Ginsberg as "a cosmic social worker" dedicating his
talents to the common welfare, "excluding no one from the warm, steady beam
of his attention." As he wrote of himself in *Howl*, "America, I'm putting my
queer shoulder to the wheel."

Kerouac's novel *On the Road*, written in 1951 about his late-1940s experiences, was not published until 1957, when it became the second manifesto
against Cold War conformity. *New York Times* reviewer Gilbert Millstein called
it "a historic occasion . . . the most beautifully executed, the clearest and the
most important utterance yet made by the generation . . . whose principal

avatar he is." Improvising like a jazz soloist, Kerouac wrote his account of cross-country quests on a one-hundred-foot roll of teletype paper in fourteen days. He had been the speed-typing champ of Greater Boston as a student, and combining that skill with his prodigious memory and sympathy, he created, ten years before Truman Capote and Norman Mailer would claim it, what came to be called the "New Journalism."

Reading his book, many experienced a flash of recognition of the frustrations underlying the booming postwar economy. In Denver, he wrote,

> At lilac evening I walked with every muscle aching among the lights of 27th and Walton in the Denver colored section, wishing I were a Negro, feeling that the best the White world had offered was not enough ecstasy for me, not enough life, joy, kicks, darkness, music, not enough night. . . . I wished I were a Denver Mexican, or even a poor overworked Jap, anything but what I was so drearily, a "White man" disillusioned.

In booming California, he finds, "LA is the loneliest and most brutal of American cities . . . [where] booted cops frisked people on practically every corner . . . all of it under those soft Southern California stars that are lost in the brown halo of the huge desert encampment LA really is."

Kerouac was terrified when he was discovered by the media. *Mademoiselle* magazine featured a piece on the San Francisco Poetry Renaissance just before *On the Road* came out. His publisher pressed him into turning out another account of life among his friends, a sequel to *On The Road* called *Dharma Bums*. A television producer rushed the series "Route 66" into production starring actor George Maharis, a near double for Kerouac. The Beats spent the next few years in Tangier, Paris, and London. In the meantime their poetry and prose circulated among a new generation of readers. What had the Beats accomplished? They had electrified the atmosphere of the cold, suspicious fifties and early sixties by their insistence on ambitious arguments, big themes, and doing something loving, raucous, or crazy to rescue American souls from consumerism and small-mindedness.

Why was San Francisco the launching pad of the Beats and their heirs, the hippies? Because San Francisco's founding, development, and physical setting gave the city a heritage of liberalism and bohemianism. This early Spanish village settlement was invaded, during the Gold Rush of 1849, by gamblers, prostitutes, rascals, and fortune-seekers of all races. The city had 537 saloons in the Gold Rush days. Historian Richard White has pointed out that, unlike Los Angeles, Portland, and Seattle, which were dominated by Midwesterners who came overland, San Francisco was dominated by Italian, Irish, and German immigrants who came by boat. By the early 1900s, the city had the most powerful labor movement in the United States. The Italians were the largest ethnic group into the 1920s, and "Chinatown" gave the city another powerful ethnic enclave with a set of values outside mainstream assimilation. As in New York's Lower East Side and Greenwich Village, strong ethnic enclaves gave exotic shelter to those mainstreamers tired of conformity and materialism. "Bohemianism," as an urban subculture of shabby intellectualism and afford-able art spaces, was first labeled in the Balkan immigrant neighborhoods of nineteenth-century Paris; Bohemia is a province of Czechoslovakia. San Fran-cisco's European and cosmopolitan working-class history made it the ideal place for American bohemianism to evolve from small subcultures into mass lifestyles. During World War II, as poet Kenneth Rexroth, who moved there in 1920, points out, half of the nation's World War II camps for conscientious ob-jectors were within hitchhiking distance of the Bay, and groups who met to dis-cuss pacifism and anarchism appeared there decades before such groups could survive in more conservative areas of the West and the rest of the country.

Another force molding the Bay Window bohemian scene was the homosex-ual presence in the art world. Gays and lesbians had made the North Beach area of the city the first openly homosexual district in the United States. North Beach was flanked by Chinatown and the Italian section, which isolated the enclave from Anglo-American dominance and insulated it from routine police scrutiny. The gay influence was an underground whose friends shared assump-tions of being despised and feared by the mainstream; their philosophy, aes-thetics, and politics were formed in oppositional dialogue with the status quo. In the 1950s it was not yet a militant mass gay scene; heavy migration of gays and lesbians to San Francisco occurred only after the sexually permissive repu-tation of the hippie life was given wide publicity in the later 1960s.

Finally, of course, San Francisco was simply the loveliest of American cities, confined on a peninsula of rounded hills surrounded by a fine bay. And Cal-ifornia was the farthest that westward-leading Americans could go—if they were to build new forms, it had to be there.

THE NEW LEFT: CAMPUS RADICALS AND COUNTERCULTURE

In the early to mid–1960s, two more social movements emerged whose most dramatic manifestations were in the Bay Area. These were the student protest movement and the hippies, two overlapping groups that shared deep roots and soon became difficult to separate. The student protest movement was broad and had a braintrust of theorists and planners who called themselves the New

Left to distinguish themselves from the hierarchical socialist and communist cultures of the 1930s and 1940s. Students for a Democratic Society (SDS) was the New Left's most focused and far-left organization. On the other hand, the hippies were a most unorganized, anti-hierarchical manifestation of a youth counterculture that decided to form its own communal culture rather than struggle with the mainstream. The New Left and the counterculture were profoundly and consciously indebted to African American models of resistance. And both took on their most militant, creative, and anarchistic forms in the West.

The New Left announced itself with a manifesto in 1962, the Port Huron Statement. Largely written by Tom Hayden of Ann Arbor, where SDS was founded, the statement rang with the insights of many thinkers but especially the young Texas sociologist C. Wright Mills. Mills wrote of the Cold War: "In both superpowers we now witness the rise of the cheerful robot, the technological idiot, the crackpot realist. All these types embody a common ethos: rationality without reason."

The Port Huron Statement proposed:

> We would replace power rooted in possession, privilege, or circumstance by power and uniqueness rooted in love, reflectiveness, reason, and creativity. As a social system we seek the establishment of a democracy of individual participation, governed by two central aims: that the individual share in those social decisions determining the quality and direction of his life; that society be organized to encourage independence in men and provide the media for their common participation.

SDS launched organizing projects among the poor in Midwest and Northeastern cities. The White middle- and professional-class students of SDS modeled their project on SNCC, the Student Nonviolent Coordinating Committee. SNCC was founded by southern Black students who had organized the first "sit-ins" in 1961 (where students sat at segregated lunch counters and endured the abuse of Whites to attract publicity). But little came of the SDS efforts to radicalize the growing population of college students, which nearly tripled between 1955 and 1970. As historian Kenneth Heineman has pointed out, Kent State (Ohio) University students had succeeded in wringing free speech codes from their administration in spring 1964, but student protest exploded into national consciousness only when a larger movement happened a few months later in Berkeley.

Berkeley student dissent had been incubating since 1960, when HUAC held hearings in San Francisco. Berkeley students crossed the Bay to protest, staging a sit-in which police attacked with fire hoses. HUAC made a heavy-handed film of this opposition, calling it "Operation Abolition" and showing it around the country to expose the student protesters as the enemy of true American values. Many activists joked that the film had recruited them to Berkeley rather than warned them against it. In 1964 many of those students had spent "Freedom Summer" in Mississippi, learning from SNCC about direct-action protest. Many had just joined with Black activists to force the San Francisco hotel industry to integrate its workforce. On October 1, 1964, two deans and the chief of the campus police ordered Jack Weinberg to stop distributing leaflets about CORE, the Congress On Racial Equality. When Weinberg refused and was arrested, a crowd gathered that soon swelled to six thousand, refusing to let the police take Weinberg away. With this attempt at censorship, the UC–Berkeley administration precipitated the Free Speech Movement (FSM), the first White student movement since the 1930s and the first to use mass direct action on a campus.

It took eight hundred arrests, police beatings, sustained political education efforts, and marathon decision making by consensus, but the Berkeley students won. The Graduate Student Association and faculty voted to support them. FSM spokesman Mario Savio, from a working-class Catholic family in the Bronx, had spent the summer learning civil disobedience from African Americans in the South. He united the Berkeley students and faculty against the administration with his oratory:

> There's a time when the operation of the machine becomes so odious, makes you so sick at heart, that you can't take part. . . . And you've got to put your bodies upon the gears and upon the wheels, upon the levers, upon all the apparatus, and you've got to make it stop. And you've got to indicate to the people who run it, to the people who own it, that unless you're free, the machine will be prevented from working at all.

Who was running and who did own the "multiversity," as Berkeley President Clark Kerr called it? The "knowledge industry," according to Kerr, should be put at the disposal of the military and the giant conglomerates of aerospace, agriculture, and the other major industries. Thus, knowledge would be the postwar engine of economic growth, "like the railroads were in the 1800s." Nearby, Stanford matched Navy research and development money with land and manpower to create the research park that became the engineering paradise Silicon Valley. In the FSM, Berkeley students exposed the sophistry that defined civil rights as "off campus business," but military–industrial development as "on-campus business." The Free Speech Movement inspired increased student organizing on campuses across the country, elevating the New Left to sudden respect. SDS chapters multiplied faster west of the Mississippi, at state colleges and universities. Western chapters and leaders were more militant, yet more libertarian, than their eastern or southern counterparts. A lasting national change forced by the FSM was the demise of *in loco parentiis,* the doctrine that school administrators should act "in the place of parents." The intense and fundamental debates staged by student protesters brought an end to 10 o'clock curfews and separate housing for men and women.

ANTIWAR PROTEST

As civil rights was the incubator and formal education for other resistance groups, Vietnam became the engine that extended radical ideas further into the mainstream. Two western presidents, Johnson and Nixon, strove not to lose this war across the Pacific. As a war supplied from western ports, Vietnam ignited opposition from western leftist and countercultural groups. In May 1965 Berkeley's Vietnam Day Committee staged the nation's first mass public opposition to the growing war. The marches and demonstrations that spread across the nation broke the illusion of public consensus that pro-war "hawks" cited to justify the escalating war. Women veterans of the Berkeley FSM staged a mass march of women on the Oakland Induction Center in 1965, planting seeds to protest their limited roles within the male-dominated protest movements.

In 1966 college administrators began sending class rankings to draft boards. Forty thousand draftees a month were being called by 1967. SDS found and published a Selective Service memo defining the agency's mission as not only inducting men into the military, but also using "pressurized guidance" to "channel" those who remained in college into defense industry careers and away from humanities and the arts. The growing opposition to this complicity between the military and higher education administrators flowed from SDS and became the driving force of mass opposition to the war among the young.

In March 1967 Stanford student body president David Harris, former Fresno "Boy of the Year," joined with David Sweeney and the Peace and Liberation Commune of Palo Alto to form what they called "The Resistance," designed as a "White SNCC." Going beyond the SDS Port Huron Statement, Harris's West Coast resistance celebrated countercultural freedom: "Our life was our art." Daniel Ellsberg traces his metamorphosis from Vietnam strategist to antiwar anarchist to an emotional speech given by Randy Kehler, leader of the War Resistance League on the West Coast. Moved to tears, Ellsberg then read Thoreau's "On Civil Disobedience," and with his children's help, photocopied the classified documents that became known as "The Pentagon Papers" when they were published by the *New York Times*.

THE HIPPIES

The hippies were the mass culture heirs of the Beats, although nearly all observers at the time described them as a wholly new phenomenon. With the Beats dispersed abroad between 1958 and the early 1960s, most of the ingredients of the hippie subculture were present in the Beat literary works. Lawrence Ferlinghetti had made those "sacred texts" widely available by opening the first paperback bookshop in the country, City Lights Books, in North Beach, a store where the barriers between authors and audiences came down. Allen Ginsberg was a major cultural evangelist who transmitted to the under-thirty crowd, during the 1970s, so much of the values and myths of the Beats. A clear sense of continuity from generation to generation was maintained by the writers Robert Creeley, John Logan, Kenneth Rexroth, Michael McClure, and Gary Snyder, anthologized and interviewed in Sixties collections and underground newspapers. Singer Janis Joplin credited Beat writers with inspiring her, and on Ginsberg's death in 1997, singers from U2's Bono to Patti Smith credited his role in their awakenings. Another indication of the western influence on national perceptions of youth cultures was the fact that *San Francisco Chronicle* columnist Herb Caen coined the names that stuck for both groups: "beatnik" meant to evoke fear of the un-American by echoing "Sputnik," the 1957 Russian satellite that shocked Americans' confidence in their superiority; and "hippie," the diminutive *-ie* perhaps a reassurance that these social dissidents were only children playing.

As with the New Left, there were young people all over the country edging in similar directions, but the Bay Area provided the most audacious and off-the-wall countercultural innovators. During the mid–sixties, hippie entrepreneurs—centered just outside of North Beach, where Haight Street crossed Ashbury—opened "free stores" that mocked consumerism. One mime troupe evolved into The Diggers, named after the seventeenth-century English Civil War revolutionaries. The Diggers gave away or burned money and made free lunches for thousands. They popularized "guerrilla theater," streetwise improvisational critiques of war, racism, and capitalistic excess. Digger alumnus Abbie Hoffman co-founded the "Yippies," a media put-on that ran a pig named Pigasus for president in 1968 and outraged Mayor Richard Daley's Chicago machine by announcing intentions to disrupt the 1968 Chicago Democratic National Convention.

Music was the artistic glue that held many segments of the counterculture together, and San Francisco's "acid rock" music scene between 1965 and 1974 was a major genre. The Jefferson Airplane, Janis Joplin and Big Brother and the Holding Company, and especially The Grateful Dead were bands whose lyrics, amplified sound, simultaneous light shows, poster art, costumes, and tribal followers made hippie expression more and more baroque and sophisticated. In 1966 a poster, designed by Family Dog commune member Stanley Mouse, featured a Plains Indian figure and announced a "Gathering of the Tribes" for a "Human Be-In." This event was planned by Berkeley political activists and Haight-Ashbury hippie delegates. Allen Cohen, editor of the underground newspaper *The San Francisco Oracle*, wrote: "A new concert of human relations being developed within the youthful underground must emerge, become conscious, and be shared so that a revolution of form can be filled with a renaissance of compassion, awareness, and love. . . . The Human Be-In is the joyful, face-to-face beginning of the new Epoch." Like the Beats, Bay Area hippies went to Europe and spread the newest bohemian culture. Chet Helms was a Texan who, along with New Yorker Bill Graham, was an architect of the San Francisco sound. Helms told Beat/Hippie historian Lee Bartlett that he took Bay Area LSD to England in 1966, giving the Beatles and Rolling Stones their first psychedelic experiences and their first look at brightly colored silk shirts. "They were all wearing black when I got there," Helms recalled. The sound and artwork of *Sgt. Pepper's Lonely Hearts Club Band* (1967) reveals the California transformation Helms triggered in the British band.

As had happened in the Beat era, however, it became painfully obvious to women of the counterculture that the new epoch would maintain most of the gender rules of the mainstream world. Women in resistance cultures were in a position similar to that of Blacks in the military and defense work: they were used and taken for granted by ostensibly progressive groups. Western women activists laid the foundations for the most recent Women's Movement by questioning their male leaders at SDS annual meetings, at the first Latino Youth Conference in Denver in 1969, and in antiwar groups. Robin Morgan, who wrote the first widely read anthology of the new women's voices, *Sisterhood Is Powerful* (1972), recalls her own path of rebellion: "My involvement went from civil rights to New Left to counterculture . . . and then to a women's movement."

For the sixties movements as a whole, polarization with the mainstream and internal excess led to a winding down. Drugs, assassinations, police brutality, and the diluting effects of mass media packaging kept the countercultural initiatives from maturing into a "loyal opposition" that could craft political alternatives to the technocratic consensus dominating the country. The police violence at the 1968 Chicago Democratic Convention, with Allen Ginsberg chanting "Om" for seven hours in the midst of chaos; the crushing of the People's Park movement in Berkeley in 1969, with a helicopter spraying nerve gas over the entire one-mile-square campus; the Kent State and Jackson State murders of unarmed student demonstrators; all were visions of Vietnam militarization come home to haunt the heartland. Bob Dylan, who dominated protest and countercultural songwriting during the sixties and seventies, embodied for a mass audience the roles of Beat poet, folk troubadour, political satirist, and continually evolving rock star. In "Desolation Row" in 1965, Dylan had anticipated the collapse of sixties idealism. His smoky voice and the surrealism of his drug experiences evoked a cynicism soon to ripple through activist circles:

They're selling postcards of the hanging; they're painting the passports brown
The beauty parlor is filled with sailors; the circus is in town
Here comes the blind commissioner, they've got him in a trance
One hand is tied to the tight-rope walker; the other is in his pants
And the riot squad is restless, they need somewhere to go
As Lady and I look out tonight, from Desolation Row . . .

Artistic renderings of opposition, like the new generation of White cultural resistance with which it was intertwined, lacked the staying power learned by Black activists over generations of persistence seeking an elusive "path to the top."

However, countercultural values filtered through the West in different ways. Seattle, despite its radical labor history, had little of the countercultural conflict San Francisco and Berkeley had. In Seattle, hippie values filtered quietly into the mainstream via eclectic institutions like KRAB-FM radio and the Free University. Via the demographics of youth, the Seattle counterculture reinforced older utopian movements and created a wave of progressive institutions, including environmental quality regulations, citizen ownership of utilities, and comprehensive planning. No other western state had "urban Cubas" (islands of liberalism) as pronounced as California and Washington; hippie values achieved much lower profiles in Arizona, Wyoming, Montana, and the Rockies and Plains states.

BLACK PANTHERS, RED POWER, AND THE CHICANO MOVEMENT

As White youth movements flourished, minority activists continued to put pressure on local governing elites. In the fall of 1966 Bobby Seale and Huey

Newton founded the Black Panthers in Oakland. Their primary goal was resistance to police brutality, and they carried shotguns and pistols as they "patrolled the police." Within a year, the Berkeley war resisters decided to move "from protest to resistance," a slogan that spread nationally. Many White activists agreed to some extent with Bobby Seale's statement: "We captured the imagination of White radicals, whose whole identification followed us." The Panthers struck a note of paramilitary intimidation in their black leather coats and black berets. The media sensationalized the guns, and many White and Black moderates stood aside. FBI counterintelligence agents and police massacres stopped the Panthers from developing in political or cultural directions. By 1968, for example, Army intelligence estimated that one demonstrator in six at the Chicago convention was an undercover agent.

The Bay Area was also the birthplace of the Native American "Red Power" movement, which arose out of a nascent "pan-Indian" culture that developed on the West Coast. Pan-Indian consciousness was itself a significant accomplishment that knitted together people from the widely disparate cultures of scores of tribes and bands, mostly from the Plains and West. This created the smallest of the nation's major ethnic groupings—"smallest" because Indians numbered some 1 percent of the national population (although in Oklahoma, New Mexico, Arizona, and California, during the Cold War era, Indian population figures would grow to represent between 5 and 10 percent of those states' total population) ; and "major" because of the tribes' historic role in resisting U.S. westward expansion. The political movement "Red Power" was born in 1969 in an occupation of the abandoned federal prison on Alcatraz Island, one mile from Fisherman's Wharf in San Francisco Bay. The movement flared into prominence when this occupation inspired the radicalization of AIM—the activists of the American Indian Movement—and then flickered into obscurity again four years later, after the second battle of Wounded Knee, South Dakota, in 1973.

Red Power was like the Indian wars of the 1870s—the clashes were fast, furious, and out of sight of nearly all other Americans. In the words of historians Robert Warrior and Paul Chaat Smith, "Like a shimmering mirage across the desert floor," the Red Power movement was "an edgy, unpredictable creature that challenged American power in a way not equaled this century before or since."

San Francisco had become a hub of urban Indians uprooted by World War II and the wars in Korea and Vietnam. Returning vets were funneled through Bay Area ports. Indian nations such as Laguna Pueblo in New Mexico established colonies in the Bay Area because of the military-support work there. In 1958 the federal Relocation Program brought a steady surge of Indians to the

Bay. Relocation was a program of assimilation and termination, devoted to erasing traditional Indian cultures, that backfired. Over 100,000 Indians were relocated nationally. Native Americans from many tribes found each other and organized picnics in Golden Gate Park that turned into a powwow circuit with dancing, drumming, and costume revival. The United Bay Area Council of Indian Affairs was one of the results of this activity. This Council planned the occupation of Alcatraz that lasted nineteen months and galvanized Indian activists around the country to action.

Most of the Alcatraz occupiers came from the Native American Studies programs that had sprung up at UCLA, UC–Berkeley, UC–Santa Cruz, and San Francisco State University, which served the more affluent students from the vast western reservations. Many of the young people were children of war veterans or industry workers and were searching for pride and identity. Seventy of the eighty who occupied Alcatraz in November 1969 were from UCLA. A ringing statement signed "Indians of All Tribes" denounced the existence of idle federal facilities when Indians were in poverty. The occupation was the founding moment of a nationwide Indian political resurgence. Activist Grace Thorpe, daughter of famed Sac and Fox Olympic athlete Jim Thorpe, said, "It made me put my furniture into storage and spend my life savings."

Urban Indian activists had founded AIM in Minneapolis in 1968. Inspired by a visit to the Alcatraz occupation the next year, AIM staged a series of actions across the nation: seizing the Mayflower II in Plymouth, Massachusetts, in 1970; nearly destroying the BIA headquarters in Washington in 1972; and occupying Wounded Knee, South Dakota, in 1973. The movement's climax happened this way: AIM leaders Dennis Banks, a Chippewa, and Russell Means, an Oglala–Lakota (Sioux), were drawn to the century-old misery at the Pine Ridge, South Dakota, reservation of the Oglala band. Pine Ridge was the poorest U.S. jurisdiction in the censuses of 1970, 1980, and 1990. The Oglala were mired in ugly infighting pitting tribal chairman Richard Wilson and his G.O.O.N. squad of thugs against young, urban-educated activists in coalition with Oglala-speaking elders. The elders accepted Means's offer of AIM's help against the BIA-supported Wilson. At the end of February 1973, Means led his troops—the "reckless, unlearned dog soldiers of AIM"—to Wounded Knee, the very site of the most infamous massacre the U.S. ever committed, against Big Foot's unarmed band on December 31, 1890.

Wounded Knee II proved to be the final act of the organized Indian movement. The AIM band found itself besieged by a huge task force of federal marshalls, FBI agents, Army counterinsurgency advisors, and local law enforcement. This task force was armed with automatic weapons, nightscopes, helicopter gunships, fighter jets, and other arms developed in the Korean and

Vietnam conflicts. But the government's most effective weapon was its prosecution strategy. Supported by the FBI's COINTELPRO (Counter-Intelligence Program), the strategy was self-defined as "disrupting, misdirecting, [and] destabilizing" a political group through the use of double-agents and disinformation. AIM leaders were subsequently ensnared in an endless series of arrests, incarcerations, and trials. During the seven-week occupation of Wounded Knee, for example, 562 AIM members or supporters were arrested. Russell Means faced eight trials in 1973. And although the Wounded Knee "Legal Defense/Offense" committee, under civil rights attorney William Kuntsler, won 92 percent of its cases, AIM crumbled under the relentless legal pressure. The controversy at Pine Ridge outlasted the occupation of Wounded Knee. Between 1973 and 1976, at least 69 AIM members or supporters were killed on the reservation, making the tiny settlement on the Plains three times as murder-prone as Detroit, then the "murder capital of the U.S."

In the end, the Red Power movement collapsed as much from its internal contradictions and divisions as from government repression. Cherokee organizer Gerald Wilkinson, whose National Indian Youth Council was based in Albuquerque, later assessed the movement's demise: it had failed to develop long-range goals and discipline and an intellectual base, like those that sustained the Black civil rights movement over decades. Still, as Warrior and Smith conclude, "It was a spectacular ride . . . a time of hope and idealism . . . a campaign of resistance and introspection unmatched in this century," one that gave thousands of Native Americans a new raison d'etre and energy. In AIM's wake, many have continued to protest the "squalid panorama" of the poorest Americans—in wealth and in health—living amid the vast resources of timber, minerals, energy production, and military operations of the western lands held in trust for them by the federal government.

As the Cold War had replaced World War II inclusion, White progressives repeatedly found examples of resistance or causes for protest in Southwest Indian and Mexican American cultures. Within conservative Los Angeles, Hollywood's film community had had an open leftist subculture from the 1930s on. When anti-Communist pressures cut out two-thirds of the "social problem" films Hollywood was making per year, leftist writers and directors found a real-life story to film: the striking Mexican American miners in the Silver City, New Mexico area. The 1951–52 Nuevo Mexicano strike against Empire Zinc Corporation became inspiration for the film *Salt of the Earth*, which was banned by Hollywood distributors but circulated for decades on college campuses. The film's feminist, class-conscious, pro-Chicano messages flowed from a collaboration between miners, their wives, and the blacklisted screenwriter, Michael Wilson, and director, Herbert Biberman. Their associate, Paul Jerrico, had met union organizers from the Silver City mines while on vacation at the Taos retreat center owned by Jenny Wells Vincent and her husband Craig. The Vincents, with links to the Beat generation, labor activism, and folksong revival, also helped with a second case of White and minority collaboration: the fight to return their sacred Blue Lake to Taos Pueblo Indians. This sixty-four-year campaign peaked in the 1960s as dozens of Whites of all political persuasions helped the Pueblo carry its fight into the Nixon White House. Their victory in 1970 helped Nixon announce his new Indian policies and marked the first time land was ever returned to an Indian tribe by the federal government. During these years, the mestizo culture of Mexican Americans awoke to protest land and cultural issues of their own.

AZTLÁN DREAMS: THE ONCE AND FUTURE MEXICO

One hundred and twenty years after annexing the northern half of Mexico in 1846, the U.S. government found itself repudiated by militant descendants of the 100,000 Mexicans trapped on the wrong side of the new boundary. Two movements arose within a year of each other, one in northern New Mexico and the other in Denver, that fired the imaginations of Mexican Americans and other Latinos across the country. Enabled partly by the same military mobility and relative affluence that affected African American and Native American protest, these Mexican American movements nevertheless had distinct and differing motives and goals.

The citizens of Rio Arriba County in northern New Mexico were descendants of Spanish settlers who had been given communal grants of land by the King of Spain. These land grants were ratified by an independent Mexico and by a conquering United States in the Treaty of Guadalupe Hidalgo in 1848. However, a century of legal chicanery had wrested most of the land from Spanish-speaking villagers and put most of it into the hands of White landowners, particularly the federal Forest Service and Bureau of Land Management. In 1965 the Forest Service revoked over half of the grazing permits held by Spanish stockowners in the Los Ojos–Tierra Amarilla area. Reies Lopez Tijerina, a Pentecostal preacher and fiery orator from Texas, emerged during 1966 as a leader who articulated and fanned the resentment that ran generations deep in the area.

Tijerina's Alianza "arrested" two federal park rangers, seized the Echo Amphitheater and campground, and renamed it San Joaquin del Rio Chama. Proudly using the name Chicano, an ancient Mexican term for the poorest of the poor, Tijerina's supporters converged on the Tierra Amarilla County

Courthouse to free an Alianza member they believed was held there. After shooting a jailer and sheriff's deputy, Tijerina's men found that their prisoner was not there. New Mexico Governor David Cargo called out National Guard troops who brought tanks, machine guns, and 20,000 rounds of ammunition. Tijerina escaped via back roads but was finally caught and tried. Moctesuma Esparza, who would later produce such landmark Chicano films as *The Ballad of Gregorio Cortez* and *The Milagro Beanfield War*, said, "Those images of tanks rumbling in New Mexico instantly galvanized us in California."

Three hundred miles to the north, at the far northern boundary of Mexican settlement, lay Denver. There, in 1966, Rodolfo "Corky" Gonzales, once the third-ranked world featherweight boxer, launched the Crusade for Justice. Chicanos were 12 percent of the Southwest population but suffered over 20 percent of the region's deaths in Vietnam. Tijerina wanted land; Gonzales wanted education and cultural dignity. "The schools advise our kids only to go into the military," he charged. Fewer than half of Mexican Americans had gone past the eighth grade; one in three was living below the poverty level. In 1967 only four Chicanos were in Congress, whereas the Chicano population would have justified thirty-six. Personifying Chicano deprivation and pride in his poem *Yo Soy Joaquin*, Gonzales wrote, "Joaquin is one of us and all of us—the life of all our people. . . . I will endure and now the trumpet sounds."

Within a year, the Chicano Movement was poised to launch a political party in protest of the disproportionate Vietnam casualties. Martin Luther King, Jr., invited Tijerina and Gonzales to join him on the Poor People's March on Washington in 1968, but King's explicit turn from race to class analysis—blaming the costs of Vietnam for stalling LBJ's Great Society social programs—was cut short by an assassin's bullet in April. In that month, ten thousand Mexican American students and their supporters walked out of six East Los Angeles-area high schools to protest racism and the lack of Hispano teachers. Their disruption of the largest school system in the United States gained nationwide coverage and marked the entry of Mexican American youth into mass sixties protest. Two years later, between twenty-five and thirty thousand Chicanos gathered in Laguna Park in East Los Angeles to protest the continuing war. Reacting to reports of a few stolen six-packs from a liquor store, dozens of riot-equipped police charged into the peaceful throngs beating people indiscriminately. Sixty were wounded and three killed. A sheriff's deputy fired a tear-gas canister into a crowded bar, killing Ruben Salazar of the *Los Angeles Times*, the best-known Chicano journalist of his day. As they had done to Black, countercultural, and Indian movements, the police sabotaged the political process. The Chicano movement had peaked, and the political party was put on hold.

ECOSYSTEM DEFENSE AND MONKEY WRENCHES IN THE GEARS

Not only mass environmentalism, but the radical varieties as well had western roots. Senator Gaylord Nelson conceived of a "national teach-in on the environment" while reading the radical magazine *Ramparts* in Berkeley. He tried out his ideas on Berkeley students, made his proposal in Seattle, and the result was Earth Day, 1970. When Denis Hayes revived Earth Day in 1990, he did it from a storefront in Palo Alto, California. With two hundred million people from 140 nations participating, it united more people around a single cause than any event to that time. Back at the famous 1955 Six Gallery poetry night in San Francisco, Beat poet Michael McClure had read a poem about bored G.I.'s machine-gunning a pod of orcas in the arctic. In a similar spirit, Earth Day protest 1970 and 1990 indicted the arms race as a key source of environmental destruction and violence toward nature.

Of all the major Cold War resistance, the radical environmental movements were least directly in debt to the Black movement; most were founded on White working-class, libertarian-anarchist traditions. Greenpeace had the most direct link to the Cold War—the group was founded by three Vancouver activists to protest U.S. detonation of a 5.2-megaton hydrogen bomb on Amchitka Island at the tip of the Aleutian Islands. Twelve protesters rented a rusty halibut boat named the Phyllis Cormack, painted "Greenpeace" on her side, and tried to disrupt U.S. Navy operations. Gale-force winds and forty-foot seas drove them back to port. On Saturday, November 6, 1971, the hydrogen bomb's blast instantly killed one thousand otters in the Bering Sea, their ears split by the shock wave. Their bodies washed up on Amchitka Island for weeks.

By 1990 Greenpeace was the best-known and most-influential environmental lobbying group in the world, with offices in twenty-seven nations, five million members, and thirty-seven campaigns ongoing around the globe, saving dolphins, stopping mining in Antarctica, and ending industrial use of chlorine. They were known for nonviolent but disruptive direct action.

The roots of the second major radical eco-movement, Earth First!, lay in the migration to New Mexico of several Cold War military veterans seeking solace in the vast panoramas of the Four Corners landscape. One of them was Edward Abbey. His father, Paul Revere Abbey, was an Appalachian Wobbly who met Eugene Debs and quoted Walt Whitman. After a tour as a military policeman, Abbey entered the University of New Mexico in 1947 to study the anarchist philosophy of Proudhon, Sorel, Bakunin, and Kropotkin. He told his best friend, writer and oral historian Jack Loeffler: "The cold war hung over us like a huge bag of doom. Wanting to escape to the wide open spaces of the Four Corners was no paranoia." Loeffler and Abbey were pals in Taos during the time when a series of northern New Mexico billboards announcing land development were cut down at night. "Growth for the sake of growth is the ideology of the cancer cell," Abbey wrote in his best-selling *Desert Solitaire* (1968). Zeroing in on the web of defense contractors and military operatives planning huge Cold War projects in the Southwest landscape, he concluded, "a patriot must always be ready to defend his country against his government."

Loeffler traces his own anarchist awakening to the predawn chill at the Nevada nuclear testing grounds when, as a twenty-one-year-old draftee in the 433rd Army Atomic Band, he played "The Stars and Stripes Forever" before 1950s bomb tests. Loeffler moved to New Mexico in 1961 with several friends from Marin County, north of the Bay Area. In July 1970 he and four friends founded the Central Clearing House in Santa Fe, to make environmental research available to grassroots groups. Their first mission opposed the Central Arizona Project, a vast network of planned strip mines, slurry pipelines, and power generation stations that would supply Colorado River water to Los Angeles and electricity to Phoenix and Tucson. The military saw the thinly populated West as one huge proving ground, and industrial contractors adapted military visions to development schemes. Nuclear designers conceived economic development "needs" for their technology: Project Gasbuggy exploded two underground bombs in New Mexico natural gas fields to boost yields, just as Project Plowshare suggested using nuclear bombs to dredge Alaskan harbors. Much of the West and Southwest was not empty, of course; it was just not heavily built-up. It was Indian country, and thus sacred, in a way the mainstream did not understand.

But the guardian of Indian sovereignty, the federal Bureau of Indian Affairs, had facilitated one-sided contracts between tribes and Peabody Coal Co. Peabody's giant earthmovers began strip-mining coal from Black Mesa, sacred to Hopi and Navajo traditionalists. "I saw an old Navajo woman faint dead away as a bulldozer leveled her hogan," says Loeffler. All sixty-three BIA reservation schools on the Navajo Reservation had signs saying, "Tradition is the Enemy of Progress." Loeffler took them all down. He supported this anarchist resistance by founding the Black Mesa Defense Fund in Santa Fe, which inspired the characters in Abbey's novel, *The Monkey Wrench Gang* (1975). "I was outraged by the violence being done to the western deserts," Abbey said in an interview. "Much more than human life had to be defended."

In 1971 New Mexico native Dave Foreman worked for the Black Mesa Defense Fund, and in 1980 he and three friends founded Earth First! The group's motto was "No compromise in the defense of Mother Earth." A loose affiliation of local chapters, Earth First! became famous for advocating the use of eco-sabotage against the machinery of development. They often quoted

Abbey that "destruction of machinery is not terrorism; but violence toward nature *is* terrorism." Working-class loggers disagreed with Earth First!'s tactic of driving long spikes into trees—or threatening to do so—to discourage cutting. The logging culture seized on this hazard to a saw man's safety as the key threat to mill towns' survival. Some Oregon and Washington Earth First! chapters repudiated spiking in the 1980s, and, by calling attention to the lumber industry's automation and selling of raw logs to Japan, were able to build a community of interest with loggers.

SANCTUARY, NUCLEAR FREEZE, AND THE
CHILDREN'S PEACE STATUE

After Vietnam, the Pentagon shifted its focus to "low intensity conflict" in the last decade of the Cold War and supported indirectly such civil conflicts as those in Nicaragua and in El Salvador. However, the western nuclear weapons labs in Los Alamos, Rocky Flats, Livermore, and Hanford continued to seek funding to develop new generations of atomic weapons. Two final Cold War movements emerged in the West: the Sanctuary Movement, offering refuge to Central Americans fleeing U.S.-aided political repression, and the anti-nuclear movements, seeking a nuclear weapons freeze, justice for those exposed to radiation, and an end to military adventurism in the West. The public drive to learn the truth about atomic testing was set in motion when Paul Cooper, a retired Green Beret with two tours in Vietnam, came down with leukemia while serving with the Idaho State Police. By the time of his death in 1978, Cooper had inspired the Committee of Survivors (with chapters in Nevada, Utah, and Arizona), the Nevada Test Site Radiation Victims Association, and the National Association of Radiation Survivors (in California). In coalition with Japanese *hibakusha* (radiation victims) and uranium miners associations, these groups pressed claims through the courts.

The Sanctuary movement was born in early 1981, when the Border Patrol and Immigration and Naturalization Service (INS) began finding middle-class Salvadorans and Guatemalans abandoned by "coyotes" (guides) and dying in the deserts of the Southwest. The Reagan Administration attitude toward the rightist regimes of Central America was set in a paper written by the "Santa Fe Group" of policy analysts. Their 1980 position paper declared that U.S. policy should counteract the leftist and populist influence of the Catholic Church's Liberation Theology. This policy cast the priests and nuns working among the poor as enemies of stability. But by 1983 Catholic sources estimated that thirty thousand civilians had been murdered in Salvador. A million refugees had fled the country. The INS was returning five hundred Salvadorans a month and granting asylum to only 2–3 percent of those fleeing the death squads. Americans opposing these policies organized secret networks, like the "underground railroad" of slave days. In Arizona, goat rancher (and Harvard Philosophy M.A.) Jim Corbett, a Quaker, was the first to demand to see Central Americans who were being held in INS detention in southern Arizona. Corbett was soon joined by John Fife, the minister of Southside Presbyterian Church in Tucson, Catholic priest Ricardo Elford, and Rabbi Joseph Weizenbaum. G. Daniel Little, director of the Presbyterian General Assembly's Mission Council, came to Tucson and spoke at Southside Church: "There comes a point where argument about consequences becomes a denial that consequences matter. We are part of a Biblical and prophetic tradition that confronts such deception by acknowledging it in ourselves, by calling for a new consciousness, and by ringing the alarm bell to wake up and pay attention to the unjust effects of our power."

A year later, thirty churches or religious communities across the country had declared themselves "public sanctuary sites," and two hundred more offered help. Democratic Governor Toney Anaya, only the second Hispano governor since 1920, declared New Mexico a Sanctuary State. In New Mexico, peace pilgrims arriving at Los Alamos on the lay-activist-led Prayer Pilgrimage for Peace in 1984 were "blessed by the archbishop at the start and photographed by the FBI at the finish." That year, the conservative *Albuquerque Journal,* known for its routine endorsement of Reagan and other conservatives, sent writer Martha Man along on a caravan taking a Salvadoran family from Phoenix to Iowa City, Iowa, to a safe home, openly inviting federal prosecution that did not come. Some seventy thousand U.S. citizens had actively broken the law to provide sanctuary. While nationwide response had been overwhelmingly supportive and the Reagan Administration did not immediately interfere, in 1985 federal prosecutors won cases against Corbett, Fife, and ten others in Phoenix and Houston.

A new generation of groups opposed to the permanent war economy hanging over vast parts of the West emerged in the 1980s. The proliferation of activist groups in the two decades since Santa Fe's Black Mesa Defense Fund is evident in the January 1991 protests at the Nevada Nuclear Test Site, hosted by the Western Shoshone Nation. The Shoshone had never signed the nineteenth-century treaty that federal authorities claimed granted the United States the right to condemn most of the Shoshone ancestral lands for munitions testing. Twenty-seven organizations based in ten western states sponsored the twenty-five hundred people who took part in 1991. Seven hundred and fifty were arrested. The protests were a form of theater, like that of the sixties guerrilla street troupes of the Bay Area. Federal marshals and local law enforcement officers contended with giant puppets, Shoshone singing and drumming, and a myriad of costumes, face paint, and props.

Though a majority of Nevadans—like westerners in general—supported in principle the Test Site and its eight thousand jobs and $800 million budget, spirited resistance had begun to emerge. The military had its way until the mid–1980s, when a wide spectrum of "strange bed-fellow" groups in Nevada began to resist the massive schemes for the MX missile. Such groups as Nevada's Rural Alliance for Military Accountability began to organize coalitions of ranchers, miners, Indians, environmentalists, and antiwar groups to protest Pentagon failure to compensate the state for the withdrawal of over four million acres of public lands and over 70 percent of Nevada's airspace for bombing ranges and electronic warfare practice.

In a final stage of Cold War resistance, three Albuquerque women enlisted elementary school children in the Peace Movement in 1990. Albuquerque peace activists knew that the Albuquerque Operations Office of the Department of Energy had responsibility for the movement of nuclear weapons throughout the nation. Carrie Gassner and Christine Luke taught a third/ fourth grade class at John Baker Elementary School. Gassner led the class through a brainstorming session on how to end war; longtime peace activist Cammie Condon put on a puppet show dramatizing the story of Sadako Sasaki. Sadako was the Japanese girl from Hiroshima who died of radiation-induced leukemia before she could finish folding one thousand paper cranes to ensure her long life. The children began meeting at Pistol Pete's Pizza and decided to build a Peace Statue in Los Alamos, home of the bomb. By 1993, sixty-four thousand kids from one hundred countries had joined to propose designs for the statue. Architect boards in each state sifted two hundred thousand drawings before a kids committee decided on a bronze, ten-foot open globe with continents made of three thousand sculptures of animals and plants contributed by kids. Los Alamos town and laboratory officials refused to accept the statue, and it now sits at the entrance to the Albuquerque Museum, where it is festooned with handwritten notes of hope and skeins of origami cranes sent by children from around the world.

And so, in our western "geography of hope," to use Wallace Stegner's phrase, Asian wars, military industrialism, working-class leftist movements, the boom of students in their teens and twenties, and traditions of Black, Native American and Mexican American cultural resistance wove together a distinctive Cold War warp and weft. The Ansel Adams landscapes had multiple claimants as military proving grounds, wilderness for its own sake, sacred homelands to Indians, and *tierra bendita* (blessed land) to Mexican Americans. As financial and political might shifted to the Pacific Rim cities of the West Coast, not only movie glamour and popular fads but modes of dissent as well flowed from West to East across the nation. The mythic pull of the West throughout American history, with its renewal and violence, pulled the Cold War along too, bringing a renewal of American opposition cultures, in fresh cycles of action and reaction, still being felt today.

BIBLIOGRAPHIC ESSAY

George Lipsitz's *Class and Culture in Cold War America* (Urbana: University of Illinois Press, 1994) covers important aspects of the transition from World War II to Cold War, particularly popular moods reflected in mass culture. Lipsitz's *A Life in the Struggle: Ivory Perry and the Culture of Opposition* (Philadelphia: Temple University Press, 1995) illuminates the evolving radicalism of a small-town Arkansas African American man whose army experience in Korea launched him on a life of social analysis and resistance in St. Louis. Michael Wilson's *Salt of the Earth: Screenplay* (Old Westbury, NY: The Feminist Press, 1978), with commentary by Deborah Silverton Rosenfelt, details the collaboration between Hollywood progressives and Chicano miners in 1950s New Mexico. Natalie Robins's *Alien Ink: The FBI's War on Freedom of Expression* (New York: William Morrow, 1992) gives the wider picture of blacklisting and FBI surveillance of writers and filmmakers.

Books about the Beats and the sixties are proliferating. Ann Charters's biography of Kerouac, *Kerouac: A Biography* (New York: Viking, 1987), is compact and comprehensive, as is her new Portable Library edition of his writings, *The Portable Jack Kerouac* (New York: Viking, 1995). Two books written in the 1970s are vivid, rich, and accurate: Barry Gifford and Lawrence Lee's *Jack's Book: An Oral Biography of Jack Kerouac* (New York: St. Martin's Press, 1978), and Bruce Cook's *The Beat Generation* (New York: Scribners, 1971). Barry Miles's biography of Allen Ginsberg, *Ginsberg: A Biography* (New York: Viking, 1990), is encyclopedic—its bibliography lists 270 books on the Beat era. Also on Ginsberg, see Gordon Ball, ed., *Allen Ginsberg: Journals Mid-Fifties 1954–1958* (New York: Harper Collins, 1995). These journals are being issued periodically. Joyce Johnson, who was Kerouac's girlfriend when *On the Road* (New York: Viking, 1957) came out, has written *Minor Characters* (Boston: Houghton Mifflin, 1983), a memoir from a female point of view, missing in virtually all work on the Beats, and winner of the National Book Critics Circle Award for biography and autobiography. Michael McClure's *Lighting the Corners: On Art, Nature, and the Visionary* (Albuquerque: University of New Mexico, College of Arts and Sciences, 1993), and *Scratching the Beat Surface: Essays on New Vision from Blake to Kerouac* (New York: Penguin, 1982), and Pierre DeLattre's *Episodes* (St. Paul, MN: Greywolf Press, 1993) are filled with anecdotes and insights from western postwar bohemianism. *The Life and Times of Allen Ginsberg* is an excellent film. Lois Palken Rudnick's *The Mabel Dodge Luhan House and the American Counterculture* (Albuquerque: University of New Mexico Press, 1996) puts bohemian eras in Taos, New Mexico, in the 1920s, 1960s, and 1990s into national context.

The definitive history of the Civil Rights Movement in the South is Taylor Branch's *Parting the Waters: America in the King Years, 1954–1963* (New York: Simon and Schuster,

1988). The later chapters of Quintard Taylor's *In Search of the Racial Frontier: African Americans in the American West, 1528–1990* (New York: W. W. Norton, 1998), cover Cold War civil rights campaigns. For New Mexico, see Albert Rosenfeld, "New Mexico's Fading Color Line: Albuquerque Shows the Way," *Commentary* 20 (August 1955): 203–11. Best on Chicano activism in the West is Carlos Muñoz, *Youth, Identity, Power: The Chicano Movement* (London and New York: Verso, 1989). A fresh retrospective by founding Chicano activists is the four-part film series, *Chicano! The Mexican-American Civil Rights Movement* (National Latino Communications Center and PBS Films, 1996). Best overview of AIM, the FBI, and Wounded Knee II is Peter Matthiessen, *In the Spirit of Crazy Horse* (New York: Viking, 1991). The best account of the entire Indian movement—a book in which the authors take pains to show that "not everything is red or White"—is Robert Warrior and Paul Chaat Smith, *Like a Hurricane: The Indian Movement from Alcatraz to Wounded Knee* (New York: New Press, 1996). In 1996 the papers of AIM founders Dennis Banks, Robert Roubidoux, and Kay Cole were donated to the University of New Mexico library. The fall 1994 issue of *American Indian Culture and Research Journal* is dedicated to new analysis of the Alcatraz takeover by participants and historians.

The best overview of major sixties movements from a West Coast perspective is Stewart Burns's *Social Movements of the Sixties: Searching for Democracy* (Boston: Twayne Publishers, 1990). Kenneth Heineman's *Campus Wars: The Peace Movement at American State Universities in the Vietnam Era* (New York: New York University Press, 1993) argues that smaller eastern and midwestern schools, not UC–Berkeley, were the incubators of student radicalism. *Berkeley in the Sixties* is a superb film about the Free Speech Movement based on period footage and interviews with participants. Timothy Miller's *The Hippies and American Values* (Knoxville: University of Tennessee Press, 1991) traces the enduring imprints of countercultural innovations, most emanating from the West Coast, on mainstream culture. Lisa Law's *Flashing on the Sixties* (San Francisco: Chronicle, 1987) is a photographic memoir of the California–New Mexico–Woodstock connections made by the Hog Farm communalists; its video version has touching interviews with most of the subjects.

Of eco-anarchists, only sketches exist. See Jack Loeffler's *Headed Upstream: Interviews with Iconoclasts* (Tucson: Harbinger House, 1989); Robert Keziere and Robert Hunter, *Greenpeace* (Toronto: McClelland and Stewart, 1972); James Hepworth and Gregory McNamee, eds., *Resist Much, Obey Little: Some Notes on Edward Abbey* (Salt Lake City: Dream Garden Press, 1985); and Jack Loeffler's "Edward Abbey, Anarchism, and the Environment," *Western American Literature* 28 (spring 1993): 43–51. For New Mexico movement participants, see Jack Kutz's *Grassroots New Mexico: A History of Citizen Activism* (Albuquerque: Interhemispheric Education Resource Center, 1989). Philip Hoose's *It's Our World, Too!: Stories of Young People Who Are Making a Difference* (Boston: Joy Street Books, 1993) has a chapter on the Children's Peace Statue.

There is one analytic book about Sanctuary: Renny Golden and Michael McConnell, *Sanctuary: The New Underground Railroad* (Maryknoll, NY: Orbis Books, 1986). Miriam Davidson, *Convictions of the Heart: Jim Corbett and the Sanctuary Movement* (Tucson: University of Arizona Press, 1988), is about the movement's Arizona roots, and Robert Tomsho, *The American Sanctuary Movement* (Austin: Texas Monthly Press, 1987) is focused on Texas activists; both are narrative accounts. On rural movements challenging the militarization of the West, and Nevada in particular, see David Loomis, *Combat Zoning: Military Land-Use Planning in Nevada* (Reno: University of Nevada Press, 1993), and A. Costandina Titus, *Bombs in the Backyard: Atomic Testing and American Politics* (Reno: University of Nevada Press, 1986), which is particularly good on the "downwinders" and their efforts to gain compensation for airborne nuclear waste exposure. *Protest Theater,* a film by Peter Goin of the University of Nevada–Reno Art Department, portrays the Nevada Test Site protests of 1991. The *High Country News* (Paonia, CO) has reported on all environmentally related movements in the West.

CHAPTER NINE

THE COLD WAR WEST AS SYMBOL AND MYTH

Perspectives from Popular Culture

❦

CHARLES KUPFER

Cultures often sanctify places where civilization's discontents can be worked out through the power of myth. Sometimes, as with Mount Olympus, the special spot is an actual topographic feature. Sometimes, it may be a realm of consciousness—a Camelot lying beyond geography. Whether such a place can be spied on a map is less important than how it serves the popular imagination. Henry Nash Smith proposed that the West existed, not only as a cartographic region, but as part of the American mind. The author of *Virgin Land* (1950) understood that tensions between fact and fancy must arise, and he identified several instances in which purportedly practical Americans lost sight of quotidian frontier knowledge while gazing upon western symbols. "Rain follows the plow," insisted the faithful, and generations of erstwhile farmers ignored ample evidence to the contrary. Aridity waved away as if by magic, the West of the imagination turned into a verdant garden where abundant rains were always in tomorrow's forecast. It took a Dust Bowl to cloud this Happy Valley vision, yet today, westerners would still recoil from that long-discarded label of the Great American Desert.

Smith knew that a large part of the West's enduring hold on our imagination comes from the powerful, ancient allure of the Garden. The Garden gave rise to an agrarian tradition that, as Smith puts it, "made it difficult for Americans to think of themselves as members of a world community." This insularity was sustained throughout much of American history because Americans could and did turn away from the Old World, preferring instead to imagine and cultivate their Garden. There, they hoped, the rest of the world could be kept at bay.

The conundrum, of course, was that in the act of settling the western lands,

Americans brought with them the despoiling aspects of their old life. Recount-ing Nathaniel Hawthorne's 1844 outing to a quiet grove near Concord, Massa-chusetts—a reverie in the woods interrupted by the fateful whistle of a far-off but fast-closing locomotive—Leo Marx illustrated that the Garden was but a temporary sanctuary. Civilization's clatter and din would find the quiet spot. *The Machine in the Garden* (1964) is Marx's explication of the inexorable intru-sion of daily concerns into the pastoral grottoes and hideaways Americans imagined on "their" frontier. Again, Americans were loathe to accept the notion that the facts of their living did not agree with the West of their imaginings.

Hiding away from the outside world is, after all, an American tradition. For the better part of this nation's first century-and-a-half, isolationism was the official diplomatic credo. With occasional military exceptions, from the Bar-bary Coast, through the Philippines, to Chateau Thierry, Americans felt it proper to mind their continental business. Usually, this involved subduing and remaking the land and its inhabitants. The West was where this often brutal process reached its apotheosis.

But, in 1946, American diplomat George Kennan wrote his famous "Long Telegram," fleshed out into an article for *Foreign Affairs* in July of the next year. "The Sources of Soviet Conduct" made it clear that, in the Second World War's wake, the United States was not likely to retreat from an inconvenient world back to a continental redoubt. Instead, the nation would find itself engaged in an open-ended systemic struggle with the Soviet Union as adversary. Kennan's article called for containing Soviet pressure, "by the adroit and vigilant applica-tion of counter-force at a series of constantly shifting geographical and political points." Containment, as the policy came to be known, would be quite a com-mitment, and it carried Americans a long way from the Garden of their west-ern dreams. Throughout its duration, in fact, the Cold War intruded into American life in countless ways, engendering anxieties and controversies. There was plenty for Americans to worry, wonder, and argue about as they dealt with fears of nuclear annihilation, agonies of remote combat, arguments over when and whether the Communist threat was real or a chimera.

"Myths are important to societies, for they play a crucial role, and certainly should not be disparaged. On the other hand, they should not be confused with reality." So wrote historian Gerald Nash in "Sharpening the Image," the epilogue to *The Twentieth Century West*, a watershed 1989 work co-authored by Richard W. Etulain. Nash's point on myth's utility is well taken. Moreover, the value of a myth can surely supersede any shaky connection to fact. Indeed, if a particular myth's worth can be judged by simultaneous durability and fungibil-ity, then the mythic West, in all its denominations, has always been indispens-able. It is a place of imagination to which a people repairs, to brood and dream productively; to consciously or unconsciously plan reactions to the sometimes duller but ever-dangerous world of reality. During the Cold War, the stresses of a worldwide nuclear showdown were dealt with and resolved in films, television programs, and books; such stories were often set in the legendary West, that handy therapeutic crucible of American myth.

Historians argue over when the Cold War started. But whatever the precise beginning date, it coincided closely with the arrival of the atomic era. What revealed itself in fire and light over Hiroshima and Nagasaki in August 1945 was tested earlier that summer in New Mexico. Paul Boyer's *By the Bomb's Early Light: American Thought and Culture at the Dawn of the Atomic Age* (1984) identifies things atomic as the new national preoccupation of the late forties. Americans peering into a future made perilous by nuclear rivalry hungered for the familiar comfort of tales from the Old West. The postwar years thus inaugurated another epoch in popular culture: the Golden Age of the Western.

Richard Slotkin, author of *Gunfighter Nation: The Myth of the Frontier in Twentieth-Century America* (1992), pinpoints 1948 as ushering in, not just the Cold War, but a remarkable twenty-five-year stretch during which Westerns dominated the film industry. Documenting this trend with statistics—Western feature production shot up from seventeen in 1947, to thirty-one in 1948, to forty-six by 1956—Slotkin also notes a correspondingly high film quality. When Americans went to the movies in the early Cold War years, chances were good they would see a Western. Moreover, since the genre's language, style, and imagery were developed in prewar years, the Western was ready to serve as a popular allegory for Cold War events. The spread of tensions across Europe, the bitter divides arising at home, and the dissipation of postwar demilitarization all coalesced into a foreboding atmosphere. Westerns reflected and deflected such ominous trends.

While movies were not necessarily created as explicit Cold War metaphors, Slotkin makes a convincing case that reciprocal influences ran between current events and film. Looking back at the Westerns of the late forties, Slotkin sees a frontier geography marked by signifying borders between civilization and savagery. Violence permeates this film landscape. The looming probability of violence on both sides of such a border mirrored a key riddle of Cold War ethics, what Slotkin acutely terms "the problem of reconciling democratic values and practices with the imperatives of power." The paradox was plain: how to square decent American views of right and wrong with the rough measures necessary to wage and win the Cold War?

Americans faced the bloody reality of that question when the Korean War broke out in 1950. Slotkin cites dead-on parallels in John Ford's *Rio Grande*, released the same year. As Colonel Kirby Yorke, John Wayne plays the epitome of a dutiful soldier. His estranged wife, played by Maureen O'Hara, grants him his due as such, even while she exclaims, "What makes a soldier is hateful to me." Reviewing Ford's heroic yet gritty portrayal of Kirby's battalion, Slotkin observes:

> We understand that these are men who do a dirty job with discipline and skill; that they are implicitly heroic but make no parade of the fact; that they defend the fort, which is a world of women and children, care and vulnerability and affection; that the Apaches are their enemies, but that they do not hate Indians.

How like official exhortations explaining why Cold War necessities forced American soldiers and spies to act harshly. When Kirby, hotly pursuing a marauding Apache band, is held up at the Rio Grande by a Mexican officer insistent on policing his own border, moviegoers might well have felt frustration akin to that of Douglas MacArthur, stymied at the Yalu River by presidential orders. Kirby's breaching of the Mexican border with the support of his superior, General Sheridan, provided onlookers a vicarious satisfaction most unlike any offered by the war in Korea. Westerns like *Rio Grande* make it clear that exigencies of war, whether cold or hot, could make "illegal actions" unavoidable, even virtuous.

This is not to say that Westerns of the fifties were ham-handed propaganda, nor that they always primped up violent men. Indeed, as film historians George Fenin and William Everson point out, such movies often showed flawed or neurotic heroes, about whom there hung an aura of Greek tragedy. For example, Henry King's *The Gunfighter* (1950) presents the inescapable kill-and-be-killed cycle faced by a professional, if reluctant duelist. As the gunfighter, Gregory Peck exhibits a weary but helpless awareness that he will never lack for challengers, and that any day, he might meet his fatal match.

Other films adeptly present the dubious viciousness at the heart of the mythical West. Kirk Douglass and Burt Lancaster play flawed heroes Doc Holliday and Wyatt Earp in John Sturges's 1956 *Gunfight at the O.K. Corral.* These are men animated by varying motivations, not all of them pristine. The alcoholic Holliday is hardly pure Hollywood glamour. The year 1954 saw William Wellman cast Robert Mitchum as a hunter tracking a cougar in *Track of the Cat*. The film follows the lead of Walter Clark's 1949 novel, as the elusive feline, unseen but ever-looming, gradually assumes transcendental status. Like the Cold War, the hidden yet ubiquitous wildcat has the power to transform those involved with it.

Some Westerns of the day consider the humanity of the enemy. Sympathetic presentations of aggrieved Indians include *Broken Arrow* (1950) and *Devil's Doorway* (1950). These films remind spectators of Native American mistreatment, while suggesting that such misfortune was natural in the hard world of the West. Such textured movies made the stock Indian villain a less credible character. The films' relative box-office success showed that Americans were not incapable of conceiving enemies as human beings, nor conflicts as complicated. Slotkin notes that Westerns of the day managed to concurrently honor the opposing cults of Cavalry, Indian, Lawman, and Gunfighter.

When critic Pauline Kael watched Gary Cooper's conflicted marshal in *High Noon* (1952), she saw his quandary and the town's cravenness as symbolic of capitalism's social shortcomings. Numerous other interpretations of *High Noon* appeared. The film attracted some complaints for its ambivalence. Nevertheless, it was a critical and popular success. Americans did not automatically reject Westerns which went beyond a standard good-versus-evil formula. At least in the cinema house, audiences were prepared to feel unsure for awhile, and to appreciate a nuanced approach.

The fusion of film, the Cold War, and the American West was not limited to cowboy movies during the 1950s. The science-fiction genre was loaded with related allegories, which were often less than oblique.

As Boyer shows in *By the Bomb's Early Light*, the Atomic Age permeated American life at the time. Nuclear fears stretched across the land, but so too did a terrible thrill at something new and awful. Merchandise tabbed "Atomic" hit the shelves, and the association was meant to attract. Marketers advertised atomic toys, clothes, and appliances. Futurists predicted a coming age of atomic conveniences. But science fiction saw a darker and threatening side of the nuclear future. The Cold War rendered the apocalypse conceivable, and Americans were fascinated by the prospect. In creating a mythology relevant to atoms and radiation, filmmakers often located their stories in the American West. A 1947 docudrama, *The Beginning or the End*, recapitulates the Manhattan Project with earnest Los Alamos physicists as the heroes. Less dry features came to dominate the genre. Dozens of truly fanciful films stand today as testament to what culture observer Susan Sontag once called the "imagination of disaster."

Alien invaders and malevolent scientists were science-fiction staples before World War II. But the creation of the atomic bomb, and the presumably ever-present Red threat, made such characters topical in postwar movies. Many "B" pictures used atomic power to unleash radioactive monsters on unsuspecting Americans. Ray Harryhausen brought forth *The Beast From Twenty Thousand Fathoms* in 1953. Awakened by nuclear testing, the Beast lays waste to New York City. The film's reception encouraged another Harryhausen effort in 1955, *It*

Came From Beneath the Sea. This time, San Francisco suffers before American soldiers destroy the creature. Monster movies were a fifties fad. Japanese filmmakers employed the formula to help their audiences exorcize atomic fears, with Godzilla, Mothra, and Rodan serving as radioactive avengers.

Even if they relied on distended freaks and exploding cities, some films rose above "B" norms, delivering deft as well as cataclysmic lessons. *Them!*, a 1954 film starring James Whitmore, presents radioactive ants attacking the Southwest. Spawned by secret bomb tests in New Mexico, the ants emerge from their desert lair to threaten Los Angeles. Peter Biskind, in *Seeing is Believing: How Hollywood Taught Us to Stop Worrying and Love the Fifties*, delivers a convincing explanation of *Them!* Biskind reveals the dual nature of scientific responsibility suggested by the film's premise: having inadvertently loosed the mammoth insects, only federal government scientists can destroy them. In the movie, much debate ensues between military and scientific experts over what weapons to use against the omnivorous enemy. In short, they were searching for a flexible response. Biskind writes of parallels between the ants and American perceptions of Cold War enemies:

> The humans of *Them!* find that their adversaries are very much like Us. If the ants are like humans, which humans are they like? In 1954, when *Them!* was made, those humans that Americans regarded as antlike, which is to say, behaved like a mass, loved war, and made slaves, were, of course, Communists, both the Yellow Hordes that had just swamped GIs with their human waves in Korea, and the Soviets, with their notorious slave-labor camps.

In the American cinematic imagination of the day, the New Mexican high desert was lonely enough to hide atomic tests and giant ants. Other western sites were similarly evocative. Nevada was the birthplace of *The Amazing Colossal Man* (1957). Mutated by radiation exposure, the behemoth leaves the Amargosa Desert to wreak vengeance upon Las Vegas. The far Alaskan Arctic was home to *The Thing*, in which a discovered UFO houses an extraterrestrial who devours human beings. Only the resolute action of the American military men at the base contains the thing-from-another-world. California was the locale for the 1956 cult classic, *Invasion of the Body Snatchers*, in which Kevin McCarthy realizes seed pods from space are turning his neighbors into conformist zombies.

The national tone shifted in the 1960s, and so too did the tenor of Hollywood. Themes brought up in the fifties were further developed. The tardy awareness that Native Americans could be something other than fierce savages took firmer hold in *Flaming Star* (1960), *The Outsider* (1961), and *Cheyenne Autumn* (1964). *The Outsider* relates the saga of Ira Hayes, an Arizona Pima who served in the Marine Corps, planting the Stars and Stripes on Iwo Jima's Mount Suribachi. Hayes, also immortalized in a Johnny Cash ballad, suffered from alcoholism after demobilization. His struggle is portrayed with sympathy. John Ford, whose 1960 *Sergeant Rutledge* addressed anti-Black racism in the cavalry, made *Cheyenne Autumn* to show audiences the Indians' view of the Old West myth. *Celluloid Weapon* authors David Manning and Richard Averson quote a blunt Ford discussing the woes imposed on Native Americans:

> Let's face it. We've treated them very badly. It's a blot on our shield; we've cheated and robbed, killed, murdered, massacred and everything else, but they kill one White man and God, out come the troops.

Science-fiction continued its apocalyptic bent. In 1962, *Panic in the Year Zero* focused on a Los Angeles family escaping nuclear attack by heading for the wilderness. The film stresses that in the wake of civilization's ruination, survival is ensured only by increasing barbarity.

No atomic holocaust tale generated greater controversy or earned more acclaim than Stanley Kubrick's oft-studied 1964 classic, *Dr. Strangelove Or: How I Learned to Stop Worrying and Love the Bomb*. A macabre comedy, gripping because of its apparent plausibility, Kubrick's satire skewers rabid anti-Communism, scientific sanguinity, political ineptitude, and the gung-ho military outlook. The mad parade towards mutual assured destruction is accelerated by memorable characters including Sterling Hayden's paranoid general, a Strategic Air Command renegade. One of the film's most famous images is that of rootin'-tootin' Slim Pickins riding a hydrogen bomb rodeo-style toward a Soviet target. *Dr. Strangelove* suggests, not too gently, that a Wild West mindset is not appropriate for a Cold War world.

Distrust of anti-Communism and the military–industrial complex motivated John Frankenheimer, director of *The Manchurian Candidate* (1962) and *Seven Days in May* (1964). The story of an abortive military coup, with a taut screenplay by Rod Serling, *Seven Days in May* sets most of the action in Washington, D.C. The covert scheme is the brainchild of a disgruntled general played by Burt Lancaster. Lancaster recruits a junta of like-minded officers and trains a strike force. This secret army is secluded in the desert near El Paso, ready to spring upon the Eastern establishment.

The sixties saw the ascendancy of another Cold War film hero, the secret agent. Although James Bond was English, he and his American CIA counterparts are reminiscent of cowboy caricatures. These celluloid spies ride the range of a Cold War world, ready to meet and dispatch any threat to the comfortable, ungrateful folks back home. Less glamorous spies, like Richard Burton in *The Spy Who Came in From the Cold* (1965), bring to mind Slotkin's description of Ford's Rio Grande soldiers as "men who do a dirty job with discipline and skill."

Vietnam influenced American views of Cold War policies and institutions. Tentatively at first, Hollywood delved into the national argument swirling around American embroilment in Southeast Asia. The Green Beret infatuation of the Kennedy administration spread into music and film. Barry Sadler's 1966 chart-topper romanticized these anti-insurgency experts in song as, "Fighting soldiers from the sky / Fearless men who jump and die / Men who mean just what they say," and who, according to the lyrics, are courage-picked examples of America's best. In this vein came John Wayne's *The Green Berets*, adapted from a 1965 best-selling book. The Duke and his fans found the movie anti-dotal to long-haired, obstreperous, countercultural youth. But by the movie's 1968 release date, a shifting national mood made *The Green Berets'* call for rededication to the Indochina conflict less than compelling.

Vietnam's shadow fell over the Western during the seventies. Two 1970 films, *Soldier Blue* and *Little Big Man*, both challenged traditional notions of American rectitude. Detailing the 1864 slaughter of a Cheyenne peace party at Sand Creek, Colorado, *Soldier Blue* drew instant comparisons to the My Lai massacre. In *Little Big Man*, Dustin Hoffman stars as a partially assimilated Indian reminiscing over frontier life. His recollections include a psychopathic General Custer, crazily exploiting military authority to sate a gnawing blood-lust. A contemporary Western, *Billy Jack* (1971), relates the struggles of a mixed-blood Indian seeking to purge his Vietnam-war experiences through good works on the reservation. Governmental and social hostility push him into violence.

Science fiction remained wedded to post-apocalyptic scenarios during the seventies, again using the West as interpretive site. In *The Andromeda Strain* (1971), the agent of mass destruction is a virus imported from space to a small western town. As with earlier films, scientists dispatched by the government offer the only hope for averting the end of the world. They converge on the beleaguered western hamlet, fighting both their own personal shortcomings and the viral spread. *The Omega Man* (1971) presents Charlton Heston as an army epidemiologist who lives through a germ war thanks to his own experi-mental vaccine. Fighting a host of mutants bent on eradicating the last traces of science, Heston roams the eerily empty streets of Los Angeles, trying to save a small survivor colony and wipe out hateful mutated Luddites.

Vietnam movies matured through the decade, with releases including *The*

Deer Hunter (1978) and *Apocalypse Now* (1979). In the latter, Francis Ford Coppola resurrects the cavalry cult. Colonel Kilgore, played by Robert Duvall, decks out his helicopter unit in Western garb, employing old-style bugle calls as his choppers rise to action. Yet, while *Apocalypse Now* trumpets the horror of war, it also contains a dose of enthrallment. Duvall's Kilgore, simultaneously besotted with two western pastimes, cavalry warfare and surfing, became a hero to many in the audience.

The reaction to Duvall's Kilgore signaled an end to morose regretfulness as the typical Vietnam war film mood. In 1980 Ronald Reagan's campaign slogan proclaimed, "It's time for a change." Reagan's electoral success stemmed in no small part from his upbeat posture and unapologetic view of the United States. Voters, filmmakers, and audiences shed the guilt and depression prevalent throughout the seventies.

Movies reflected this attitudinal shift. Hollywood's Vietnam veterans, formerly traumatized characters like the wheelchair-bound Jon Voight of *Coming Home*, started meting out after-the-fact punishment to Red villains. Sylvester Stallone in the *Rambo* series, and Chuck Norris in the *Missing in Action* films, alternated solitary wilderness training with one-man anti-Communist missions. Appalled critics panned these movies, sometimes bundling complaints about White House policies into their reviews. In his study of eighties' film themes, scholar William J. Palmer deplores what he calls the "American Cowboy movie star personality cult of Ronald Reagan." As in *Dr. Strangelove*, a Wild West persona was seen as dangerous in the modern world. Disarmament activists at home and abroad took up the "Dangerous Cowboy" lament, referring to the tough-talking Californian president. "Cowboy" became pejorative when used by Reagan's opponents. Anti-administration contrarians insisted that a cowboy mentality dominated Reagan's Washington, and they said it threatened detente and world peace.

In fact, Soviet–American relations did worsen during the early eighties. Wars in Afghanistan and Central America, Olympic boycotts in 1980 and 1984, the Soviet downing of a Korean airliner in 1985, and leadership changes in the Kremlin infused the first half of the decade with an air of superpower confrontation. Several films took on the Evil Empire directly. *Firefox* (1982) stars Clint Eastwood as a retired ace pilot, called away from his western mountain retreat to steal a hot new MiG fighter. *Red Dawn* (1984) features a group of Colorado teenagers in a guerrilla band resisting a Soviet–Cuban invasion of the United States.

Based on fact, *The Falcon and the Snowman* (1985) recounts the pro-Soviet espionage of two young American men. Their spying stems from disillusionment with what they see as American governmental malfeasance. One of them eluded FBI pursuers for months by holing up in Idaho's border country. *The Right Stuff* (1983), a film version of Tom Wolfe's popular book, recalls Soviet–American competition in space. Its portrayal of the space race and the New Frontier of the early sixties relies more on nostalgia than anti-Soviet bromides. One of the film's best performances is delivered by Sam Shepard, the actor/playwright whose own productions often explore hidden pains alive in the modern West. Shepard's Chuck Yeager, celebrated test-pilot, is a dashing yet taciturn western hero living true to an old/new frontier code.

Profound changes transformed the Communist world by the end of the decade. *The Hunt for Red October* (1990), adapted from Tom Clancy's best-selling book, dramatizes the defection of a Red Navy nuclear submarine commander. One of his officers dreamily repeats his lifelong wish to settle in Montana. This technological thriller was a hit even as the Cold War world broke up. President George Bush spoke of the search for a New World Order at the dawn of war in the Persian Gulf. The international scene shifted into flux. Hollywood, like Washington, would henceforth search for post–Cold War paradigms.

The Cold War and nuclear age were not the only eras born soon after the Second World War. At least as significant in terms of everyday life was the arrival of television as an American institution. Although the infant medium dated its birth back to experiments earlier in the century, it was only during the late forties that TV developed beyond curiosity level. Disparaged as a vast wasteland by some, television nevertheless was frequently incisive during its phase of rapid growth. Like its senior cousin, film, television often treated Cold War and western themes, sometimes simultaneously.

Emerging from radio roots, television looked to "B"-formula Western programs. William Boyd's *Hopalong Cassidy* started its run in 1949. Other theatrical Westerns followed. Strictly for the younger set, "Buffalo Bob" Smith's *Howdy Doody* cultivated the first TV generation, beginning in 1947.

The medium was famously disparaged as an "idiot box." Its millions of devotees were similarly scorned by arch-eyebrowed sophisticates. But such snobbery had no net effect on television's popularity. Nor was it especially accurate. The nascence and development of television and the Cold War paralleled each other, and in some ways the living-room screen was well positioned to capture the global spectacle and bring it into American lives. If commercialism and the immediate ratings and sponsor-driven pressures of TV limited its artistic boundaries, then the episodic nature of many programs countervailed. The sheer abundance of shows, and the assemblage of creative personalities seeding the fresh medium, made television an often fertile ground for thematic growth. The Cold War was a regular topic, even as TV gained a reputation for light popular entertainment.

Television did not rely solely on thrills and laughs. During the fifties, public affairs programs grasped the Cold War nettle. No journalistic figure played a more important role in this regard than westerner Edward R. Murrow. North Carolina-born but raised in Skagit County, Washington, Murrow's unimpeachable stature as a reporter made him a natural host for *See It Now*. Guests on the show included President Truman and Soviet Premier Nikita Khrushchev. Investigative reports on Joseph McCarthy in 1953 and 1954 ensured the notorious Wisconsin senator's wrath, but slowed the pace of his movement. Murrow's colleague, folksy Texan commentator John Henry Faulk, famously defied his own blacklisting.

Diplomacy became programming during Khrushchev's 1959 tour of the United States. His every move filmed by network cameras, Khrushchev's visit culminated in a Hollywood banquet during which the pains of the blacklist were conveniently ignored. The sumptuous affair, shown in the nation's living rooms, blurred the distinction between news and entertainment.

Public affairs shows remained vibrant during the sixties. Some of the best presentations looked into the American West with a questioning eye. Murrow's "Harvest of Shame" documented the plight of migrant farm workers in 1960. In 1961 NBC presented *The Real West*. Compiled from old photographs, *The Real West* debunked the romance of frontier settlement. Another NBC production, *End of the Trail*, carried the story further, recounting westward expansion from an American Indian perspective.

Cold War subjects were a main feature of several shows during the late fifties and early sixties. Like film, television experienced a science fiction boom. The Bomb was virtually a cast member of *The Twilight Zone*, debuting in 1959. Harrowing atomic war scenarios cropped up regularly, as did spooky tales of the Old West. In one episode, writer/producer Rod Serling combined these two favorite themes. "The 7th is Made Up of Phantoms" (1963) tells the tale of a Montana National Guard tank unit training near the Little Big Horn. The modern-day soldiers are magically transported back in time to 1876, where they are slain by ghostly Indians.

Prime-time Western series dominated fifties and sixties television. *Gunsmoke*, *Bonanza*, *Wagon Train*, and *The Virginian* all won high ratings. Such programs rarely dealt with contemporary social issues. However, there were occasional forays in that direction. *The Big Valley* included an episode in which an anarchist Basque shepherd is unfairly persecuted by xenophobic Stockton, California, townsfolk. A local attorney defends him against the hostile community, which eventually confronts its own prejudice. Such plots were exceptional. Western shows during the tumultuous sixties were generally dished up as a respite from the decade's controversies.

Not that such respites were ideology free-zones. On the contrary, as cultural historian Gary A. Yoggy shows in "Prime Time Bonanza!"—a trenchant chapter of editor Richard Aquila's 1996 book, *Wanted Dead or Alive: The American West in Popular Culture*, a hero code was at work, especially in Westerns aimed at children. Yoggy convincingly paints the heroes of such programs—many first aired in the fifties—as cowboys converted into chaps and spurs-wearing knights, bringing to bear putatively medieval values such as diligence, patriotism, mercy, bravery, and resolution. Such attributes, combining martial prowess with humaneness, fit into American conceptions of the national characteristics needed to prevail against the Communist danger. Seeing these attributes embodied in attractive heroes offered American viewers reassurance in a threatening time.

Escapism was also the lure in spy dramas during those years. *Mission Impossible*, *I Spy*, *The Saint*, and *The Man from U.N.C.L.E.* were programs showing Cold War espionage as the domain of alluring agents pulling off daring capers. Always on the lookout for exotic or amusing contrivance, such shows sometimes decked out their spies in cowpoke garb, with plots set in the American West. Even *Mister Ed*, the talking horse from Los Angeles, regularly foiled foreign agents from enemy lands. *The Wild, Wild West* managed to combine an old frontier look with the new frontier of espionage, spinning elaborate yarns about two secret service agents afoot in the 1870s west.

But here again, as with the Westerns, spy programs were never message-free. The basic premise was outfoxing the other side. The virtues that allowed American agents and their British cohorts to prevail over dour enemies from behind the Iron or Bamboo Curtains were similar to the attributes of TV cowboys. Viewers found attractive combinations of confidence and humility, humor and purpose, handsomeness and modesty, dedication and flair. To these could be added a dose of good-old-American technological know-how; clever gadgets designed for dirty work in the service of the country's cause. The Gatling Gun and six-shooter helped take the West, and high-tech gizmos used by Red-White-and-Blue spies no doubt help win the Cold War fight—at least on TV.

The Old West gave way to the New West as the sixties gave way to the seventies. *Little House on the Prairie*, a family-intended drama derived from the Laura Ingalls Wilder novels, lasted throughout the decade. But cowpoke shows were seen only in reruns. Eventually, soap operas like *Dallas* and *Falcon Crest* established prime-time's view of western life. *Dallas* was a worldwide obsession.

The oil-rich Ewing family of South Fork Ranch served as cultural ambassadors representing Hollywood's version of high life and drama in exotic Texas.

Two other programs of the eighties fused Western and Cold War themes, attracting considerable critical reaction. *The Day After*, a 1983 televised movie, caused much hoopla. Director Nicholas Meyer characterized the drama as a huge public service announcement he felt a moral obligation to make. *The Day After* chronicles the travails of Kansas City residents during and after a nuclear attack. Its doomsday drama was not novel, but coincided with renewed fears over the arms race. Its broadcast followed by live discussion groups, *The Day After* was a prime-time venting of popular atomic anxiety. The second drama dealt with a rather different postwar scenario. Airing in 1987, *"Amerika"* set forth life in "Heartland," a Soviet-occupied American puppet state. This miniseries sparked critical opprobrium from those worried that its anti-Russian tone was unduly provocative. Kris Kristofferson plays the hero, who tries to reignite the spark of patriotism in a beaten, divided America.

Cold War era Americans in search of entertainment from or about the West knew they could find plenty in movie theaters or on television screens. But they also made tracks to libraries and bookstores, for authors had long used the West as inspiration. Readers knew that there was nary a dearth of imaginative western literature. Rendering western experiences—or pseudo- experiences—into written narrative was of course a hoary tradition long before the Cold War. Another tradition antedating the Cold War was the tendency of cultural guardians back East to disparage stories seen through western eyes, or told in western tongues.

Western literature was plentiful, but the richness and diversity of books blending legend with fact, history with fancy, was rarely acknowledged by those inclined to look askance at things western. If high-toned establishmentarians lumped all such literature under a "cowboys and Indians" label, they missed the essential value of what Michael L. Johnson, author of *New Westers: The West in Contemporary Culture*, so wonderfully terms, "That muddle. . . . Literature with a centaur-like mythical-historical makeup." Johnson ably rounds up divergent brands of western literature, from shoot-'em-up exercises in macho chauvinism to anti-cowpoke novels awash with revisionist sensibilities. He also guides readers to Richard W. Etulain, whose own research tells the tale of the development of respectable western literary study.

In "The Historical Development of the Western," from *The Popular Western: Essays Towards a Definition*, co-authored by Etulain and Michael T. Marsden in 1974, Etulain described the origins of the Western Writers of America. Born in the early fifties, this group gave western authors support and exposure. Elsewhere—as Johnson recalls—Etulain pinpoints the dawn of serious academic treatment occurring in the next decade, with the establishment of the Western Literary Association, the Popular Culture Association, and the Southwestern Literary Association. In their respective works, Etulain and Johnson both dissect the broad themes and particular differences afoot in the genre during the Cold War years. Both identify counter strains—some authors responding to the West's arid spaciousness, others reacting to a provincial culture, some discovering or rediscovering Native American mindsets, and still others picking up the myth of the Garden, as articulated earlier by Henry Nash Smith.

One fact that scholars such as Etulain and Johnson make clear is that there need be no iron boundaries between Western novels and histories; nor between popular and serious works. Wallace Stegner, with whom Etulain memorably speaks in *Conversations with Wallace Stegner on Western History and Literature* (1983), most famously proves the point, for his works frequently cover all these angles—novels rich in history that are serious and popular. Inspired by this fusion, other scholars continue to explore it, including New Western historian Patricia Limerick. Limerick's essay, "What Raymond Chandler Knew and Western Historians Forgot," from *Old West, New West: Centennial Essays*, edited by Barbara H. Meldrum (1993), proposes the popular detective novelist as "the first uncle of western American history." What earns Chandler Limerick's nomination is, foremost, his storytelling ability. There is undeniable logic at work here. The West has always been story-telling territory. Since the Cold War was the paramount story of its time, storytellers—popular writers, for example—treated both themes with regularity.

Spy thrillers and gunfighter potboilers often make bestseller lists. Other books forthrightly combine Western and Cold War subjects. Many of the trends common to film and television's handling of these issues are present in such works. Authors, like directors, found science fiction attractive during the fifties. Rife with metaphor, the genre enabled writers to ruminate on matters such as nuclear war and the race into space. While science fiction writers wrote atomic-based stories well before 1945, the Bomb made such stories more believable. Fact-based novels, such as Pearl Buck's *Command the Morning* (1955), elaborated on the Manhattan Project. The secrecy cloaking the work of atomic science inspired stories from science-fiction luminaries such as Philip K. Dick, Theodore Sturgeon, and Robert Heinlein. Magazines like *Astounding Science Fiction* and *Thrilling Wonder Stories* provided a forum for creative minds to speculate on possibilities of the new age. Sometimes, their fictional musings were close enough to fact to inspire official disquietude. Federal authorities persuaded *Bluebook Magazine* not to run Paul Wylie's "The Paradise Crater," a story about a secret Nazi atomic project in the Nevada desert. Comic books, so fond of lurid speculation on war, technology, and horror, came under congressional scrutiny during the 1950s as grown-ups fretted over corrupted youth.

Authors often put the United States on the receiving end of atomic attack. *When the Rockets Come* (1945), by Robert Abernathy, tells of war between Russian-speaking Martians and English-speaking terrestrials. Pat Frank's *Forbidden Area* (1956) makes the point that nuclear war must destroy, not conquer. Such works generally turn to rebuilding life on a fresh frontier, whether in the far reaches of the West or the farther reaches of space. In fact, the lure of post-apocalyptic renewal attracted writers all through the Cold War's duration. *Warday*, a 1984 novel, recounts a road journey through an American West devastated by nuclear missiles and rebuilt under foreign authority.

The West, atomic birthplace and military stronghold, presents a portentous if obvious juncture between conflicting concepts of land and power. Given Native American suffering, it is unsurprising that some of the finer popular fiction exploring such themes exhibits indigenous sensibilities. Frank Waters, a student of various Southwestern peoples, wrote *The Woman at Otowi Crossing* in 1966. This novel examines Los Alamos through the disparate eyes of a physicist, an anthropologist, a witch, and a medicine man. Peggy Pond Church's 1960 book *The House at Otowi Bridge: The Story of Edith Warner and Los Alamos*, remains one of the most deeply pleasing relevant works. A remembrance of the earth-shaking transformation of New Mexico from the twenties through the fifties, Church's book recaptures her subject's relationships with neighboring Indian people, with physicists at work on the atomic frontier, and with the eternal plateau landscape valued by both groups for such different reasons.

This attenuated cord between Native American worldviews and Cold War–driven American science was anticipated in historian Mari Sandoz's *Crazy Horse: Strange Man of the Oglalas* (1942). In giving face to the legendlike warrior, Sandoz showed readers the antipathetic tensions radiating between Indian "medicine" and western "progress." There was a dire incompatibility of outlooks, which authors like Church, Waters, and Edward Abbey would draw out.

Abbey, the unapologetically radical ecologist, wrote prolifically. He drew strength and zeal from the power of western land, so tangible in *Desert Solitaire* (1968). But his opposition to the alteration—or degradation—of these lands by dams or other "symbols of progress" led him to pen *The Monkey Wrench Gang* in 1975. This rambunctious novel of humor and sabotage was a cult favorite, serving as a sort of how-to scripture for deep ecology advocates aiming to interrupt construction projects they saw as ruining a non-boundless, fragile West. If dams and developments hurt the land, then military testing grounds were even more contentious. The use of western tracts as test ranges attracted opposition from writers. Richard Misrach's *Bravo 20: The Bombing of the American West* (1990) is a late–Cold War look at the Nevadan desert's mutation from ecosystem into lunar-cratered bomb pit. Such works show that the Cold War process of land transformation by ordnance begun at Los Alamos remains underway.

Los Alamos—its implications and influences—also provides a topic for Martin Cruz Smith, a part–American Indian author. Smith achieved commercial success with *Gorky Park* (1981), a murder mystery set in Moscow that inspired a hit feature film. But it is two other novels, *Nightwing* (1977) and *Stallion Gate* (1986), that dwell upon the use of sacred western lands for destructive ends. *Nightwing* tells of a Hopi shaman's attempt to wipe out the blight of modern life he sees staining his birthplace. His weapon is ancient magic, his intentions eschatological, as he rises from his kiva to unleash a plague of vampire bats. Smith's shaman is chilling, yet matter-of-fact:

> Well, this world is supposed to end with atomic bombs, that's what some of the other priests say. I've been waiting for it but I don't think it's going to happen very soon. You can't depend on that. So, I'm going to end it now.

Stallion Gate also draws power from the tension between Native lore and modern science. Its protagonist is Joe Pena, a Pueblo G.I. during World War II—and childhood friend of Robert Oppenheimer—who is assigned to monitor the private affairs of Manhattan Project scientists. The novel's progression depends on the gradual awakening of Pena's Native American consciousness, and his growing opposition to the atomic test. Pena believes that the desert of spirits and wild horses cannot withstand the heat of nuclear fission.

Deeply sensitive explorations of this theme flow from the pen of Laguna Pueblo novelist Leslie Marmon Silko, author of *Laguna Woman* (1974), *Ceremony* (1977), *Storyteller* (1981), and *Almanac of the Dead* (1991). Silko's writings earn both popular and critical attention. *Ceremony* tells of the loss of self suffered by a Native American G.I. after World War II. His reawakening comes only from a return to his spiritual heritage and ancestral lands and ways. *Almanac of the Dead*, a layered and furious work, takes such ideas to more intense extremes, spinning desert spirits, modern politics, old oppression, and contemporary rebellion into a tapestry that is at once postmodern and ancient in its lushness. The story swirls around a prescient Indian seer who updates the Quetzalcoatl myth of the Aztecs, predicting the violent overthrow of White modernity and a restoration of usurped ancient power.

Silko's apocalyptic discontents with contemporary times, capitalism, and commercialism are manifest. But she is not the only writer at work weaving together Cold War life and the West. Her example proves that voices worth hearing on the subject and likely to gain the popular ear are not restricted to traditional pop culture realms. In a postmodern age, the lines dividing high from popular art are down along with the Berlin Wall. To amplify the point, consider the January 1995 issue of *Outside* magazine. *Outside* usually directs its readers toward the West's finer hiking and skiing destinations. But there is no discordance in the magazine's praise of two rising young poets, Campbell McGrath and Catherine Bowman, held up as avatars of the "7–11" school, so named because their work revolves around a western landscape comprising ageless values and tawdry modernity.

It is likely that this fresh duo, branching out of poetry's precious ghetto and using popular language, will help frame the literary renderings of the post–Cold War West. McGrath writes in a rock-and-rolling Guthriesque style about the Cold War's effect on Southern California in "Nagasaki, Uncle Walt, and the Eschatology of the American Century." From his volume, *American Noise*,

> Like all good stories it starts with a bang: August 6, 1945 / America's Century begins in fire and ends, like any respectable act of creation, in something resembling ash. . . . Dan'l Boone and frozen dinners in the family room. . . . For those reared in the shadow of the Fat Man / anything less than global thermo-nuclear destruction seems laughable, wimpy, . . . We could enter the arc-lit freeway slipstream / and climb the desolate escarpments to the higher desert / looking down at the city sprawled like a uranium nebula . . . a vast untranslatable energy / against the furrows of dust as pale and frangible as ash.

Such explorations constitute a poetic supplement to the acid insights penned by Joan Didion in *Slouching Towards Bethlehem* (1968). Didion's tales of modern California—"Love and death in the Golden Land"—dissect human foibles in a West struggling with and against its fabled legacy, especially in a state haunted by hunters of a Golden Dream.

Rock-and-roll music, while heavily influencing writers like Didion and McGrath, is not always thought of as having Cold War context. Instead, more basic concerns such as sex, cars, and obnoxious parents are rock theme favorites. But politically motivated music can accompany teen perspective. No rock-and-roll-era musician touched on Cold War western themes to more enduring effect than Bob Dylan. Albums such as *John Wesley Harding* and *Highway 61*

Revisited escape the pitfall into which much protest music falls, remaining relevant after particular controversies fade. Dylan's themes of war, peace, freedom, and wandering fit a western ethos of independence and renewal.

Cultural historian and rock-and-roll expert Richard Aquila makes an acute analysis of western myths and their place in popular music. "A Blaze of Glory: The Mythic West in Pop and Rock Music," is his chapter-long elucidation from *Wanted Dead or Alive*. "By tapping into shared memories of the alleged western experience," Aquila writes, "the mythic west provided solutions that might be applied to social problems as well as wartime enemies. . . . The myth had always portrayed life in simple terms, as a struggle between good and evil that American good guys always win."

Rock had its share of good guys and cowboy heroes, as did country-and-western music. But perhaps the most abiding western rock image of the sixties was that of the tanned and toothsome Surfer Girls and Boys. The Beach Boys, Jan and Dean, and other bands made it brightly plain that, in a world bathed in tensions and strife, the best living took place on America's sunny beaches and fast-track drag strips, where romance was hot, surf was heavy, and cars were slick. California, the land of regnant youth, was the object of a worldwide yearning that the dreary Communists could never hope to copy or surpass. So alluring was the California Dream, so lingering was the warmth of the sun, that attacking it all as excess in their signature 1976 hit "Hotel California" was the Eagles' way of bidding the sixties' ethos adieu. But even then, one wonders whether the Eagles' many foreign fans, whose grasp of English and rock allusion might not be as strong as their familiarity with American myth, understood that the tune whose words they mouthed actually bemoaned what the Golden State lifestyle had purportedly become.

Other rock-and-roll rejections of western myth attacked the fate of the land's original inhabitants. Cree songstress Buffy Sainte-Marie was a staple of the sixties protest circuit. But even in rebelling, singers such as Willie Nelson, and his Austin, Texas, peers, fell under an established and convenient western label—that of the Outlaw. Rejecting one western myth often means falling under the purview of another.

Sports is another realm of popular culture in which the West and Cold War occasionally met, sometimes memorably. American–Soviet sporting collisions were rather rare, because most spectator attention in the United States remains focused on domestic games. But the Olympics did provide regular superpower athletic competition. The medal race between the USA and USSR was a subplot of most quadrennial contests. In the 1964 games, Native American Billy Mills was an upset gold medallist. The distance-runner became a modern Indian hero, the "Running Brave." Fans and commentators treated the United

States ice hockey team's 1980 upset over the Soviets as a miracle, as well as a victory for Uncle Sam.

Perhaps the most symbol-laden Olympic event occurred during the 1984 games at Los Angeles. The boycotting USSR team's absence hovered over the games like a phantom, yet the 1984 Olympics were exuberant in tone and reception. The victories won by American athletes helped, but at least as important was the overall national mood of that reelection year: sunny and self-assured. As that year's campaign slogan announced, it was "Morning again in America." Southern California seemed the appropriate place for an international festival of American splendor. In *American Noise*, poet McGrath observed the unselfconscious irony of the opening and closing ceremonies. He writes of the sun-kissed, cheerfully inaccurate Golden West pioneer theme in the poem, "Almond Blossoms, Rock and Roll, the Past Seen as Burning Fields":

> They chose to reenact the national epic, westward expansion, only due to certain staging restrictions the covered wagons full of unflappable coeds rolled from west to east, a trivial, barely noticed flaw.

Perhaps the eastward rush of those ersatz Conestogas was appropriate. There issued out of the West a tide of American culture, surging over the world. It was a circling wave unmindful of its own contradictions and complexities, but no less inexorable for that. It was a running flood of symbolism, sweeping mere fact before it. It inundated those who watched, whether their gaze was rapt or averted.

Some years ago, at an academic conference, a Pulitzer Prize–winning scholar whose work on the American West spans four decades offered a definitive answer to peers quarreling over the geographical parameters of the West. Answering their arguments over whether the West included the Plains, or the Coast, or Texas, William H. Goetzmann contended that nit-picking over cartographical boundaries is pointless. The true and most accurate location of the West is in the collective American consciousness, what Goetzmann refers to as "The West of the Imagination," in a book of the same name. His point is apt, for it speaks to the indomitable signifying powers of symbol and myth. Moreover, it allows for flexibility, understanding that there are many imagined Wests, always changing, and often drastically different from each other.

In *The West of the Imagination*, Goetzmann explores several generations of writing, painting, and photography. His thesis holds sway in the national active imagination—the popular culture world of movies, television, and literature. The Cold War may be over, but myths look backwards as well as forwards. Without a doubt, Americans will continue working to make sense of their transforming Cold War experience. It will come as no surprise when that experience is filtered through the ever-shifting yet somehow constant West. Both the Cold War and the American West are likely to be reinvented together in unexpected ways. Popular culture will surely continue to facilitate this perpetual synthesizing of fact and myth.

BIBLIOGRAPHIC ESSAY

Readers commencing Cold War study might find relevant material intimidating for its sheer abundance. Certain broadly historical works make fine starting points, however. Several of the following take note of cultural developments in the United States, even if their broader focus is diplomacy or strategy. Anyone considering containment must read George Kennan's seminal article, "The Sources of Soviet Conduct," *Foreign Affairs* 25 (July 1947): 566–82. *The Tragedy of American Diplomacy*, rev. ed. (New York: Dell, 1972), by William Appleman Williams, is the foundation work of the Wisconsin revisionist school, whose reexamination approach fits in with the sixties ethos. Later refinements of the revisionist case are found in Walter LaFeber, *America, Russia, and The Cold War 1945–1980* (New York: Knopf, 1981); and the works of Thomas G. Paterson, including *On Every Front: The Making of the Cold War* (New York: W. W. Norton, 1979). Robert W. Tucker's *The Radical Left and American Foreign Policy* (Baltimore: Johns Hopkins University Press, 1971) is a contemporaneous critical evaluation of revisionism.

Robert Dallek's *The American Style of Foreign Policy: Cultural Politics and Foreign Affairs* (New York: Oxford University Press, 1983) is persuasive and speaks to American behavior modes as well as to diplomacy. For recent investigation, see Peter W. Rodman's *More Precious Than Peace: The Cold War and the Struggle for the Third World* (New York: Scribner, 1994). Balanced and accessible are John Spanier, *American Foreign Policy Since World War II* (Washington, D.C.: CQ Press, 1991) and Stephen Ambrose, *Rise to Globalism: American Foreign Policy Since 1938* (New York: Penguin, 1991). Robert A. Divine's *Since 1945: Politics and Diplomacy in Recent American History* (New York: McGraw Hill, 1985), and William G. Hyland, *The Cold War: Fifty Years of Conflict* (New York: Times Books, 1991) are valuable. The most outstanding survey is John Lewis Gaddis, *The Long Peace: Inquiries into the History of the Cold War* (New York: Oxford University Press, 1987). Gaddis's new book, *We Now Know: Rethinking Cold War History* (New York: Oxford University Press, 1997), is an instant classic. All include ample bibliographies.

Readers looking for histories that are more explicitly cultural should start with Paul Boyer, *By the Bomb's Early Light: American Thought and Culture at the Dawn of the Atomic Age* (New York: Pantheon, 1984). This major book effectively presents interdisciplinary scholarship. The comprehensive *Gunfighter Nation: The Myth of the Frontier in Twentieth-Century America* (New York: Harper Perennial, 1993), by Richard Slotkin, is a valuable film reference packed with well-researched observations. The preceding discussion relies on Boyer and Slotkin, as well as on Philip French's *Westerns: Aspects of a Movie Genre* (New York: Oxford University Press, 1977); George N. Fenin and William K. Everson, *The*

Western From Silents to the Seventies (New York: Penguin, 1977), and David Manning White and Richard Averson, *The Celluloid Weapon: Social Comment in the American Film* (Boston: Beacon Press, 1972).

Peter Biskind's *Seeing is Believing: How Hollywood Taught Us to Stop Worrying and Love the Fifties* (New York: Pantheon, 1983) cogently and convincingly analyzes postwar science fiction films. See also Jeff Rovin's *A Pictorial History of Science Fiction Films* (Seacaucus, NJ: Citadel Press, 1975). Martha A. Bartter's *The Way to Ground Zero: The Atomic Bomb in American Science Fiction* (New York: Greenwood Press, 1988) is a remarkable work deserving wider notice. Bartter's detailed conclusions inform this essay's look at science fiction literature. *Hollywood Films of the Seventies: Sex, Drugs, Violence, Rock 'n' Roll & Politics* (New York: Harper & Row, 1984), by Seth Cagin and Philip Dray, is brief but perceptive. Forceful analysis permeates William J. Palmer, *The Films of the Eighties: A Social History* (Carbondale: Southern Illinois University Press, 1993), from which the preceding chapter draws when discussing movies of the Reagan era.

Television histories are plentiful, if not uniformly useful. Erik Barnouw, *Tube of Plenty: The Evolution of American Television* (New York: Oxford University Press, 1982), and Norm Goldstein, *The History of Television* (New York: Portland House, 1991) are helpful. More academic in tone is Jeremy Tunstall's *The Media Are American: Anglo-American Media in the World* (New York: Columbia University Press, 1977). The best history of television Westerns is Gary A. Yoggy, *Riding the Video Range* (Jefferson, NC: McFarland, 1994). *In Search of Melancholy Baby* (New York: Vintage, 1989), written by the Russian émigré Vassily Aksyonov, gives a refreshing look at American popular culture.

The novels of Leslie Marmon Silko, Frank Waters, Edward Abbey, and Martin Cruz Smith are vital fiction bearing on the Cold War and the American West. Indispensable nonfiction includes Joan Didion's *Slouching Towards Bethlehem* (New York: Washington Square Press, 1968, 1981) and Tom Wolfe's *The Right Stuff* (New York: Farrar, Straus, & Giroux, 1979). Joel Garreau's *Edge City: Life on the New Frontier* (New York: Doubleday, 1991), and *The Nine Nations of North America* (Boston: Houghton Mifflin, 1981) are unusual and impressive. The most notable "7-11 Poetry School" works to date are Catherine Bowman (of Texas), *1-800-Hot-Ribs* (Salt Lake City: Gibbs-Smith, 1993) and the Campbell McGrath trio: *Capitalism* (Hanover, NH: Wesleyan University Press, 1990), *American Noise* (Hopewell, NJ: Ecco Press, 1993), and *Spring Comes to Chicago* (Hopewell, NJ: Ecco Press, 1996). Richard Aquila edited and contributed to *Wanted Dead or Alive: The American West in Popular Culture* (Urbana: University of Illinois Press, 1996). Lively and rigorous, this is a singular collection of insightful essays. Aquila's masterful chapter, "Blaze of Glory," underpins my discussion of popular music. Michael L. Johnson's *New Westers: The West in Contemporary American Culture* (Lawrence: University Press of Kansas, 1996) is excellent.

The works of Richard W. Etulain inform the entire field of western literary study and history. *A Bibliographic Guide to the Study of Western American Literature* (Lincoln: University of Nebraska Press, 1982) and *The American West in the Twentieth Century: A Bibliography* (Norman: University of Oklahoma Press, 1994) are well organized for the reader's benefit. *The Twentieth-Century West: Historical Interpretations* (Albuquerque: University of New Mexico Press, 1989), edited by Etulain and Gerald D. Nash, is already a standard. *Conversa-*

188   Charles Kupfer

tions With Wallace Stegner on Western History and Literature (Salt Lake City: University of Utah Press, 1990) speaks for itself. See Etulain's chapters on western culture in *The American West: A Twentieth-Century History* (Lincoln: University of Nebraska Press, 1989), by Michael P. Malone and Etulain. The book also has an extremely valuable bibliography. Etulain's *Reimagining the Modern American West: A Century of Fiction, History, and Art* (Tucson: University of Arizona Press, 1996) captures the cycles of change wheeling across the West.

New Western history readers benefit from two anthologies, *Trails: Toward a New Western History* (Lawrence: University Press of Kansas, 1991), edited by Patricia Limerick, Clyde A. Milner II, and Charles E. Rankin, and *Under an Open Sky: Rethinking America's Western Past* (New York: W. W. Norton, 1992), edited by William Cronon, George Miles, and Jay Gitlin. See also the chapter, "The Imagined West," in Richard White's *"It's Your Misfortune and None of My Own": A History of the American West* (Norman: University of Oklahoma Press, 1991), and Barbara H. Meldum, ed., *Old West-New West: Centennial Essays* (Moscow: University of Idaho, 1993).

Henry Nash Smith's *Virgin Land: The American West as Symbol and Myth* (New York: Vintage, 1950, 1957) has influenced generations of scholars. *The Machine in the Garden: Technology and the Pastoral Idea in America* (New York: Oxford University Press, 1964, 1967) is Leo Marx's landmark work of American Studies. William H. Goetzmann and William N. Goetzmann, *The West of the Imagination* (New York: W. W. Norton, 1986), is an elegant, compelling, and intelligent companion to their television series of the same name. It is an excellent entry point to the many books of William H. Goetzmann, which include his Pulitzer Prize–winning *Exploration & Empire: The Explorer and the Scientist in the Winning of the American West* (Austin: Texas State Historical Association in cooperation with University of Texas at Austin's Center for Studies in Texas History, 1966, 1993). Taken together, Goetzmann's volumes form an essential and unrivaled body of work on the American West.

CHAPTER TEN

ALASKA AND HAWAI'I
The Cold War States

༜

JOHN WHITEHEAD

In March 1946, just as Winston Churchill delivered his "Iron Curtain" speech presaging the onset of the Cold War, the Gallup organization announced that mainland Americans registered a 60 percent approval for the admission of Hawai'i as a state; a few months later, in September, a similar poll showed a 64 percent approval for the admission of Alaska. This was the first time a majority of Americans had shown such interest in the two territories. In a previous poll, conducted in January 1941, Gallup found that only 48 percent approved of statehood for Hawai'i; Alaska did not attract the pollster's interest at all before the war. Residents of the two territories evidently agreed with the interest shown on the mainland. Hawai'i had voted 2–1 for statehood in a 1940 plebiscite, and Alaskan voters favored statehood by slightly less than a 3–2 margin in a 1946 plebiscite. The approval rating for the two held constant in a succession of Gallup surveys repeated over the ensuing dozen years. Alaska and Hawai'i finally entered the union as the forty-ninth and fiftieth states, respectively, in January and August 1959. With their admission, America's quasi-colonial territorial system, which began with the creation of the Northwest Territory in 1787, came to an end after 172 years.

During the thirteen years from 1946 to 1959 in which the territorial system came under its final scrutiny and dissolution, the Cold War burst into flame. Those first embers of fear implanted in the European "Iron Curtain" spread to Asia and the Pacific with the 1949 "loss" of China, the Korean Conflict of the early 1950s, and the mounting hysteria that the Communist menace threatened both coasts of the United States. The "battle for statehood," as residents of Alaska and Hawai'i called their home-rule quest, and the growth of the Cold

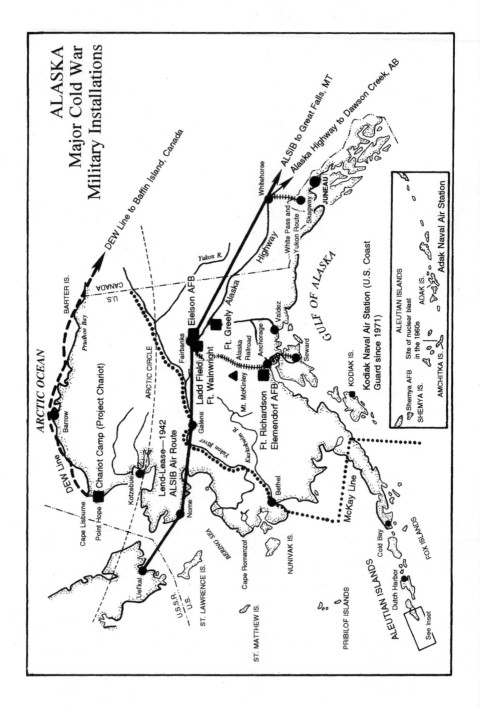

ALASKA
Major Cold War
Military Installations

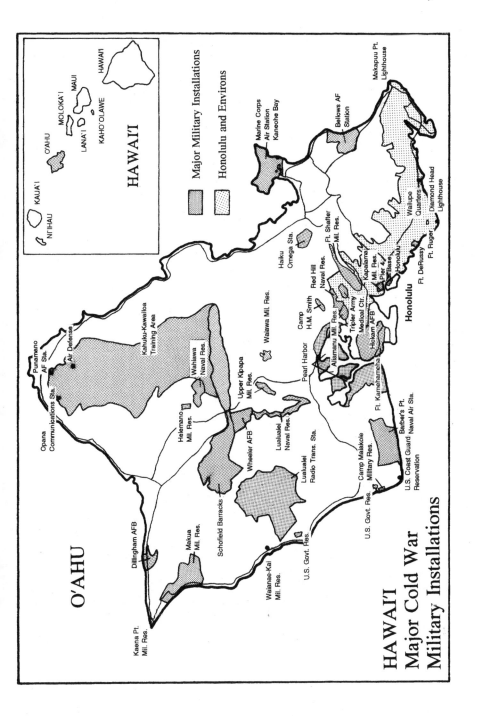

O'AHU

Kaena Pt. Mil. Res.

Dillingham AFB

Makua Mil. Res.

Schofield Barracks

Waianae-Kai Mil. Res.

U.S. Govt. Res.

U.S. Govt. Res.

Opana Communications Sta.

Punamano AF Sta.

Air Defense

Kahuku-Kawailoa Training Area

Helemano Mil. Res.

Wahiawa Naval Res.

Wheeler AFB

Lualualei Naval Res.

Upper Kipapa Mil. Res.

Lualualei Radio Trans. Sta.

Camp Malakole Military Res.

Barber's Pt.

U.S. Coast Guard Reservation

Naval Air Sta.

Ft. Kamehameha

Waiawa Mil. Res.

Haiku Omega Sta.

Pearl Harbor

Camp H.M. Smith

Aliamanu Mil. Res.

Hickam AFB

Red Hill Naval Res.

Tripler Army Medical Ctr.

Ft. Shafter Mil. Res.

Kapalama Mil. Res.

Pier 4

Honolulu

Ft. DeRussy

Waikiki

Quarters

Ft. Ruger

Diamond Head Lighthouse

Marine Corps Air Station Kaneohe Bay

Bellows AF Station

Makapuu Pt. Lighthouse

□ Major Military Installations

░ Honolulu and Environs

NI'IHAU

KAUA'I

O'AHU

MOLOKA'I

LANA'I   MAUI

KAHO'OLAWE

HAWAI'I

HAWAI'I

HAWAI'I
Major Cold War
Military Installations

War did not occupy the same time span coincidentally. They built on each other. The full incorporation of Alaska and Hawai'i into the American body politic was an integral part of the extension of a permanent military defense perimeter thousands of miles into the far north and mid–Pacific. Joseph Farrington, Hawai'i's territorial delegate to Congress, advocated in 1946 that Hawai'i's admission "would serve notice on the world anew that the Central and West Pacific constitute a defense zone to the U.S." Cold War policy also confirmed Alaska as a prime national defense outpost shielding the Pacific Coast as well as the continental interior from Soviet air attack across the Arctic Circle. Cold War policy and the "battles for statehood" were so interwoven that we may well call Alaska and Hawai'i the Cold War States.

The strategic military defense posture of the two new states was not a new creation of the Cold War, but a reinvigoration of the position Alaska and Hawai'i had acquired in World War II—much as the Cold War itself was an extension or reinvigoration of the global problems inherited from World War II. To understand the effect of the Cold War on Alaska and Hawai'i, a brief background on their role in World War II is necessary.

THE TRANSFORMATION OF ALASKA AND HAWAI'I IN WORLD WAR II

Prior to World War II Congress was well aware of Hawai'i's strategic military significance. By 1940, over $125 million had been invested in defense installations there; total military personnel stood at 29,830, with annual defense expenditures reaching $60 million. Hawai'i had become "the Gibraltar of the Pacific," but the American military had not yet overwhelmed or transformed the islands. The mainstays of Hawai'i's economy were still sugar and pineapples, with annual defense revenues amounting to about 25–35 percent of the islands' income. Military personnel constituted only 7 percent of the islands' 427,884 residents.

In Alaska the pre-war buildup was negligible. Though World War I air ace General Billy Mitchell forcefully told Congress in 1935 that Alaska was the key to the air security of North America, his efforts, along with those of Alaska's territorial delegate, fell on deaf congressional ears. By late 1939, only 524 military personnel were stationed in the territory out of a total population of 72,500. Annual defense expenditures amounted to less than $1 million. Finally, in the spring of 1940 Congress made its first new military appropriation for Alaska—$4 million to be used for a cold-weather testing laboratory in Fairbanks. Over the next year funds for new airfields in Alaska were appropriated, and troop strength rose to 3,000 by early 1941.

The Japanese bombing of Pearl Harbor in December 1941, the ensuing attack at Dutch Harbor on the Alaska Peninsula in June 1942, and the subsequent capture of Kiska and Attu islands in the Aleutians transformed the two territories into major theaters of the Pacific War. Though Hawai'i suffered no further military attack after Pearl Harbor, it remained the center of Pacific mobilization for the duration of the war. The presence of the Japanese at Attu and Kiska placed Alaska in the brink of battle until the late spring and summer of 1943, when the two Aleutian islands were retaken by American troops. While the war raged, the presence of the military, in terms of both population and monetary expenditures, transformed the two territories.

In Alaska total defense expenditures—both capital construction and operating expenses—exceeded $1 billion between 1941 and 1945. Airfields, army forts, and naval installations were constructed at over thirty separate locations, with the largest permanent concentration being in Anchorage and Fairbanks. The construction activity included the building of the 1,671-mile Alaska/Canada (ALCAN) Highway during the summer and fall of 1942. That year also saw the inauguration of a new air system, known as ALSIB, to ferry planes bound for Russian Siberia from Great Falls, Montana, via Alaska as part of the U.S. Lend–Lease program. The transportation grid created by ALCAN and ALSIB would have pronounced effects on the future development of the territory. Alaska, which had previously been linked to the West only by sea routes to Seattle and San Francisco, now had road and air routes that connected the territory to inland western states. The air bridge to Russia confirmed the strategic position that would set the stage for Alaska's role in the Cold War.

During the heavy fighting of the Aleutian campaign, Alaska's military population reached a peak of 152,000 in 1943 and pushed the territory's total population to a new high of 233,000, a figure that would not be seen again until after statehood. From 1941 to 1945, over 300,000 troops passed through the northern outpost. The human wave that swept through Alaska had a permanent effect on the territory. The military buildup led to substantial urban development and transformed the sleepy railroad town of Anchorage into a military headquarters city. Military expenditures and other wartime measures overwhelmed the prewar goldmining/salmon packing economy. The territory's gold mines were formally closed by a federal war emergency order in 1942.

The war's effect on Hawai'i was as dramatic as on Alaska. The number of troops stationed in the islands rose to a staggering 442,160 in 1944 and boosted Hawai'i's total population to 858,945, a figure that would not be seen again until 1974. Over the course of the war, almost one million troops passed through the islands. Along with those coming to the islands, some 40,000 troops from Hawai'i left the islands to fight in the war. Almost half were Americans of

Japanese ancestry (AJAs), including those who belonged to two famous all-AJA units, the 100th Infantry Battalion and the 442nd Regimental Combat Team. These units were among the most highly decorated in the war. Their combat record changed American mainland attitudes about AJAs and influenced the role these citizens would play in Hawai'i's postwar development.

Military expenditures in Hawai'i were as overwhelming as the human wave. New military construction, estimated at over $400 million during the war, included fifty army reservations and twenty-six navy stations on the island of O'ahu. Total military expenditures, including payrolls, raised the total federal outlay in the peak year of 1944 alone to $800 million! As in Alaska, wartime activity and construction enhanced urban concentration. The importance of O'ahu and Honolulu grew relative to the outer, predominantly sugar-planta-tion, islands. While pineapple and sugar production continued during the war, their value was dwarfed by the military economy.

At the war's end in 1945, residents of both territories feared the impact of a military demobilization and wondered what the future would hold. Whatever that future might be, it was clear that the war had not left Alaska and Hawai'i the same places they had been five years earlier. Gwenfread Allen, the major chronicler of Hawai'i's war years, noted that "from the moment bombs fell on Pearl Harbor in World War II, these isolated islands became an integral part of the fabric of the nation at large." The official U.S. Army account of the war in Alaska expressed a similar transformation: "Never before, not even at the time of the gold rushes, was the Territory so advertised. Americans who seemed to have forgotten the existence of the northern possession rediscovered Alaska." The Gallup poll results in 1946 signified that mainland Americans clearly recognized and endorsed the role World War II played in the transformation of the two once-distant territories.

COLD WAR ALASKA AND THE FORTY-NINTH STATE

In Alaska the handful of years between the demobilization from World War II and the buildup for the Cold War caused a great deal of initial confusion and uncertainty. Troop levels fell from their 1943 peak of 150,000 to 50,000 in 1945, and then to 19,000 in 1946. The territory's overall population stood at 99,000 that year. There was little confidence that Alaska could quickly return to its prewar economy. The output of canned salmon, the territory's largest commer-cial export, dropped to a twenty-year low in 1946; no one knew if the gold-mining operations closed during the war would reopen. Some hoped that veterans would stay in the territory as homesteaders; federal legislation passed in 1945 made specific land grants available to them. The future looked bleak in 1946, as Alaskans voted in that October referendum for statehood.

The precise decision-making procedures that led the military to remain in Alaska after World War II are unclear. Army publications are vague and basically state that Alaska's location on the Great Circle air route dictated its strategic importance. By early 1947 it is clear that the new Department of Defense had made such a decision and created the Alaskan Command (ALCOM)—the first unified army, air force, and navy command in the nation. The unified command was headquartered in Anchorage at Fort Richardson, thus assuring the future of Alaska's largest city as a military headquarters. The first duties of the new command centered on demobilization rather than Cold War buildup. The Aleutians were not considered a major theater for future Cold War activities; the closure of airfields and bases there was a top priority of ALCOM. Even while the demobilization continued, Alaska's overall importance as a strategic air center was reemphasized; report after report noted that the shortest air route for a Soviet attack on the United States was via the polar route. New military construction resumed in Anchorage and Fairbanks in 1947, and by 1948 troop strength had returned to 27,000, out of an overall territorial population of 120,000.

In 1949 Alaska's defensive position was underscored by events in the state of Washington. Territorial Governor Ernest Gruening learned that the Defense Department wanted to move a substantial portion of Boeing's Seattle operations to the company's factory in Wichita, Kansas. This would shield the production of military aircraft from Soviet air attack. Gruening flew to Seattle and in conjunction with the Seattle Chamber of Commerce proposed what he thought was a wiser strategy: build a string of radar stations across the arctic coast of Alaska to warn of any Soviet air intrusion. There would then be time for the Air Force to respond before enemy planes could threaten Seattle—particularly if air bases in Alaska were enlarged. According to Gruening, the plan to move Boeing was dropped; three years later, preparations to construct the radar line, known as the Distant Early Warning Line or DEW Line, began.

With the 1949 "loss" of China and the onset of the Korean War in 1950, Alaska's defensive position in the Pacific theater of the Cold War emerged with full force. Over the next decade, and particularly between 1950 and 1952, a renewed military buildup in the territory matched the World War II construction boom. Construction for the Cold War centered on a relatively small number of installations that would serve as permanent defense sites. The two principal sites were Anchorage (Elmendorf Air Force Base and a new Fort Richardson) and Fairbanks (Ladd Field, renamed Fort Wainwright in 1961, and Eielson Air Force Base.) The Kodiak Naval Air Station was reinvigorated, and Fort Greely, a training center for cold-weather combat, was established ninety miles south of Fairbanks at Big Delta. The Aleutians were not totally abandoned; major defense installations, which had been initially demobilized after World War II, were reestablished at Adak Naval Air Station and Shemya Air Base, a remote eight-square-mile island that lay halfway between Anchorage and Tokyo, and only 280 miles east of Russia. In addition to these major facilities, a number of smaller air stations were established.

The overall financial scope of the increased military activities was staggering. Total Department of Defense expenditures (including construction and operations) reached $449 million in 1949–50 and hit a peak of $512 million in 1952–53. Armed forces personnel grew to 50,000 in the 1952–55 period and pushed Alaska's total population to 220,000. Including civilian workers, the Department of Defense employed 51.5 percent of Alaska's workforce in 1952. The Cold War was clearly the dominant economic force in the territory.

National defense strategies now included the DEW Line. Planning for the radar shield began in the summer of 1952 with a military–scientific study group convened at the Massachusetts Institute of Technology. The 3,000-mile line would stretch along the Arctic coast from Point Barrow, Alaska, to Baffin Island, Canada, with some fifty separate installations. The first test site was constructed at Barter Island, Alaska, in 1953, and the project, whose final cost totaled almost $500 million, was completed in 1957. In addition to the DEW Line, the military constructed the Aircraft Control and Warning System (AC&W), as well as an internal communication system linking Alaska with the "lower 48" states called "White Alice." The White Alice system later became Alaska's civilian communication system, known as Alascom. Like the ground and air transportation systems constructed in World War II, the enhanced Cold War communication system further tied Alaska to the interior American West with a reporting link to Continental Air Defense Command (CONAD) headquarters in Colorado Springs.

In the mid– to late-1950s, Alaska truly became a Cold War military territory. Alaska's expanding population and economic growth was fueled almost exclusively by military personnel or civilians engaged in military construction. Gold mining, which staged a limited comeback after World War II, and salmon canning, which now showed the impact of sustained overfishing, declined steadily in the last half of the decade. By 1960, some observers placed the total military investment in Alaska since 1940 (World War II and Cold War installations) at $3 billion! Though there was a fear that a "bust" could follow the construction "boom," Alaska boosters pointed out that the maintenance and operation of the new, permanent Cold War defense and communication installations would provide a sustained multimillion dollar annual economy.

The 220,000 population the territory reached in 1955 held firm over the next five years and was even further concentrated in urban areas. Anchorage (with suburbs) grew from 11,200 (19,866, including suburbs) in 1950 to 44,200 (66,562) by 1960. Fairbanks rose from 5,700 (8,171, including suburbs) to 13,300 (19,378) in the same period and became the airlift staging area slope for equipment shipped to the DEW Line. Not only did the Cold War expand Alaska's urban communities, it shifted the concentration of population away from the southeastern panhandle to the military, or "railbelt," axis along the Alaska Railroad from Anchorage to Fairbanks. The ethnic makeup of the new military population also changed Alaska. Prior to World War II, Alaska's population was roughly 50 percent Alaska Native and 50 percent non-Native, or Caucasian. By 1950, the proportions were roughly 25 percent Native and 75 percent non-Native; a decade later the figures were 20 percent Native and 80 percent non-Native. Not only were there more Caucasians, as well as the first substantial numbers of African Americans, there was a new kind of non-Native Alaskan. The old-time "pioneers," or "sourdoughs," were quickly outnumbered by the new military arrivals, who had a decidedly different value system. As Alaskan economist George Rogers has noted, "The people who came with military Alaska were not independent self-sufficient pioneers of past centuries, but members of mid–twentieth century America's urban-industrial society. They required and expected the same standards of community living and services available elsewhere, and the economic prosperity which accompanied their coming made it possible to meet these demands." Though there was tension at times between the "sourdough" Caucasian community and the new military population, many of the sourdoughs left mining or fishing to work as civilians on the military posts.

The Cold War defense buildup was the crucial factor in securing statehood for Alaska. In 1946 congressional opposition to statehood was based on Alaska's small population, its uncertain economy, and the belief that Alaska could not financially support a state government. The Cold War gave Alaska its needed population and economy, and it shaped the two in ways that were both subtle and dramatic. Unlike the prewar mining and fishing industries, the military did not entwine itself in territorial politics or seek special favors from the legislature. When Alaskans held a constitutional convention in 1955–56 to draft a charter for the future state, they were not lobbied by the military for special favors. At a fortieth anniversary reunion of that convention, held in February 1996, the delegates were asked if the Cold War military buildup was on their minds when they wrote the constitution. At first, they responded "No, they didn't think of it at all." But later in the conversation various delegates kept coming back to the issue of the military impact. Finally, Jack Coghill, a delegate who later served twice as Alaska's lieutenant governor, explained that the military buildup "freed the population." For the first time, people came up from the "lower 48" who were not "under the thumb of the mining and fishing industries." In Coghill's mind, the military buildup provided the precondition for statehood by "producing a free people."

The impact of those new free people became even more evident as the statehood movement gained force in the mid–1950s. Letter-writing campaigns by military personnel stationed in Alaska to their "home state" congressmen formed a major lobbying activity for statehood. Some of those congressmen knew Alaska firsthand from military service during World War II. Senator Richard Neuberger of Oregon had worked on the Alaska Highway and had served as an Army pilot. He wrote numerous magazine articles on Alaska's role as a vital military defense center for the nation and was a key supporter of the statehood legislation that finally passed the Senate in June 1958. Later that year, Alaskans were asked to approve statehood in a plebiscite mandated by Congress in the statehood legislation. Military personnel, who were allowed to register and vote if they indicated a desire for permanent Alaska residence, joined in the 5–1 positive vote. This overwhelming majority for statehood elicited the eternal wrath of certain antistatehood "sourdoughs," like Fairbanksan Joe Vogler, who claimed until his death in 1993 that the positive plebiscite carried only because of the military vote.

The only drawback of the military presence to statehood was the fear by President Dwight Eisenhower that some of Alaska's federal defense installations might be compromised by state sovereignty. Though Eisenhower never explained why defense would be more compromised in a state than a territory, the final statehood bill demarcated a section of western and northern Alaska bounded by the "McKay Line" in which land could be withdrawn for defense purposes and placed under federal rather than state jurisdiction. As of the present day, no such withdrawals have been made. With Alaska's entry into the union in January 1959, one could reasonably argue that the Cold War placed the forty-ninth star on the flag and gave the United States its first "defense state."

COLD WAR HAWAI'I: COMMUNIST OUTPOST OR SHOWCASE FOR AMERICANISM?

In Alaska both the World War II and Cold War military presence were seen in positive terms by its residents, save for those few old-time pioneers who lamented the vanishing "last frontier." The military brought population and prosperity to the territory and created the conditions that made statehood

possible. Throughout the 1940s and 1950s, Alaska's territorial government remained under civilian control. There were no rumors that the military saw
sinister forces in the North that would necessitate emergency military rule
or martial law. In Hawai'i the scenario was different. Though the military
brought prosperity to Hawai'i in World War II, it also brought martial law that
extended from December 1941 to October 1944. A major reason that so many
islanders favored statehood by 1945 was to preclude any recurrence of military
rule. Martial law would be much more difficult to establish in a state than a
territory.

Though Hawai'i experienced a rapid demobilization after V-J day and saw
its population drop from 814,000 in 1945 to 545,000 in 1946, the territory still
retained the requisite population and economic base to become a state. Hawai'i's political establishment rushed to spur Congressional action for admission. In early 1946 a congressional subcommittee arrived in the Islands and
began hearings on statehood. After the delegation reported favorably on admission, the U.S. House of Representatives passed the first bill for Hawai'i
statehood in June 1947. Islanders now hoped that nothing would halt the
statehood bill in the U.S. Senate. These hopes were soon dashed. Before the
Senate could act, the territory found itself embroiled in the Cold War quag-
mire of anti-Communist hysteria. Hawai'i was branded a Communist outpost,
and the statehood movement was derailed for a decade.

The first flames of anti-Communist hysteria had local roots that were
quickly fanned to a fever pitch by mainland politicians. With the war's end, a
substantial portion of Hawai'i's nonmilitary population had reasserted an economic and political agenda begun in the late-1930s and early-1940s. The nascent prewar labor movement that was put on hold by World War II quickly
reemerged to organize Hawai'i's agricultural and dock workers. In 1945 the
territorial legislature passed the Hawaii Employment Relations Act, which
extended collective bargaining to agricultural workers. Unionization of the
Islands' sugar, and later, pineapple workers proceeded rapidly. After a seventy-
nine-day sugar strike in 1946, the unions claimed a major victory in both
recognition and wage increases from the locally owned "Big Five" corporations
that controlled both the plantations and the docks. Organization of the dock
workers eventually led to a crippling 177-day strike in 1949. The union involved in organizing both plantation and dock workers was the San Francisco–
based International Longshoremen's and Warehousemen's Union (ILWU).
Even before the war, ILWU leaders, particularly Union President Harry
Bridges, were accused of being members of the Communist party. The Communist label was also attached to the chief organizer of the union in Hawai'i,
Jack W. Hall.

The anti-Communist fireworks erupted in November 1947 when the Democratic territorial governor, Ingram Stainback, announced that there was a Communist plot to take over Hawai'i, with the ILWU being a major actor. Stainback quickly implemented President Truman's civilian loyalty program and vowed to purge public employees with a Communist connection.

After 1947, anti-Communist hysteria gained force every year, causing real alarm to those advocating statehood. In 1948 Stainback upped his anti-Communist attack and claimed that Communists and the ILWU were trying to take over the local Democratic party. The 1949 dock strike led to strident charges, both locally and from the mainland, that the strike was Communist inspired. Senator Hugh Butler issued a report that Communism held a firm grip on the Islands, with ILWU leader Harry Bridges being the Communist dictator of Hawai'i. Butler, who had earlier stalled Senate action on the 1947–48 statehood bill, now recommended that all congressional consideration of statehood for Hawai'i be suspended until the Communist menace was thoroughly under control.

To counter the anti-Communist hysteria in 1949, the territorial legislature authorized a Constitutional Convention to be held in April 1950. Hawai'i's lawmakers also invited the House Un-American Activities Committee to hold hearings in the Islands concurrently with the convention. These two events, they hoped, would highlight the level of democracy in the Islands, present Hawai'i as a "showcase for Americanism," and dispel Butler's accusations.

Despite the charges of Butler and other anti-Communist foes, Hawai'i still had supporters in Congress. In March 1950 the House once again passed a statehood bill for Hawai'i. The Constitutional Convention/HUAC hearings that followed the House vote produced mixed results for statehood in the Senate. The convention produced a "model constitution," but two of its members were expelled for alleged prior Communist affiliation. At the HUAC hearings, thirty-nine witnesses refused to answer "yes" or "no" to any questions concerning prior affiliation with the Communist party—and fourteen of the so-called "Reluctant 39" were delegates to the convention. Even though HUAC reported no major Communist menace in the Islands, the cause of statehood was not advanced. The outbreak of the Korean War in June 1950, even more than the events in the Islands, diverted the Senate's attention, and the vote for statehood in the upper house languished once again.

The fallout from the HUAC hearings led to a schism within the local Democratic party and to federal charges of contempt against the Reluctant 39. Calm might have returned in early 1951, when a federal court acquitted all thirty-nine. Shortly after the blanket acquittal, however, Jack Kawano, a former ILWU official and one of the thirty-nine, now offered firsthand knowledge of the Communist underpinnings of the union. He traveled to Washington to explain his findings to HUAC. Kawano's new testimony led to the arrest and trial of seven suspected Communists in Hawai'i, including Jack Hall, for violation of the 1940 Smith Act, which outlawed any attempt to advocate the overthrow of the U.S. government. The Smith Act trial resulted in the conviction of Hall, though he was quickly released from jail on appeal. The conviction was ultimately reversed.

The anti-Communist hysteria in Hawai'i did not subside until the mid–1950s. The anti-union element of the alarm gradually declined, as the Big Five firms and the ILWU found ways to work together. Of even greater importance was the superb record of Asian American soldiers from Hawai'i, many of whom were ILWU members, in the Korean War. The battlefield casualty rate for "Hawaii boys" was three times the national average, and the 426 men killed-in-action was four times the national average on a per capita basis. Nor were there any desertions among Hawai'i veterans. Statehood supporters issued pamphlet after pamphlet in the mid–1950s that stressed the Korean War record and portrayed Hawai'i's AJA veterans as pillars in the "showcase for Americanism." Despite the efforts of the new pamphleteers, the statehood movement had been effectively stymied by the mid–1950s. Statehood legislation for Hawai'i would not regain congressional favor until 1959.

While anti-Communist hysteria captured the Islands' political life in the first five years after World War II, the onset of the Korean War focused attention on Hawai'i as a staging and training area for Cold War Pacific conflict. Military leaders, particularly General Douglas MacArthur and Admiral Chester Nimitz, had never been as concerned with the alleged Communist menace in the Islands as Senator Butler and other members of Congress. Even the FBI noted that Hawai'i's Communists "just don't rate."

There had never been any doubt that Hawai'i would remain a central Pacific defense area after World War II. As in Alaska, a unified command, the U.S. Pacific Command (CINCPAC), was created in January 1947 and headquartered in Honolulu. The question was simply the scope of its role. Postwar demobilization reduced federal expenditures from that record $800 million in 1944 to $147 million in 1950; the territory's population continued to drop, from 545,000 in 1946 to 497,000 by 1950. The number of active-duty military reached a low that year of 20,000–21,000—a return to the level of the 1930s.

The Korean War arrested that decline. Annual military spending in the Islands rose over the next decade to $338 million by 1959 and exceeded the value of Hawai'i's sugar and pineapple exports by almost $100 million. Active-duty military now numbered over 50,000. With dependents, the military population was closer to 110,000 or between one-fifth and one-sixth of the total

622,000 population. Including civilian defense employees and their families, the portion of the population dependent on defense activities was roughly 200,000. As in World War II the military presence during the Cold War was concentrated almost exclusively on the island of O'ahu, further enhancing the urban dominance of Honolulu in the territory. Armed forces personnel substantially augmented the Caucasian presence in the territory and accounted for the overwhelming portion of the African American population.

Increased construction in the Islands during the 1950s, both military and civilian, led to new linkages with the mainland. With the arrival of California industrialist Henry J. Kaiser, Hawai'i's economy became less dominated by the old *haole* Island families. Kaiser soon became the single largest individual investor in the Islands. As in World War II, the constant arrival and departure of troops during the Cold War increased mainland knowledge of the Islands. This led to increased tourist travel and to the eventual migration of mainland veterans back to the Islands.

Despite the anti-Communist hysteria, Hawai'i in the 1950s became better known and less strange to Americans as a result of the Cold War. Though the Hawai'i statehood movement had been temporarily derailed, the overall Pacific military buildup that led to Alaska's admission in January 1959 swept Hawai'i back into the political mainstream. Once Alaska was admitted, any lingering congressional opposition to Hawai'i collapsed. With Alaska in the Union, Hawai'i could no longer be opposed as a noncontiguous territory. If federal defense installations were not compromised by statehood in Alaska, they would not be compromised by statehood for Hawai'i. The Hawai'i statehood bill passed both the House and Senate in less than three months after the Eighty-Sixth Congress convened in 1959. With the addition of the fiftieth star to the flag in August 1959, the second Cold War state joined the union.

THE COLD WAR AFTER STATEHOOD—1959–1995

The Cold War was not over in 1959, and its impact in both Alaska and Hawai'i did not end that year. It would continue to influence the two new states for the next three decades. In the first decade after statehood the military's importance actually grew in both states. The escalation of the Vietnam War in the 1960s and 1970s once again emphasized Hawai'i's role as the center for Pacific defense operations. Military expenditures in the islands rose from $373 million in 1960 to $675 million in 1970 and on to $1.4 billion by 1980. Hawai'i's military population (including dependents) rose in the 1960s to peaks of over 130,000, then stabilized in the 1970s at approximately 125,000. Readers of Robert McNamara's *In Retrospect* (1995) will certainly remember the Secretary of Defense's numerous trips to CINCPAC headquarters in Honolulu to plan strategy for the Southeast Asian war. And thousands of American servicemen in that conflict will remember trips either to Trippler Army hospital or to Hawai'i's beaches for "R & R." The end of the Vietnam War in 1975 also led to the migration of over 3,400 Vietnamese to Hawai'i by 1980. Since that time, Hawai'i's total military population has remained stable at the 125,000 level.

While the military maintained a prominent role in Hawai'i after 1959, it was soon surpassed by a new wave of people sweeping into the islands—tourists. The arrival of the first jet airliner in 1959 inaugurated the age of mass worldwide tourism to Hawai'i. The annual number of tourists visiting Hawai'i (and staying overnight) stood at 31,000 in 1941. The prewar level was not reached again until 1948. The number first surpassed 100,000 in 1955 and reached 171,000 in 1958, the last pre-jet year. The numbers quickly exploded to 243,000 in 1959 and soared to 1.5 million a decade later. The advent of jumbo jets further stimulated the tourist onslaught, which reached 4 million in 1979—four times the number of soldiers who had passed through Hawai'i in all of World War II. Annual tourist expenditures rose from the prewar level of $12 million in 1940 to $24 million in 1950. Over the next decade tourist dollars zoomed to $131 million in 1960 and then to $595 million in 1970. Tourist spending surpassed the military in 1972 ($840 million vs. $732 million) and reached $2.9 billion in 1980—double the military economic impact.

Tourism surpassed the military just as the military had earlier surpassed sugar and pineapples. The visitor impact on Hawai'i was even more pervasive. Overcrowding in general and the constant presence of civilian transients in the Islands were a great concern. Unlike the military installations that were confined to urban O'ahu, tourism spread to the outer islands. On Kaua'i, Hawai'i, and particularly Maui, the conversion of agricultural lands into resorts and condominium complexes seemed to threaten the overall atmosphere and culture of the Pacific paradise. Throughout the Islands tourism led to an increase in land and housing prices that threatened to dispossess many permanent Island residents. In the eyes of many islanders, the Cold War buildup had been much less overwhelming than the tourist onslaught.

What tourists did to overshadow the military in Hawai'i, oil did in Alaska—and in roughly the same time period. As in Hawai'i, the military presence continued to dominate Alaska in the first years of statehood. Though the active-duty military population fell from 50,000 in the mid–1950s to 33,000 by 1960, the military still constituted 33 percent of Alaska's workforce in 1960. Defense expenditures of $268 million were the single largest item in the new state's economy.

As the new state searched for ways to diversify its economy, another aspect of the Cold War culture, non-defense nuclear activity, was initially hailed by many Alaska boosters. Beginning in 1958 and continuing into the early 1960s the Atomic Energy Commission and Edward Teller, the nation's leading nuclear advocate, attempted to "sell" Alaskans on a scheme in the national Project Plowshare program known as Project Chariot. Teller proposed an underwater nuclear explosion at Cape Thompson in Northwest Alaska to demonstrate the engineering capability of atomic power. The explosion would carve a man-made harbor and make possible the export of minerals from that section of the new state. Teller's intent was not so much to help Alaska as to find a spot on American soil where he could develop a nuclear engineering capability to be used on the Panama Canal. The project soon came under attack from native Alaskans and local, as well as lower-48, scientists over potential environmental hazards. Though the AEC withdrew the project in 1962, the protests to Chariot had dramatic repercussions. Environmentalist Barry Commoner noted that his participation in the protest to Chariot led to his involvement in the modern environmental movement. The environmental studies demanded by local scientists were a precursor for the Environmental Impact Statements later required by the National Environmental Protection Act of 1969. Native protest led to the creation of the first all-Native newspaper in Alaska, The Tundra Times, and to the first unified organization of Alaska's different native groups, the Alaska Federation of Natives, in 1962.

Though Chariot was abandoned, the use of Alaska as a nuclear test zone was not. The lonely, uninhabited island of Amchitka in the Aleutian chain, which had been a fortified defense post in World War II, was chosen by the Department of Defense and the AEC to test nuclear warheads considered too large for detonation at the Nevada test site. One purpose of the proposed tests was to distinguish between the seismic signals from earthquakes and those from underground nuclear explosions. Three major tests were conducted in 1965, 1969, and 1971. The latter test known as "Cannikin" aroused the protest of environmentalists and Native groups. One group of protesters, who arrived on a ship named Greenpeace, soon formed an environmental activist group by the same name. Despite the protests, the explosion went ahead and produced a shock equivalent to a 7.0 Richter scale earthquake. The 1971 Amchitka blast proved to be an ending rather than an acceleration of nuclear testing in Alaska. From 1958 to 1971 events in distant Alaska were vital components in the growing national concern over environmental pollution. Alaska helped fan the nation's environmental movement and was also a staging area for major Native political movements.

Various military and military/scientific projects underpinned Alaska's quest for a permanent economy in the first decade of statehood. Alaska finally headed away from military dependence in 1968, when the Atlantic Richfield Company (ARCO) discovered oil on land owned by the state at Prudhoe Bay on the Arctic slope. In 1969 a sale of oil leases brought $900 million to the state, a revenue inflow that exceeded annual military expenditures for the first time. After a number of setbacks, presidential approval for the construction of the Trans-Alaska Oil Pipeline was given in 1973. Work began in 1974. For the next three years, Alaska's economy boomed with this $8 billion dollar project, the first major nonmilitary construction project in Alaska's history.

In June 1977 the first oil from Prudhoe Bay flowed through the pipeline and launched Alaska's future as an oil-rich state. By 1980, Alaskans proudly announced that for the first time in the state's history, federal tax revenues derived from Alaska exceeded the flow of federal funds into Alaska. Some members of the Alaska legislature even proposed that the state secede from the national union and end its sudden new subsidization of the federal budget! Alaska had finally emerged from its dependence on both the federal government and the military sector. The number of active-duty personnel had steadily fallen, from 30,000 in 1970 to 22,000 by 1980. Including dependents, the military accounted for roughly 14–15 percent of the state's 400,000 population. About 11 percent of Alaska's workforce was now dependent on military employment, compared to 33 percent in 1960 or the 51 percent in 1952. As in Hawai'i, the permanent military presence spawned by the Cold War remained, but it was no longer the dominant, all-pervasive factor that it had been in the years before statehood.

By 1980, oil and tourism overshadowed the military in the two "Cold War states" of Alaska and Hawai'i. But the military presence and the military role as Pacific Rim defenders remained a prominent and permanent part of their economies and cultures. In both states the number of military personnel remained remarkably constant from 1980 to 1990, and in fact served as a stabilizing element in the labor force. With the close of the Cold War in the late-1980s and early-1990s, neither state has faced the dramatic demobilization that was so feared after World War II. Alaska and Hawai'i have actually seen their military significance grow, and the two have become united as a Pacific defense perimeter. In 1989 a reconstituted Alaskan Command, which had undergone a number of reorganizations since its creation in 1947, was placed under CINCPAC, headquartered in Honolulu. Pacific defense functions in non-U.S. locations have been transferred to the Alaska/Hawai'i perimeter. The eruption of Mt. Pinatubo in 1991 and the subsequent closing of Clark Air Force Base and Subic Bay Naval Base in the Philippines led to the transfer of training and medical operations to Alaska. Though the fear of Soviet Air attack has lessened, Alaska's congressional delegation has continued to emphasize the state's strategic location as the only air center equidistant from potential trouble spots in both Asia and Europe.

In the rounds of base closures and realignments triggered by the end of the Cold War from 1988 to 1995, Alaska and Hawai'i have been much less impacted than other Pacific regions, particularly less so than California. Only the Barbers Point Naval Air Station has been closed in Hawai'i. In Alaska, the Adak Naval Air Station, Shemya Air Force Base, and Fort Greely have been closed or realigned. With the closure of Adak and Shemya, the military significance of the Aleutians dating from World War II has come to an end, at least temporarily. But the Cold War buildup of the Anchorage–Fairbanks railbelt corridor remains intact.

Oddly enough, one of the few significant pullbacks triggered by the end of the Cold War has been in civilian aviation. When Soviet airspace was closed to western air carriers, European airlines flew to Japan via the Great Circle route and stopped in Anchorage, and to a lesser extent Fairbanks, for refueling. In the 1970s and 1980s, Anchorage International Airport became a major hub for such flights. With the opening of Russian airspace in the late-1980s and early- 1990s, European airlines have rerouted their passenger flights to Japan over Russia. By the early 1990s virtually all Japan–Anchorage–Europe passenger service had stopped, though cargo flights from Europe to Japan via Alaska are still maintained. Passenger flights from Anchorage to the Russian Far East have been inaugurated, but they do not match the traffic on the Cold War Europe/Japan routes.

THE EXTENSION OF THE COLD WAR WEST TO ALASKA/HAWAI'I

The permanent military frontier spawned by the Cold War quite definitely changed the remote territories of Alaska and Hawai'i and integrated them into the nation. Their joint statehood in 1959 was the most dramatic testimony of their Cold War transformation. But did these Cold War changes also integrate the two more fully into the American West—or extend the region to include them?

The transportation and communication routes generated by both World War II and the Cold War tied Alaska to the interior West via the Alaska Highway, interior air routes, and communication lines such as the DEW Line connection. Alaska emerged as a defense shield to protect the West from Soviet air attack. It became the region's far northwestern boundary. The boom in air travel, both military and commercial, between Hawai'i and the mainland during the Cold War used West Coast cities as its base. Hawai'i became not only the far western defense boundary, but also the far western tourist boundary of the region.

While Alaska and Hawai'i were more fully integrated into the western region, they simultaneously joined a much wider global space outside of the region. The thousands of military personnel who came to Alaska and Hawai'i did not migrate from the West, they came from all parts of the nation. Hawai'i moved further into the global arena with the expansion of tourism. Though cheap airfares from the West Coast were an early mainstay of the tourist trade, the first jet to land in Hawai'i in 1959 was not an American carrier, but a Quantas jet inaugurating an air route from San Francisco to Australia. And though tourists from the western region have been the single largest group coming to Hawai'i, the islands have also attracted significant numbers of Japanese tourists and investors.

This globalizing trend in the two far western states was part and parcel of the overall Cold War transformation of the West that extended the region northward and westward. As the West increasingly acquired the function of Pacific Rim defender and military contractor for the nation during the Cold War, Alaska and Hawai'i became integral parts of that western function. With the military downsizing since 1989 the Alaska/Hawai'i defense perimeter has seized a larger portion of that function relative to other areas of the West. Reacting to the dramatic base closures in California, an aide to governor Pete Wilson announced in 1995, "I certainly hate to think they [the Base Realignment and Closure Commission] have sort of an anti-California approach. . . . Are people saying we no longer need to be the guardian of the Pacific and the Pacific Rim?" If a major function of the West is to be the "guardian of the Pacific and the Pacific Rim," then Alaska and Hawai'i are clearly a part of the region—and an increasingly important part of it. In transforming the West, the Cold War integrated Hawai'i and Alaska into the world, the nation, and the West. And the Cold War West assumed greater national and global roles as it extended to Alaska and Hawai'i.

BIBLIOGRAPHIC ESSAY

The impact of the Cold War in Alaska and Hawai'i has received only cursory attention, and as yet no comparative treatment, in the general secondary literature of each state. The following references are divided by state.

Hawai'i

The economic and political impact of World War II on Hawai'i is covered well in Gwen-fread Allen, *Hawaii's War Years, 1941–1945* (Westport, Conn., Greenwood Press [1971, c1950]). No comparable overview exists for the Cold War period. General overviews that mention the Cold War impact include Bryan H. Farrell, *Hawaii: The Legend That Sells* (Honolulu: University of Hawaii Press, 1982); Lawrence Fuchs, *Hawaii Pono: A Social History* (New York: Harcourt, Brace, Jovanavich, 1962); Thomas Kemper Hitch, *Islands in Transition: The Past, Present, and Future of Hawaii's Economy* (Honolulu: First Hawaiian Bank, 1992); Edward Joesting, *Tides of Commerce* (Honolulu: First Hawaiian Bank, 1983).

The impact of the anti-Communism movement and the coming of statehood in Hawai'i is well treated in Roger Bell, *Last Among Equals: Hawaiian Statehood and American Politics* (Honolulu: University of Hawaii Press, 1984); Buck Buchwach, *Hawaii USA: Communist Beachhead or Showcase for Americanism?* (Honolulu: Hawaii Statehood Committee, 1957); T. Michael Holmes, *The Specter of Communism in Hawaii* (Honolulu: University of Hawaii Press, 1994).

Hawai'i is well served by general demographic and statistical reports that cover the military impact on the state's economy and population. Particularly helpful volumes include Eleanor C. Nordyke, *The Peopling of Hawai'i* (Honolulu: University of Hawaii Press, 1989); Robert C. Schmitt, *Historical Statistics of Hawaii* (Honolulu: University of Hawaii Press, 1977); and the University of Hawaii, Department of Geography, *Atlas of Hawaii*, 2nd ed. (Honolulu: University of Hawaii Press, 1983). Readers looking for statistics on the military in Hawai'i should be aware of a few caveats. Prior to 1954, statistics were kept only for shore-based active-duty personnel. In 1954, this was augmented for the first time with data for military personnel stationed in Hawaii but physically aboard ship. The "afloat" personnel adds about 15,000–20,000 to the annual "total military personnel figure." Data on dependents were also not kept until 1954. All figures quoted for World War II and for the period 1945 to 1954 are only for shore-based active-duty personnel. From 1954 to the present, the category "total active duty military personnel" includes those both ashore and aboard ship. And from 1954 to the present, the category "total military population" includes military personnel—ashore and aboard ship—plus total dependents. Where figures differ from source to source, I have relied on those published in Schmitt and Nordyke.

Alaska

Several military-oriented overviews of Alaska touch on the economic and political impact of the Cold War, though more emphasis is generally placed on World War II. For the immediate changes that World War II brought to the North, see Jean Potter, *Alaska Under Arms* (New York: Macmillan, 1942). Potter was a reporter for *Fortune* magazine. For broader surveys, see U.S. Army, Alaska, *The U.S. Army in Alaska*, USARAL Pamphlet 360–5, 1972 (previous editions in 1969 and 1965 appear as *The Army's Role in the Building of Alaska* and *Building Alaska with the Army*); Penny Rennick, ed., special issue entitled "World War II in Alaska," *Alaska Geographic* 22, no. 4 (1995); Jonathan Nielson, *Armed Forces on a Northern*

Frontier: The Military in Alaska's History, 1867–1987 (New York: Greenwood Press, 1988); John Chloe, *Top Cover for Alaska: The Air Force in Alaska 1920–83* (Anchorage: Air Force Association, 1984); George W. Rogers, *The Future of Alaska: Economic Consequences of Statehood* (Baltimore: Johns Hopkins Press, 1962). Within Rogers' book, the brief historical overview section entitled "Military Alaska" provides the most persuasive case that the population and political culture of the territory were changed by the arrival of a permanent military establishment. Readers can find the same "Military Alaska" section in David T. Kresge, Thomas A. Morehouse, and George W. Rogers, *Issues in Alaska Development* (Seattle: University of Washington Press, 1977). The construction of the Alaska Highway received considerable attention at the time of its fiftieth anniversary in 1992. See particularly Heath Twichell, *Northwest Epic: The Building of the Alaska Highway* (New York: St. Martin's Press, 1992). Twichell's father was an army engineer during the highway's construction. For perspective on the impact of the highway in Canada, see K. S. Coates and W. R. Morrison, *The Alaska Highway in World War II: The U.S. Army of Occupation in Canada's Northwest* (Norman: University of Oklahoma Press, 1992).

From the late-1940s to the early-1960s a popular "guide to Alaska" literature emerged that well documented the impact of the Cold War on the new state and territory. It particularly pointed to the dominant presence of the military in Alaska's two major cities, Anchorage and Fairbanks. Among the best sources are two books spaced a decade apart by Herb Hilscher and Miriam Hilscher, *Alaska Now*, rev. ed. (Boston: Little, Brown, 1950), and *Alaska U.S.A.* (Boston: Little, Brown, 1959). Herb Hilscher was a member of the 1955–56 Alaska Constitutional Convention. Another guide that devotes considerable attention to the Cold War impact is Harry Kursh, *This is Alaska* (Englewood Cliffs, NJ: Prentice Hall, 1961).

The construction of the DEW Line and other specific Cold War military projects has attracted some attention. See Richard Morenus, *DEWLINE: Distant Early Warning: The Miracle of America's First Line of Defense* (New York: Random House, 1957). Territorial governor and later U.S. Senator Ernest Gruening describes his role in proposing the DEW Line to protect the Seattle plants of the Boeing Company in his autobiography, *Many Battles: The Autobiography of Ernest Gruening* (New York: Liveright, 1973). For a catalog of military construction in Alaska, see Lyman Woodman, *The Army Corps of Engineers in Alaska Starting in 1896 and History of its Alaska District During 1946–74* (Anchorage: Elmendorf Air Force Base, 1976).

The impact of Cold War nuclear activity in Alaska and the dramatic story of Project Chariot is well told in Dan O'Neill, *The Firecracker Boys* (New York: St. Martin's Press, 1994). For a general discussion of the environmental history of Cold War Alaska, see Peter A. Coates, *The Trans-Alaska Pipeline Controversy: Technology, Conservation and the Frontier* (Bethlehem, PA: Lehigh University Press, 1991). The two extensive Alaskan environmental studies that were precursors for the Environmental Impact Studies later required by the National Environmental Protection Act of 1969 are Norman J. Wilimovsky and John N. Wolfe, eds., *Environment of the Cape Thompson Region, Alaska* (Oak Ridge, TN: U.S. Atomic Energy Commission, 1966), and Melvin L. Merritt and R. Glen Fuller, *The Environment of Amchitka Island, Alaska* (Oak Ridge, TN: Technical Information Center, Energy

Research and Development Administration, 1977). For a brief background to the origins of Greenpeace, see Greenpeace Foundation, *Greenpeace Report 1976* (Vancouver, B.C.: Greenpeace Foundation, 1976).

General statistical surveys are less well compiled on Alaska than on Hawai'i. I was able to piece together a statistical portrait of military spending and population from O. Scott Goldsmith, *Federal Revenues and Spending in Alaska* (Anchorage: Alaska Statehood Commission, 1981); and from annual reports (for fiscal years 1983, 1984, 1987, 1988, 1989, and 1990) entitled *Impact of Military Spending on the Economy of Alaska*, prepared for the Alaskan Command by the Cost Analysis Branch of the 21st Tactical Fighter Wing, Elmendorf Air Force Base, Alaska. For the most recent news on base closings in Alaska and Hawai'i, I have relied on news releases in the *Fairbanks Daily News-Miner*, and statistics supplied by the U.S. Senate Committee on Appropriations. The fortieth reunion of the Alaska Constitutional Convention delegates was held February 4, 1996 at the University of Alaska Fairbanks and was attended by the author.

THE COLD WAR WEST
A New Image?

℘

KEVIN J. FERNLUND

The American West is of all America's regions the most imagined. There are many reasons for this fact—historic, mythic, aesthetic, religious, and environmental. Certainly one of the most enduring and powerful of these images is of the West as the "old frontier." By "old," western historians mean typically that period between the end of the Civil War and the start of the twentieth century. This is the Old, or Wild West, of cowboys and Indians and many other colorful figures, from buckskin-clad scouts to Mormons joined in polygamous unions. This unique stock of characters have all been made popular over the years through dime novels, Wild West shows, motion pictures, and television programs. Historically, the late nineteenth century was a period of special significance to the nation. At the end of the Civil War in 1865, Americans in both the North and South turned to the West as the section of the future, where the country could reinvent itself. The idea of the West as America's land of promise, where things would be different, strongly took hold at this time and remained unshaken well into the twentieth century.

As the essays in this volume make clear, however, the region did not remain as the country's frontier. On the contrary, by virtue of its unique environment, its geographic location, and its highly concentrated urban settlement, the American West, within less than a century, moved from the edge of things to the center of one of the great struggles for power, in which the civilizations of the world faced the horrible prospect of total destruction. In coming to terms with this change, the West's image as a place apart, of new beginnings, and a stern moral code, which lingered in a myriad of popular forms, was forced to accommodate another, much darker, and often ambiguous image as a staging area for global war and nuclear Armageddon. This recent historic situation, needless to say, bears very little resemblance to the West's mythic past.

But if we set aside the mythic dimension and focus on the West's European American origins, then it becomes clear that the region has always figured prominently in the calculus of European and American statesmen. It has been a place, after all, long valued for its strategic location. In the 1590s, decades after Coronado's failure to find the elusive Seven Cities of Gold, the Spanish grew interested in the West, which was their "north," only after they feared the encroachment of other European powers in that quarter. The result was the colonization of New Mexico and the subsequent exploration and colonization of the American Southwest and Pacific Coast in an ambitious effort to create a wide buffer zone between the silver mines of Zacatecas and the outside world. Later, the French, English, Russians, and Americans each vied for advantage in the region.

During the 1800s, Americans would make the region their own. From the Lewis and Clark expedition in 1804–06 to the construction of the Panama Canal some ten decades later, the West was regarded as vitally important to U.S. security and the key to the nation's growing hemispheric and global ambitions. Thus, when the United States assumed the mantle of "defender of the free world" after World War II, the West's place in global strategy did not require invention; it was a long-recognized fact. It was no surprise, then, that during the Cold War the American West would take its place in the front lines of a protracted international struggle in which the stakes, given the advent of nuclear weapons, were never higher. Taking into account this larger historical perspective, it is clear that the Cold War West is but the region's most recent manifestation as a strategically significant part of the world.

In separating myths from realities, students of the Cold War in the American West will uncover a region with many ties to its past. Indeed, since Frederick Jackson Turner announced in 1893 that the frontier had "closed," interpretations that view the West in terms of the westward movement have, not surprisingly, gradually lost their relevance. New perspectives that see the West in strategic and global terms, however, will perhaps be more helpful to historians as they increasingly start their narratives and analyses with the premise that the West is a place rather than a process—a view that makes more and more sense in light of contemporary concerns. For in the twentieth century, the West has become a mature, fully developed, and completely integrated region, but one that has remained distinctive owing to its environment, colorful history, and enduring sense of romance and promise. Yet, despite the West's modernization, it has continued to play a role in world affairs not unlike the one first cast for the region by Spanish statesmen four centuries ago. In this respect, the continuities with the past are striking. During the Cold War, the West's past met the future, and its myths collided with reality. It is not clear, so soon after the fall of the Berlin Wall, what will emerge out of this jumble of fact and fiction. What is clear is that the Cold War has been a costly experience—in ways that we still do not fully understand. And, in the event of another cold war, it is doubtful that the region will be so willing and able to accept the fate assigned to it thus far by history.

CONTRIBUTORS

TIMOTHY M. CHAMBLESS is an Associate Instructor in the History department, the Political Science department, and in the English Language Institute at the University of Utah, where he received his Ph.D. in 1987. His dissertation is "Muckraker at Work: Columnist Jack Anderson." He has also taught courses at Weber State University and Salt Lake Community College.

RIC A. DIAS is an Assistant Professor of History at Northern State University in Aberdeen, South Dakota. His dissertation is " 'Together We Build': The Rise and Fall of the Kaiser Steel Corporation in the New Deal West." He has submitted several articles on western topics.

KEVIN J. FERNLUND is an Assistant Professor of American History at Valley City State University, North Dakota. He received his Ph.D. from the University of New Mexico in 1992. Currently, he is turning his dissertation, "William Henry Holmes: Explorer of the Americas from the Yellowstone to the Yucatan, 1872–1895," into a book.

STEVE FOX is the Project Administrator for the New Mexico Endowment for the Humanities. He received his Ph.D. in American Studies from the University of New Mexico in 1988. He has taught in several departments at UNM and written about Southwest cultural topics. He is also the author of *Toxic Work: Women Workers at GTE-LenKurT* (1991), and "Boomer Dharma: The Evolution of Alternative Spiritual Communities in New Mexico," in *Religion in Modern New Mexico*, ed. Richard W. Etulain and Ferenc Szasz (1997).

A. YVETTE HUGINNIE is an Assistant Professor in American Studies at the University of California, Santa Cruz. She teaches courses on U.S. Race and

Ethnicity, the American West, and U.S. Labor history. Her research interests include turn-of-the-century race, labor, and immigration history. She is currently finishing a manuscript on race, class, and politics in Arizona.

CHARLES KUPFER is finishing his Ph.D. at the University of Texas at Austin. His dissertation is "We Felt the Flames: American Responses to Blitzkrieg, Summer, 1940." His research interests are cultural and political history, especially overseas reactions to the United States.

KEVIN LEONARD is an Assistant Professor of History at Western Washington University. His dissertation, "Years of Hope, Days of Fear: The Impact of World War II on Race Relations in Los Angeles," won the W. Turrentine Jackson Award for the best dissertation on any aspect of the western United States in the twentieth century.

MARÍA E. MONTOYA is an Assistant Professor in the Department of History and the Program in American Culture at the University of Michigan. Her book, *Children of the Land: Property, Power, and Resistance on the Maxwell Land Grant,* will be published by the University of New Mexico Press.

JACQUELINE V. NOLAN holds B.A.'s in Ethnology and Geography from Mary Washington College, and an M.A. in International Studies from the University of Wyoming. She is currently employed by the National Park Service as the Geographic Information System Coordinator for the George Washington Memorial Parkway. She has freelanced in cartography since 1979.

MARK STOLL teaches history at Texas Tech University. His book, *Protestantism, Capitalism, and Nature in America,* was published by the University of New Mexico Press in 1997. Author of several papers and articles on religious topics, Stoll received his Ph.D. in 1993 from the University of Texas.

MICHAEL WELSH is an Associate Professor of history at the University of Northern Colorado. He has written on ethnicity, environment, and education topics. Among his publications are *Dunes and Dreams: A History of White Sands National Monument* (1995); *A Special Place, A Sacred Trust: Preserving the Fort Davis Story* (1996); and *U.S. Army Corps of Engineers: Albuquerque District, 1935–1985* (1987).

JOHN WHITEHEAD is a Professor of History and Director of the Honors Program at the University of Alaska Fairbanks. He has compiled an oral history of the participants in the constitutional conventions of Hawai'i (1950) and Alaska (1955–56). He is the author of "Hawai'i: The First and Last Far West," *Western Historical Quarterly* (May 1992), and he is the author, with Arrel Morgan Gibson, of *Yankees in Paradise: The Pacific Basin Frontier* (1993).

INDEX

Abbey, Edward, 159–61, 165, 181

African Americans, 68; discrimination against, 51–52, 58–60; migration of, 36–39, 48, 54–55; protests by, 140–42, 148–49, 153–54

AJAs (Americans of Japanese ancestry). *See* Asian Americans

Alaska, 206–10; "battle for statehood," 189–90, 192, 194–99; resource exploitation in, 21, 196, 203–5; during World War II, 192–94

Albuquerque, 81–82

American Indians. *See* Native Americans

American West, defined, 31, 48, 185–86

Americans of Japanese ancestry (AJAs). *See* Asian Americans

anti-Communism, as effective political philosophy, 107–12; in Hawai'i, 199–201; of religions, 121–26, 128–30

anti-gay purges, 31, 45–46, 63

anti-nuclear movement. *See* protesters, anti-nuclear

anti-war groups. *See* peace movements

apocalypse, atomic-age, 122–23, 129–30

architecture, 15–16, 23, 73, 82–83

Arizona, 141–42; Phoenix, 19

Armageddon, atomic-age, 122–23, 129–30

armed services personnel, 30, 32–34, 77; homosexuals, 45–46, 63, 66–68

artists. *See* films; popular culture

Asian Americans, 69; assimilation of, 62–63; discrimination against, 51–54, 58–60; immigration of, 41–43, 53, 63, 203; as soldiers, 194, 201

"battle for statehood." *See* Alaska; Hawai'i

Beat generation, 143–47, 151–53, 164

Berkeley Free Speech Movement, 139, 149–50, 165

Bible Balloon project, 124–25

Black Panthers, 153–54

bohemianism, 147, 164

Caen, Herb (columnist), 151

CALC (Clergy and Laity Concerned), 127, 131-32

California, Berkeley, 139, 149–50, 165; defense cutbacks in, 83, 96–99; fundamentalists in, 133–34; growth of, 32–33, 44, 75–77, 92–95, 142–43; San Francisco, 146–47

Cammermeyer, Margarethe, 66–68

campus radicals. *See* students

Catholics, 120, 136; anti-Communist stance of, 121–23; opposition of, to Cold War, 126–28; to Reagan administration policies, 130–35

Central Americans. *See* Hispanics

Chicanos, 156–58, 165

Children's Peace Statue, 139, 143, 163, 165

Chinese Americans. *See* Asian Americans

Christian Right. *See* fundamentalists

Church of Jesus Christ of Latter-Day Saints, 120–21, 132, 136

Civil Rights Movement, 64, 164–65. *See also* African Americans

Clergy and Laity Concerned (CALC), 127, 131-32

Clergy and Laymen Concerned about Vietnam (CALCAV). *See* Clergy and Laity Concerned

colleges, protest movements at. *See* students

Colorado, Colorado Springs, 17–18, 23, 95; Denver, 17–18, 26, 79–80

Communism. *See* anti-Communism

consumerism, 20, 59–60

countercultures. *See* resistance cultures

defense industry. *See* armed services personnel; military installations

Denver, 17–18, 79–80

desert, Great Plains, 12–13, 90; transformation of, 13–16, 24–27, 167–68 (*see also* suburbanization; urbanization)

Dharma Bums (Kerouac), 146

DEW Line (Distant Early Warning Line), 195-97

discrimination, gender, 58, 145, 152; job, 29, 37–39, 47, 55, 58–59; racial, 64, 68, 74, 84, 123–24, 164–65 (*see also* homosexuals; *names of specific groups)*

Distant Early Warning Line (DEW Line), 195-97

"down-winders," 104, 166

Dylan, Bob, 153, 183–84

Earth Day, 159

Earth First!, 143, 159–61

eco-movements. *See* environment, protection of

88 Reasons Why the Rapture Will Be in 1988 (Whisenant), 129–30

Eisenhower, Dwight D., 18–19, 46, 198

El Salvadorans. *See* Hispanics

emigrants. *See* immigrants

employment, 32, 57–59, 69, 140; discrimination in, 29, 37–39, 47, 55, 58–59. *See also* armed services personnel; unions

environment, 12–13, 25–26, 165–66; degradation of, 11, 14–15, 18, 104, 112–14, 116; protection of, 106–7, 114–16, 143, 159–63, 181, 204. *See also* resource exploitation

Española Valley, 16

families, research on, 61–64, 70

"Federal City" (Albuquerque), 81–82

Ferlinghetti, Lawrence, 151

Filipinos, immigration of, 41–43

films, 105, 156–57; espionage, 173–76; science fiction, 171–74; Westerns, 169–71, 173–76. *See also* popular culture

Fort Kirtland (New Mexico), 81–82

Fort Riley (Kansas), 78–79, 81

Four Corners area, 22–23

Free Speech Movement (FSM), 139, 149–50, 165

Front Range (mountains), 9, 17–18, 26

fuel exploration. *See* resource exploitation

fundamentalists, 133–36; anti-Communist stance of, 122–26, 128–30

Garden, the (isolationism), 167–68

gays. *See* homosexuals

gender and sexuality. *See* families, research on; homosexuals

Ginsberg, Allen, 143–46, 151, 153, 164

Goldwater, Barry, 104, 109, 115

Gonzales, Rodolfo "Corky," 158

Great American Desert. *See* desert
Great Plains, 12–13, 90
Greenpeace, 143, 159, 165, 204
growth networks, 103–4; defined, 77–78;
    Denver, 79–80; Junction City, Kansas,
    78–79, 81; Moreno Valley (California),
    83; San Antonio, 78, 80–81
Gunbelt, 95–96

"hard-winter West," 35–37, 47–48
Hawai'i, 53–54, 203, 206–8; "battle for
    statehood," 189, 191–92, 198–202; during
    World War II, 192–94
highways, development of, 18–20, 26, 73–
    74, 112
hippies, 147–48, 151–53, 165
Hispanics, 15–16, 137; immigration of, 43–
    44, 133–34, 143, 161–62, 165–66. *See also*
    Mexican Americans
Hollywood. *See* films
homosexuals, 31, 49, 70, 147; in armed ser-
    vices, 45–46, 63, 66–68
House Un-American Activities Committee
    (HUAC), 108, 110, 126, 200–201; opposi-
    tion to, 142, 148–49
Houston, 19–20, 60
Howl (Ginsberg), 144–45
HUAC (House Un-American Activities
    Committee), 108, 110, 126, 200–201
Hunthausen, Raymond (archbishop), 130–
    31, 136

immigrants, 31–32; Asian, 41–43, 53, 63,
    203; Hispanic, 40–41, 43–44, 49; and
    Sanctuary Movement, 133–34, 143, 161–
    62, 165–66. *See also* migrants
in loco parentis, demise of, 150
Indians. *See* Native Americans
Inman, James E., as prototypical migrant,
    29–30, 34–35
interstate highway system. *See* highways,
    development of

isolationism, 167–68
Italian Americans, 61

Japanese Americans. *See* Asian Americans
Jews, 123–26
John Birch Society, 125
Johnson, Lyndon, 108–9
Junction City, Kansas, 78–79, 81

Kansas, 78–79, 81
Kennan, George F., 3–4, 168
Kerouac, Jack, 143–46, 164
Korean War, 76, 110, 126, 136, 201–2; influ-
    ence of, on films, 169–70
Koreans. *See* Asian Americans

labor. *See* armed services personnel; em-
    ployment; unions
Late Great Planet Earth, The (Lindsey), 129
Latin Americans. *See* Hispanics; Mexican
    Americans
legislation, Base Closure and Realignment
    Act (1990), 114; Flood Control Act
    (1944), 89; full-employment (1946), 29–
    30; G.I. Bill (1944), 89; Immigration Re-
    form and Control Act (1986), 41; Inter-
    state Highway and Defense Act (1956),
    19, 112; Luce-Cellar bill (1946), 53;
    McCarran-Walter Act (1952), 53; New
    Mexico Civil Rights Act (1955), 142; Taft-
    Hartley Act (1947), 56; Wilderness Act
    (1964), 106–7
Leonard, Charles "Chuck," as prototypical
    migrant, 34–36, 47–48
lesbians. *See* homosexuals
Lindsey, Hal, *The Late Great Planet Earth,*
    129
Loeffler, Jack, 159–60
"Long Telegram" (Kennan), 168
Los Alamos, 14–16, 25–26, 139, 163

McCarthyism, 112, 125–26, 142, 177
McGovern, George, 104

Manhattan Project, 14–16

March Air Force Base (Southern California), 83, 85

Marcos, Ferdinand, 41–42

Mexican Americans, 22–23, 69; discrimination against, 54–55, 58–60; immigration of, 40–41, 49; protests by, 156–58, 165

migrants, 31–32; African American, 36–39, 48, 54–55; Native American, 39–40, 154–55; prototypes of, 29–30, 34–36, 47–48. *See also* immigrants

"mild-winter West," 34–37, 46–48

military-industrial complex. *See* military installations; urbanization

military installations, architecture of, 15–16, 82–83; buildup of, 11, 25, 75–78, 89, 91–92; in Alaska, 192–98, 203–6; in Albuquerque, 81–82; in the Gunbelt, 95–96; in Hawai'i, 192–94, 198–203, 205–6; closures, 80–81, 83, 85, 92, 96–97, 114, 206–7; distribution of, 8, 101–4; opposition to, 79–80, 94, 104, 149–50, 159–60, 166. *See also* California; growth networks; MX antiballistic missile system; peace movements; Texas; urbanization

missiles, 5–6, 12–13, 27. *See also* MX antiballistic missile system

Monkey Wrench Gang, The (Abbey), 160, 181

Moreno Valley (California), 83

Mormons, 120–21, 132, 136

MX antiballistic missile system, 114–15, 136; opposition to, 131–32, 163

National Committee for a Sane Nuclear Policy (SANE), 131–32

Native Americans, 15–16, 49, 58, 62–63, 68; effects of resource exploitation on, 22–23; migration of, 39–40, 154–55; portrayals of, in popular culture, 170–73, 177, 181–84; protests by, 132, 154–57, 160, 162–63, 165

Nevada Test Site, 14

New Deal, 74, 88–89

"New Journalism," 146

New Left, 147–50

New Mexico, 26, 142, 162; Albuquerque, 81–82; Los Alamos, 14–16, 25, 139, 163

New Right politics, 65–68

Nixon, Richard, 107–8, 110

Norris, J. Frank (fundamentalist minister), 122–24

nuclear facilities, environmental impact of, 9–11, 14–15, 25–26, 112–14, 116; opposition to, 161–63, 166, 181–83, 204; Rocky Flats, 9–11 (*see also* peace movements)

nuclear threat, influence of, on popular culture, 168, 171–73, 179–81

oil. *See* resource exploitation

Oklahoma City, 19

On the Road (Kerouac), 145–46

Oppenheimer, Robert J., 14–15, 99

peace movements, 126–28, 130–33, 135–37; student, 128, 133, 139–40, 143, 150–51, 163, 165

Peace Statue, 139, 143, 163, 165

Phoenix, 19

politicians. *See also* Eisenhower, Dwight D.; Reagan, Ronald; anti-Communist, 107–12; New Right, 65–68; pro-defense, 103–6; pro-environment, 106–7, 114–16

popular culture, 167–69, 185–88; literature, 143–47, 151–53, 179–83; music, 183–84; sports, 184–85; television, 146, 176–79. *See also* films

population growth, 19–20, 26, 44, 81–82, 105–6; causes of, 16–18, 31–32, 34–36, 46–48, 90–91. *See also* buildup of; California; growth networks; military installations; Texas; urbanization)

Port Huron Statement, 148

Project Chariot, 204

Project Plowshares, 21

Protestants. *See* religions

protesters, 143; African American, 140–42, 148–49, 153–54; anti-nuclear, 161–63, 166, 181–83, 204; Berkeley Free Speech Movement, 139, 149–50, 165; Mexican American, 156–58, 165; Native American, 132, 154–57, 160, 162–63, 165. *See also* environment, protection of; peace movements; resistance cultures

racialized groups. *See names of specific groups*
racism. *See* discrimination, racial
Randolph, A. Philip (union organizer), 140
Reagan, Ronald, 94, 108, 113–15, 117, 175; policies of, opposed, 130–35, 143, 161–62, 165–66; and religious right, 128–29
"Red Power" movement, 154–57
refugees. *See* immigrants
religions, 119–21, 135–37; anti-Communist stance of, 121–26, 128–30; opposition of, to Cold War, 126–28; polarization of, during Reagan administration, 130–35; Sanctuary Movement, 133–34, 143, 161–62, 165–66
religious right. *See* fundamentalists
Reluctant 39, in Hawai'i, 200–201
resistance cultures, 164–66; Beat generation, 143–47, 151–53, 164; hippies, 147–48, 151–53, 165; New Left, 147–50; precursors to, 140–43; Sanctuary Movement, 133–34, 143, 161–62, 165–66; in San Francisco, 146–47; women in, 145, 150, 152, 163–64. *See also* environment, protection of; peace movements; protesters
resource exploitation, 20–24, 26–27, 89, 196, 203–5
Rocky Flats Environmental Technological Site, 9–11

Saint George, Utah, 14
Salt of the Earth (film), 156–57
San Antonio, 78, 80–81

Sanctuary Movement, 133–34, 143, 161–62, 165–66
SANE (National Committee for a Sane Nuclear Policy), 131–32
San Francisco, resistance cultures in, 146–47
sexuality and gender. *See* families, research on; homosexuals
Smith, Gerald L. K. (fundamentalist minister), 123–26
"Sources of Soviet Conduct" (Kennan), 168
South Koreans. *See* Asian Americans
students, 139, 147–50, 155, 165; and peace movements, 128, 133, 139–40, 143, 150–51, 163, 165
suburbanization, 11, 16–20, 23–24, 26, 59–60, 81–83. *See also* urbanization
"sunbelt West" ("mild winter West"), 34–37, 46–48

Termination policy, against Native Americans, 62–63
Texas, 32–33, 44, 75–76, 92; Houston, 19–20, 60; San Antonio, 78, 80–81
Tijerina, Reies Lopez, 157–58
Titan Missile Museum, 6
Titan II missiles, 5–6
Tunney, John, 32–33, 49
Turner, Frederick Jackson, 72, 84–85, 104–5

Udall, Stewart L., 115–16
unions, 55–57, 140, 156–57, 199–201
urbanization, 71–72, 75–77, 84–85, 197; history of, in American West, 72–75. *See also* growth networks; suburbanization
urban sprawl. *See* suburbanization; urbanization
Utah, 14, 93–94, 111

Vietnamese. *See* Asian Americans
Vietnam War, 65, 202–3; influence of, on films, 174–75; opposition to, 127–28, 150–51

War of the Worlds (Wells), 119

Waste Isolation Pilot Project (WIPP), 14, 16, 27

Waters, Maxine, 36–39, 49

Whisenant, Edgar, *88 Reasons Why the Rapture Will Be in 1988*, 129–30

White Sands Missile Range, 14

WIPP (Waste Isolation Pilot Project), 14, 16, 27

women, in labor market, 57–58, 140; in resistance cultures, 143, 145, 150, 152, 163–64

World War II, impact of, on American West, 2–4, 25, 74–75, 84, 87–89, 98–100; territories during, 192–94

Wounded Knee II, 155–56, 165